Advances in Computer Vision and Pattern Recognition

Founding editor
Sameer Singh
Rail Vision Europe Ltd.
Castle Donington
Leicestershire, UK

Series editor
Sing Bing Kang
Interactive Visual Media Group
Microsoft Research
Redmond, WA, USA

More information about this series at http://www.springer.com/series/4205

Tong Lu • Shivakumara Palaiahnakote
Chew Lim Tan • Wenyin Liu

Video Text Detection

Springer

Tong Lu
Department of Computer Science
  and Technology
Nanjing University
Nanjing, China

Chew Lim Tan
National University of Singapore
Singapore, Singapore

Shivakumara Palaiahnakote
Faculty of CSIT
University of Malaya
Kuala Lumpur, Malaysia

Wenyin Liu
Multimedia Software Engineering
  Research Center
City University of Hong Kong
Kowloon Tong, Hong Kong SAR

ISSN 2191-6586   ISSN 2191-6594 (electronic)
ISBN 978-1-4471-7009-9   ISBN 978-1-4471-6515-6 (eBook)
DOI 10.1007/978-1-4471-6515-6
Springer London Heidelberg New York Dordrecht

Springer is part of Springer Science+Business Media (www.springer.com)

Preface

With the increasing availability of low cost portable digital video recorders, we are witnessing a rapid growth of video data archives today. The need for efficient indexing and retrieval has drawn the attention of researchers towards handling the video databases. However, efficiently handling video content is still a difficult task in the pattern recognition and computer vision community, especially when the size of the database increases dramatically. A lot of ideas have been proposed, but like other frontiers in this community, there is no reliable approach that has theoretical grounding in video content analysis.

Fortunately, studies have shown that humans often pay their first attention to text over other objects in video. It is probably due to the ability of humans to simultaneously process multiple channels of scene context and then focus the attention on texts in video scenes. This fact makes video text detection a feasible and probably the most efficient way for indexing, classifying, retrieving and understanding the visual contents in videos. This can be further used in transportation surveillance, electronic payment, traffic safety detection, sport videos retrieval, and even commercial online advertisements. One example is video-based license plate recognition systems, which are accordingly necessary to help improve the convenience of checking vehicle status at roadside and designated inspection points efficiently. Another example is online video advertising. Driven by the advent of broadband Internet access, today's online video users face a daunting volume of video content from video sharing websites, personal blogs, or from IPTV and mobile TV. Accordingly, how to develop advertising systems especially considering contextual video contents through efficient video text detection techniques has become an urgent need.

Actually, video text detection has not been systematically explored even though people have developed a lot of optical character recognition (OCR) techniques, which are considered as one of the most successful applications in the past decades. For example, to explain a typical Google street video scene view, popular visual understanding methods detect and identify objects such as car, person, tree, road and sky from the scene successfully. However, regions containing text tends to be ignored. It is probably due to the fact that text from video is sometimes difficult to detect and recognize. The performance of OCR thereby drastically drops when applied to video texts which are either artificially added (*graphic text*) or naturally existing on video scene objects (*scene text*). There are several reasons for this fact. First, the variety of color, font, size and orientation of video text bring difficulties to OCR techniques. Second, video scenes exhibit a wide range of unknown imaging conditions which in general add sensitivity to noises, shadows, occlusion, lights, motion blur and resolution. Finally, the inputs of most of the OCR engines are well segmented texts which have been distinguished from background pixels. Unfortunately, the segmentation of video text is much harder.

This book tries to systematically introduce readers to the recent developments of video text detection for the first time. It covers what we feel a reader who is interested in video text detection ought to know. In our view, video text detection consists of a general introduction to the background of this exploration (Chap. 1), pre-processing techniques (Chap. 2), detection of graphic text from video (Chap. 3), detection of scene text from video (Chap. 4), post-processing techniques such as text line binarization and character reconstruction (Chap. 5), character segmentation and recognition (Chap. 6), video text applications and systems in real-life (Chap. 7), video script identification (Chap. 8), multi-modal techniques which have been proved to be useful for video text detection and video content analysis (Chap. 9), and performance evaluation of the video text detection algorithms and systems (Chap. 10). A reader who goes from cover to cover will hopefully be well informed. However, we also tried to reduce the interdependence between these chapters so that the reader interested in particular topics can avoid wading through the whole book. We present theoretical material in a succinct manner. The reader can easily access to a more detailed up-to-date set of references of the methods discussed for further reading. Thus we are able to maintain a focus on introducing the most important solutions of video text detection in this book.

We are indebted to a number of individuals both from academic circles and industry who have contributed to the preparation of the book. We thank Hao Wang, Zehuan Yuan, Yirui Wu, Run Xin and Trung Quy Phan for collecting materials and their experimental evaluations on particular methods introduced in this book.

Special thanks go to Simon Rees for providing us this chance, and for the commitment to excellence in all aspects of the production of the book. We truly appreciate his creativity, assistance, and patience.

Nanjing, China   Tong Lu
Kuala Lumpur, Malaysia   Shivakumara Palaiahnakote
Singapore, Singapore   Chew Lim Tan
Kowloon Tong, Hong Kong SAR   Wenyin Liu
April 04, 2014

Contents

Chapter 1
Introduction to Video Text Detection

Text plays a dominant role in video viewing and understanding as text carries rich and important information relevant to the video contents. Studies have shown that humans often pay first attention to text over other objects in a video. In fact, visual attention model is built in some computational approaches to text detection [1]. Essentially, text detection pertains to the segmentation of text regions in a video frame by identifying exact boundaries of text lines. Text detection plays a vital role in subsequent steps, namely, text localization, text word segmentation, and text recognition. This chapter serves to introduce the problems and challenges in video text detection. A brief historical development of video text detection will next be covered followed by a discussion of its potential applications.

1.1 Introduction to the Research of Video Text Detection

With the increasing availability of low-cost portable digital cameras and video recorders, there are large and growing archives of multimedia data, such as photos and videos since 1990 [2–5]. As a result, the need for efficient indexing and retrieval has drawn the attention of researchers toward handling the huge multimedia databases. However, how to index and retrieve the information efficiently, when the size of the database increases dramatically, is a big question. Another challenge is how to label and annotate events recorded in the video based on the semantics. Content-based image indexing is the process of attaching labels to video/images based on their contents. Video content can be seen as two major categories: *perceptual content* and *semantic content* [2]. Perceptual content includes attributes such as color, intensity, shape, texture, and their temporal changes, while semantic content includes objects, events, and their relations. Several methods based on low-level perceptual content for image and video indexing have already been reported [2]. However, these methods do not have the ability to annotate the video based

© Springer-Verlag London 2014
T. Lu et al., *Video Text Detection*, Advances in Computer Vision
and Pattern Recognition, DOI 10.1007/978-1-4471-6515-6_1

on semantics, and hence, there is a semantic gap. Therefore, studies on semantic image content in the form of text, face, vehicle, and human action have attracted recent interests. Among them, text in images/videos is of particular interest as (1) it is very useful for understanding the content of an image, (2) it is easy to extract compared to other semantic contents, and (3) it is useful for applications such as text-based image search and automatic video logging. The semantic gap refers to the different interpretations and meanings of the extracted low-level features (e.g., texture, color, shape, etc.) by the users with respect to applications. For instance, retrieving exciting events from sports video with low-level features is not simple because the extracted low-level features may not yield meaning of exciting events (high-level features). Text in video can be used to fill this gap because in many videos, there is a considerable amount of text. Video text can thus help to improve the effectiveness of content-based image and video retrieval systems [2–5].

When we look at traditional document image analysis, in the early 1960s, optical character recognition (OCR) was taken as one of the first clear applications of pattern recognition. Today, for some simple tasks with clean and well-formatted text, document analysis is viewed as almost a solved problem [5]. In this way, great progress has been made in processing printed characters against clean background such as scanned document pages where it is easy to separate text (foreground) from the background. Today, more and more information is transformed into digital forms. Visual texts appear in many forms of digital media, such as images and videos. Unfortunately, these simple tasks do not meet the most common needs of the users of multimedia document analysis today. It is evident that when the video images are fed to the current OCR, the character recognition rate typically ranges from 0 % to 45 % due to limitations of the current OCR and the nature of video images [6].

Compared with the text in a typical document, the text in a video frame is in a much smaller quantity. However, these texts in video often give crucial information about the media contents. They usually appear in the form of names, locations, products' brands, scores of a match, date, and time, which are helpful information to understand the video content. The text in the images and videos can be superimposed on arbitrary backgrounds or embedded on the surfaces of the objects in the scene with varying font, size, color, alignment, movement, and lighting condition. Hence, text detection and extraction are extremely difficult. The aim of research on text detection and recognition in images and video focuses on finding a proper way to extract different types of text from videos with arbitrary, complex backgrounds. It will not only extend the application of OCR system into wider multimedia areas but also help people further understand the mechanism of the visual text detection and recognition.

A large number of approaches, such as connected component based, texture based, edge based, and other methods [2–6], have been proposed. Some of these methods have already obtained impressive performance. A majority of text detection and extraction approaches in the literature are developed based on scanned document nature. Although most of them can be adopted for video images, detecting and

Fig. 1.1 Examples of graphics text video fames

Fig. 1.2 Examples of scene text video frames

extracting text in video present unique challenges over that in document images, due to many undesirable properties of video for text detection and extraction problems. Fortunately, text in video usually persists for at least several seconds, to give human viewers sufficient time to read it [4]. This temporal nature of video is very valuable and can be well utilized for text detection, extraction, and recognition in videos.

There are two types of text in video. The first type is caption text which is artificially superimposed on the video during the editing process as shown in Fig. 1.1, where the video frames have graphics/caption/artificial/superimposed text. The second type is scene text which naturally occurs in the field of view of the camera during video capturing as shown in Fig. 1.2, where scene text appears with different backgrounds, orientations, fonts, etc. Figure 1.2 shows that scene text is much more challenging than caption text due to varying lighting, complex movement, and transformation. Text detection and extraction from video are challenging and interesting because of the following variations in the properties of video text.

Text in videos can have many variations with respect to the following properties [2].

1. Geometry

   (a) Size: Although the text size can vary a lot, we can make certain assumptions, depending on the application domain.
   (b) Alignment: The caption texts appear in clusters and are usually in horizontal orientation. Sometimes they can appear as nonplanar text as a result of special effects. On the other hand, scene text can be aligned in any directions and can have geometrical distortions (e.g., perspective distortions).

2. Color: The characters tend to have the same or similar colors. This property makes it possible to use a connected component-based approach for text detection. Most of the research reported till date has concentrated on finding text strings of a single color (monochrome). However, video images and other complex color documents can contain text strings with more than two colors (polychrome), i.e., different colors within one word, to attract visual attention.

3. Motion: The same characters usually exist in consecutive frames in a video, with or without movement. This property is used in text tracking and enhancement. Caption text usually has uniform motions, e.g., horizontally or vertically. On the other hand, scene text can have arbitrary motion due to camera and object movement.

4. Edge: Most caption and scene texts are designed to be readable. Thus, there are usually strong edges at the boundaries of text and background.

5. Compression: Many digital images are recorded, transferred, and processed in a compressed format. Thus, a faster text extraction system can be achieved if one can extract text without decompression.

To solve this video text detection and extraction problem, the method is generally divided into the following stages: (1) text detection, finding regions in a video frame that contains text; (2) text localization, grouping text regions into text instances and generating a set of tight bounding boxes around all text instances; (3) text tracking, following a text event as it moves or changes over time and determining the temporal and spatial locations and extents of text events; (4) text binarization, binarizing the texts bounded by text regions defining boxes and marking text pixels with one and background pixels with zero (or vice versa); and (5) text recognition, performing OCR on the binarized text image. A block diagram showing the above stages is given in Fig. 1.3. Among these stages, text detection and text localization are important and have attracted much research attention because the final text recognition accuracy depends on these steps.

Fig. 1.3 Block diagram of
the text extraction system [2]

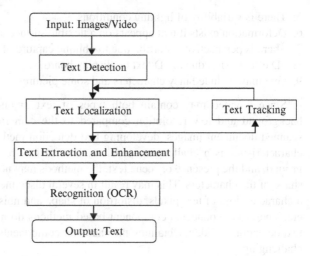

1.2   Characteristics and Difficulties of Video Text Detection

As mentioned in the previous section, a video may contain both graphics and scene text. Since graphics text is manually edited, graphics text can have good clarity and contrast and is often in the horizontal direction without much distortion [3]. Therefore, to detect graphics text, the method can take advantages of the following properties or characteristics similar to those of text in scanned document image:

1. Text is always in the foreground and is never foreground occluded.
2. Usually it is with suitable lighting condition, which is scene independent.
3. The values of the text pixels are distributed according to limited rules.
4. Size, font, spacing, and orientation are constant within the text region.
5. Text is normally aligned horizontally.
6. All text pixels in the same text line have the same or almost the same color.
7. Text pixels have a higher contrast compared to its background.
8. Most of the time, text appears at the bottom of the frame.
9. Text is grouped as sets of words rather than isolated characters.
10. Text is either stationary or linearly moving in horizontal or vertical direction.
11. The background is usually uniform for moving text.
12. The same text appears in several consecutive frames.
13. Text has low resolution.

On the other hand, scene text exhibits the following characteristics:

1. Text may be embedded within objects with cluttered background.
2. There is variability of size, font, color, orientation, style, and alignment, even within the same word.
3. Part of the text may be occluded due to object and camera movements.
4. There may be complex movement in the scene.

5. There is variability of lighting conditions.
6. Deformation exists if text appears on a flexible surface such as clothing.
7. There is perspective distortion due to oblique capture of the camera.
8. 3D effect exists due to 3D text on display board.
9. Text may include fancy characters and some pictures.

Since a video may contain both types of text in one frame, with complex background and low resolution compared to the camera-captured document or scanned document images, developing text detection methods based on the above characteristics is a challenging problem. Due to low resolution, complex background, and the presence of scene text, the methods may not be able to preserve the shape of the characters. This may result in several disconnected components within a character, loss of text pixels, distortion of shape and noisy pixels due to shadow, etc. Therefore, connected component-based methods do not give good results for text detection in video. Obtaining the character components without losing shape is challenging.

Several methods have been developed based on contrast information and texture of text by defining text as a special texture to overcome the problems of low contrast and complex background. As long as text has high contrast and regular patterns based on the shapes of the character components, these methods give good results. However, handling the variation in fonts, size, occlusion, and text-like features in background is still a challenging problem.

Machine learning-based methods often use classifiers, which are trained on labeled samples and/or unlabelled samples, to classify pixels as text and non-text by using features described. Due to unconstrained variation of non-text regions, these methods use a large number of samples to cope with these variations. This leads to more computational burden. In addition, choosing samples for non-text pattern is not straightforward.

To enhance low-contrast text in video, some methods propose to use temporal frames to sharpen text pixels on the basis that temporal frames contain the same text for a few seconds and the text is static. Simple operations such as averaging, median, minimum, and maximum are not sufficient to increase the contrast of text pixels as these operations sometimes blur the edges instead of sharpening them due to small variation in intensity values. Another issue is that choosing the number of temporal frames to improve the quality of the image is not adequately addressed. Some methods choose the number of frames randomly in a rather ad hoc way. This leads to poor results. In addition, there is no validation algorithm to measure the quality of the image given by the method. Therefore, the use of temporal information is still a research problem for text detection and tracking through enhancement.

Some methods are developed based on edge strength and gradient information on the basis that edge strength is high at or near the edge of a text stroke. This assumption makes the algorithms more efficient and accurate compared to texture-based and connected component-based methods. Defining edge strength and gradient for pixels in cluttered backgrounds is the main problem for these methods. Therefore, although these methods are fast and give good results, they also produce more false positives because the defined properties may also be satisfied by objects like leaves, windows of buildings, etc.

Some authors proposed methods by combining different features and properties of text such as color and edge strength with different classifiers, to classify between text and non-text. Though the methods may give good results with the right choice of features, current challenges with these methods lie in finding which features contribute to the classification results. In other words, there is no clear basis in combining different classifiers.

Most methods and researchers generally assume horizontal text lines. They tend to ignore the problem of text lines appearing in arbitrary orientations in video because of the complexity in dealing with varying text orientation. Most methods developed to address this issue are based on grouping of connected components using textual features and nearest neighbor criteria. As long as the space between text lines is sufficient, these methods work well. Otherwise, they may end up in grouping two nearby text lines and the background between them into one region.

In summary, although many methods have been developed, none of them give perfect solution to text detection, especially for 3D texts and texts affected by severe perspective distortion. More details on the respective methods will be discussed in Chaps. 2 and 3.

1.3 Relationship Between Video Text Detection and Other Fields

Text detection involves several fields, namely, computer vision, image processing, pattern recognition, document image analysis, artificial intelligence, multimedia, and system design to make a complete system and a working model.

Text detection in video is an extension of document analysis in the sense that the word text is to be extracted and recognized just like a document analysis task. Text analysis, layout analysis, and text recognition with the help of OCR are the successful applications in document analysis. As discussed in Sects. 1.1 and 1.2, text in video share the same properties as text in documents. The process of separating foreground (i.e., text) and background in video for text recognition is the same as that in document analysis. To improve video text recognition, most researchers use binarization methods in document analysis with modification. The only difference is that text in document images has high resolution and high contrast and with clean background, whereas text in video can have any resolution and contrast and can be embedded in a complex background. Thus, text detection for document analysis has to be further extended and enhanced for video text.

When we consider a video frame as an image, then we need to perform image processing operation in order to extract the features to detect text. The above features/characteristics are extracted using image processing tools and techniques such as gradient computation, edge detection, color analysis, wavelet coefficients analysis, Fourier coefficients analysis, morphological operations, etc.

Nowadays, many researchers make use of recent methods in computer vision to extract features for video text detection. Examples are SIFT, HOG, SURF, super pixels, and MSER. According to the literature, these features are stable features compared to traditional features as they are robust against distortion and geometrical transformation. These features are now widely used for text detection in video, and it is a trend in this field.

Feature extraction is meaningful when it does some classification and recognition. The classification and recognition are done by pattern recognition-based methods such as supervised classifiers (SVM, neural networks, Bayesian, etc.) and unsupervised classifiers (clustering, discriminative analysis, etc.). Features are extracted in the same way, but supervised learning requires labeled samples while unsupervised learning can be applied to unlabeled samples. To facilitate text detection, preprocessing such as classification of text and non-text pixels and identification of true text blocks are done by pattern recognition methods.

The applications of video text detection require real-time systems. For instance, by detecting and recognizing text and road signs automatically, a system can help the visually impaired to walk on roads. Therefore, text detection and recognition requires support of hardware and graphical user interface in order to be of practical use.

Sometimes, recognition of characters, words, and text lines may not be sufficient to develop intelligent systems. Therefore, methods should be capable of studying user feedback, data, and context automatically to understand real-world situations. For this, text detection method requires knowledge-based and other artificial intelligence approaches.

Text detection is part of multimedia applications which involve information retrieval and events retrieval. As discussed earlier, content-based image retrieval methods are good for retrieving images based on some similarity and dissimilarity measures with the query image. However, they are not adequate in retrieving whole events containing video clip as similarity/dissimilarity measures fail to capture the semantics of the video contents. Text detection and recognition can be used together with video features such as audio and motion for automatic annotation of video events. For example, to retrieve an event related to birthday, analyzing image contents alone will not necessarily identify it as a birthday event. However, detection and recognition of text such as "Happy Birthday" and a personal name on the cake or some decorative banner will enable identification of a birthday event. In this way, text detection and multimedia fields complement each other.

1.4   A Brief History of Video Text Detection

The origin of video text detection research may be traced to document image analysis because of its core techniques in optical character recognition (OCR). The need for optical character recognition, in fact, arose well before the advent of digital computers which were invented to represent and process information that traditionally appeared on papers. Patents on optical character recognition, for reading aids for the blind and for input to the telegraph, were filed in the nineteenth century, and working models were demonstrated by 1916. However, the field of document image analysis itself is only about 40 years old [6, 7]. OCR on specifically designed printed digits (OCR fonts) was first used in business in the 1950s. The first postal address reader and the social security administration machine to read typewritten earnings reports were installed in 1965. Devices to read typeset material and simple hand-printed forms came into their own in the 1980s, when the prices of OCR systems dropped by a factor of 10 due to the advent of microprocessors, bit-mapped displays, and solid state scanners.

Some of the early stages of processing scanned documents were independent of the type of document. Many noise filtering, binarization, edge extraction, and segmentation methods could be applied equally well to printed or handwritten text, line drawing, or maps. Half-tone images require specialized treatment. Connected component analysis is often the starting point here. Once a document is segmented into its constituent components, more specific techniques are needed. Traditionally, the field has been divided into two areas, namely, processing of mostly text documents and processing of mostly graphics documents. Pages of mostly text documents are segmented into columns, paragraph blocks, text lines, words, and characters. OCR then converts the individual word or character images into a character code like ASCII or Unicode. But there is much more to a text document than just a string of symbols. Additional and sometimes essential information is conveyed at the same time by long established conventions of layout and format, choice of type size and typeface, italic and boldface, and the two-dimensional arrangement of tables and formulas. To capture the whole meaning of documents, document image analysis must extract and interpret all of these subtle encoding schemes.

Engineering drawing, maps, music scores, schematic diagrams, and organization of charts are examples of mostly graphics documents. Line drawings are decomposed into straight lines and curve segments, junctions, and crossings before high-level components, such as dimensions, center lines, and cross-hatching, can be interpreted. Maps may require color separation and association of text (labels) with many symbols. Line drawings typically contain a great deal of lettering that must be located, perhaps isolated and recognized.

There are two major approaches to document image analysis, namely, top-down versus bottom-up analysis. In mostly text document processing, top-down analysis attempts to find larger components, like columns and paragraph blocks before proceeding to the text line and word levels. Bottom-up analysis forms words into text lines, lines into paragraphs, and so on. Because black pixels are usually a much smaller fraction of a line drawing than of text, most techniques for graphics are bottom-up approaches. The distinction is elusive because both methods must access individual pixels, runs, or connected components.

Document image understanding is the formal representation of the abstract relationships indicated by the two-dimensional arrangements of symbols within a document. Domain-specific knowledge appears essential for document interpretation.

To the best of our knowledge, no one has ever attempted to develop systems to interpret arbitrary documents. Both model-driven and data-driven approaches have been investigated. Models have been developed for formulas, equations, business forms, tables, flow charts, mechanical drawings, circuit schematics, music symbols, and chess notations. Some of these models reflect the properties of natural language, while others have domain-specific constraints, like correspondence between a dimension statement and the radius of an arc, the rule that determines whether an equation is properly formed, and relationships between the fields of an invoice.

Since the 1960s, much research in document processing has been done based on optical character recognition. Some OCR machines which were used in specific domains started to appear in the commercial market. The study of automatic text segmentation and discrimination started about three decades ago. With the rapid development of modern computer technology and the increasing need for large volume of data, automatic text segmentation and discrimination have been widely studied since the early 1980s [9–11]. In the period of 1980–1995, a lot of methods were proposed, and many document processing systems were proposed. About 500 papers were presented at the international conference on document analysis (ICDAR' 91, ICDAR' 93, and ICDAR's 95), and there were special issues of journals such as Machine Vision and Applications that specifically dealt with document analysis and understanding. There was a rapid growth of papers that dealt with new development in this area as shown in the references.

Within another decade, optical disks and tape cartridges had attained sufficient capacity, at a reasonable price, for storing thousands of document images in the form of compressed bitmaps. Interest grew quickly in converting them to computer-searchable form. In 1999, document imaging, i.e., electronic document storage without sophisticated image manipulation, is a billion-dollar business, but document analysis, when considered as document image interpretation, is still only a small part of it. This is where document image analysis had gained increasing attention from researchers who found new applications where document image analysis played a vital role. With such rapid increase in applications, document images have become a powerful medium for transferring knowledge. In fact, much knowledge is acquired from documents such as technical reports, government files, newspapers, books, journals, magazines, letters, and bank checks, just to name a few. The acquisition of knowledge from such documents by an information system can involve an extensive amount of handcrafting. Such handcrafting is time consuming and can severely limit the applications of information systems. Actually, it is a bottleneck in information systems. Thus, automatic knowledge acquisition from documents has become an important subject [8]. One of the most interesting applications where document image analysis is essential is postal automation.

The increasing volume of mails handled by the postal services, coupled with the rising labor costs, has made postal automation imperative. It is widely recognized that the most viable solution to the problem of postal automation is a machine vision system which can parse and interpret the addresses on incoming mail pieces and sort them appropriately. Automatic sorting machines for letters have been in existence for several years. The technology of OCR used in such systems is well established though correct recognition rate has been reported to be only about 55 % [12]. The main reason for this poor performance is the inability of the recognition system to locate the address block correctly. Automatic sorting of other mail pieces, such as color magazines and parcels, becomes even more challenging because of the random positioning of pasted address labels as well as graphics and other printed materials present on these objects. On most magazine covers, the color of the pasted or printed address label is white and quite different from the background. In these situations, it is easy to identify the address blocks based on its color and size properties. However, when the address label is pasted or printed in a region of similar color, the problem of automatically identifying the address block becomes more difficult.

Several approaches have been proposed for solving the problem of automatic address block location on mail pieces. A good review of these approaches can be found in [13]. Among them, a texture segmentation method based on multichannel Gabor filters has been used successfully [14]. The same method is extended in [12] to deal with more complex images of magazines covers. This method is robust to variations in orientation and scale of relatively low-resolution input images. It also can deal with handwritten as well as printed address blocks. The address block segmentation on mail pieces led to the exploration of a new area in document image analysis, namely, locating text in complex background images, such as CD cover, book cover, etc., amidst challenges in universal image understanding system. In a complex image, characters cannot be easily segmented by simple thresholding, where the color, size, font, and orientation of the text are unknown.

Image segmentation into coherent regions is an important preprocessing step before applying an object recognition method. In the case of document image analysis, prior to OCR, the characters must be extracted from the image. Applications of locating and recognizing text include address localization on envelopes, scanning and understanding a printed document, and identifying products (such as books, CDs, canned food, etc.) by reading the text on their covers of labels. Another application area of a text understanding system is in image database retrieval, where the capabilities of usual textual database system are extended to image databases. Given a user's request, the system must retrieve all images in the database which match a text pattern (or generally, any kind of image pattern). A query by image content (QBIC) database system allows retrieval of images from the database based on image content. An example of QBIC is a trademark image database which allows checking of possible infringement by searching whether new trademark is very similar to any of the thousands of existing trademarks in the database. Incorporating text recognition in such a QBIC system enhances and facilitates faster retrieval of similar trademarks as many trademarks contain text in addition to logos.

Detecting and extracting text over complicated background such as in trademark images and in other document page images in general can be a challenging task. A simple thresholding will only work if the background is plain and uniform in color. Considering a full-page document, page layout segmentation is necessary to discriminate text areas from figures (half tones). The difference between text and figures is obvious to a human reader. It is, however, difficult to formalize for an automatic system, and therefore, various heuristics have been used in different page segmentation methods.

The most intuitive characteristic of text is its regularity. Printed text consists of characters with approximately the same size and the same stroke thickness. Characters are located about the same distance from each other, they are organized into lines of the same height, and the lines usually form columns that are justified from the two sides. Such regularities have been used implicitly by considering text regions as having a certain texture with frequency components distinct from those of a grayscale figure. The regular alignment of characters into lines and columns has been used explicitly, where text lines are assumed to form rectangles with distinct shapes, and different lines are to be separated by white regions with no black pixels. These methods have been successfully applied to obtain page layout of technical journals. To extract characters from a more complex scene, the connected components approach has been used in [15]. The image is first segmented into candidate character regions using adaptive thresholding and connected component analysis. A component then can be accepted as a character (or a part of character) by applying additional heuristics or simply classifying it with an OCR system which has a reject option for noncharacter class. We note that in a general setting, it is impossible to extract text or characters from a complex scene without first recognizing it. However, feeding an OCR system with all possible components in an input image is not reasonable because a typical image may contain thousands of components. Therefore, the approach is to segment the image into text/non-text as best as possible and then let the OCR system do the detailed refinement. With this intention, Zhong et al. [16] propose two approaches for extracting text. The first approach is based on segmenting the color image into connected components of uniform color and using various heuristics to reduce the number of candidate characters. The second approach locates the text line rather than individual characters by using difference of spatial gray value variance inside the text regions and the background. A hybrid method, which combines the two approaches, is then proposed to extract text from complex scene images.

Over the past 40 years, document image processing and understanding have progressed beyond the initial work on OCR. Today, the field has covered many different areas including preprocessing, physical and logical layout analysis, optical and intelligent character recognition, graphics analysis, form processing, signature verification, and writer identification. The research results have found many practical applications, including office automation, forensics, and digital libraries. For many years, the methods mainly focused on scanned document images because that was perhaps the only most widely used device available for document image capture. Therefore, traditionally, document images were obtained by scanning from pseudo-binary hardcopy paper manuscripts with a flatbed, sheet-fed, or mounted imaging device. In the last decade or so, however, a new and popular mode of document image capture has emerged, namely, through the use of digital cameras, PC-cams, and cell phone cameras. Although they cannot replace scanners, these devices are small, light, and easily integrated with networks and are much more handy for many document capturing tasks in less constrained environments. Unlike scanned document images, camera-captured document images are subject to distortion such as uneven illumination, folded pages, perspective vision, etc. As a result, document image analysis has to deal with a new set of research problems arising from camera-based document images in recent years.

The industry has sensed this direction and is shifting some of the scanner-based OCR applications onto new platforms. For example, XEROX has a desktop PC-cam OCR suit, based on their Cam Works project, aimed at replacing scanners with PC-cams in light workload environments. The digital Desk project turns the desktop into a digital working area through the use of cameras and projectors. Meanwhile, another new set of problems arises from camera-based images not from document images but rather outdoor pictures as some natural scenes contain text such as road signs, billboards, building signs, and advertisements. While techniques for text extraction and recognition for document images may appear applicable to natural scene text, it was realized that scene text presents new challenges due to problems such as complex background and perspective distortion. Since then, there has been active research in natural scene text extraction and recognition. While scene text analysis involves a single image, a related research problem is how the techniques may be applied to scene text in image sequences in video. Video scene text detection presents even greater challenges because of the low resolution of video images. A survey paper in 2003 on camera-based scene text detection [5] projected future interests of the document analysis community in video scene text detection. While scene text detection in video is relatively new and challenging, there is actually another kind of text present in video images which is comparatively easier to deal with than scene text in video. This kind of text pertains to graphics texts artificially added into video frames as video captions, movie titles, film credits, news flashes, etc. These texts tend to be prominent with uniform background. Way back in the later part of 1990s, there were already attempts to extract graphics text from video. Kim in 1996 [17] was probably the first to propose to locate graphics text in video by exploring the color information of text components using color clustering in a color histogram in the RGB space. Since several threshold values needed to be determined empirically, this approach was not suitable as a general-purpose text localizer. Shim et al. [18] used homogeneity of intensity of text regions in video images. Pixels with similar gray levels are merged into groups based on heuristics. These heuristics work well as long as the text has uniform-sized fonts and components. Lienhart et al. [19, 20] treated text regions as connected components based on the fact that text components have the same or similar colors and sizes. The input image was therefore segmented based on the monochromatic nature of text components using a split-and-merge algorithm. Their primary focus was on caption text, such as pre-title sequences, credit titles, and closing sequences, which exhibit a higher contrast with the background. This made it easy to use the contrast difference between the boundary of the detected components and their background in the filtering stage. There were many other methods [21–30] developed during the late 1990s to early 2000s that mainly aimed at graphics text extraction.

Recent research interests are now directed at the ability to deal with both graphics and scene texts present together in the same video stream. Shivakumara et al. [31–39] have proposed a host of methods to deal with graphics and scene text. Scene text often suffers from complex background in addition to the problem of low resolution that plagues both the graphics and scene texts. Thus, their methods essentially use edge-enhancing techniques such as wavelet or Laplacian operators to identify text edges amidst interfering background.

While many video text detection methods have traditionally assumed horizontal or vertical alignment of text, there are recent attempts to tackle the problem of multi-oriented text in video. Shivakumara et al. [40–43] proposed several techniques to deal with this problem. One of the techniques makes use of boundary growing based on a nearest neighbor concept. Another method leverages on skeletonization. These methods allow text to grow in an arbitrary direction rather than basing on horizontal or vertical projection.

The above historical development has led to the present-day intensive research in video text detection. This is the main objective of this book to introduce to the reader this exciting field of research in meeting challenges in locating and recognizing graphics and scene text in video. The subsequent chapters of this book will provide all the necessary details of the respective methodologies.

1.5   Potential Applications

Today, an enormous amount of information is stored in various kinds of digital forms including images and videos. TV broadcasting, the Internet, and digital media have revolutionized modern-day living with a deluge of multimedia information. One particular problem is the difficulty in managing a wide range of information sources. The ability to extract text from multimedia information has practical applications in dealing with information overload. The following are some examples of such applications.

Text-Based Image and Video Indexing: Efficient descriptors are needed for indexing and retrieving of images and videos. Low-level features-based content representations, such as color and texture, are difficult for users to input as keys for indexing and retrieving. In addition, indexing and retrieving methods based on these low-level features are not as efficient as text-based search engines. In contrast, most of the high-level content descriptions, such as human face, body, physical objects, and activities, in images and videos are not only difficult to be represented but also not amenable to matching for the purpose of retrieval. On the other hand, as a form of high-level representation, text provides more precise and explicit meaning and easier description of the content than low-level and other high-level visual features. Text therefore provides a natural means for indexing and retrieving by using text-based search engines and OCR system.

A powerful source of information is the text contained in images and videos. Superimposed captions in news videos usually provide information about the names of related people, location, subject, date, and time. Captions also often provide an abstract or summary of the program. This information is often not available in other media like audio "track." Titles and credits displayed at the beginning or end of movies provide information like names of actors, producers, contributors, etc. Captions in sports program often contain the names of teams, players, scores, etc. Text information can also be found in the scene, e.g., the players' ID numbers and names, the names of the teams, brand names, locations, and commercials. Displayed maps, figures, and tables in video contain text about locations, temperatures, and certificate items. Titles, logos, and names of programs displayed in video are important for annotation with respect to the program types and titles. License plates and brand names of vehicles and text on paper documents such as CD covers, books, and journals in a video stream are also valuable sources of information.

Many websites today display images, photographs, and videos on their web pages. If the text in these images and videos can be detected and recognized, they will provide added indexing information for search engines to reach these websites. Both the text-based searching and matching technologies are mature technologies. Text-based search engines have been well developed to address the problem of automatic and efficient document retrieval. Coupling text-based search engines with video text recognition using OCR technologies will therefore provide a promising solution for indexing and retrieving images and videos and hence enhancing the search capability of search engines. However, current OCR technologies, though very successful for document images, are not able to recognize text in images and video due to complex background in natural scenes and low resolution in video. Results in video text recognition research will have wide implication to future video and image search and retrieval.

Content-Oriented Video Coding: Besides indexing and retrieval, another application of media text detection and recognition is content-oriented multimedia coding. Since text carries clear information to the viewers, text texture should be carefully processed when images and videos are compressed. The text texture can be extracted from images and videos as a kind of visual object and encoded with special algorithms to achieve higher compression rate or image quality. Furthermore, text objects can be recognized into text and applied in MPEG-4 SNHC (synthetic and natural hybrid coding) with proper synthesis algorithms. Media text detection and recognition offers an opportunity to extract text objects in video.

Applications on the Internet and Digital Libraries: Media OCR can be applied to the Internet and digital libraries. Typical applications in these areas include the following:

- Transcription and acoustic output of text for blind WWW users
- Conversion of documents into electronic versions
- Conversion of paper-based advertisement into electronic form to automatically generate its electronic equivalent for WWW publication

Assisting Visually Impaired People: Text in video can be used for assisting the visually impaired to walk on roads. For instance, they can wear a device which is capable of capturing texts of sign boards, street names, etc. The text recognition algorithm helps in converting text into speech. The main challenge is that texts on sign boards and street names are usually scene text which can have any orientations, background, and distortion. The text recognition algorithm should be invariant to those distortions.

Traffic and Cargo Movement Monitoring: Recognition of text on vehicles' number plates can be of use in traffic monitoring, such as in checking of traffic offenses, road toll and parking fee charging, accident management, and so on. Container cargos carry identification texts which are amenable for text recognition to facilitate cargo movement control and monitoring as part of the container port management system.

Assisting Tourists: Video text detection and recognition is useful in guiding tourists to visit sightseeing venues. With the help of GPS and Google maps, tourists can easily find the locations of interest. For each location, they can find several street names, building names, park names, etc., along with directions of the road map. With built-in machine translation capability, text recognition from road signs or billboards in a foreign country can be automatically translated after text extraction to assist tourists in navigating in unfamiliar roads.

Automation in Supermarkets: In supermarkets or malls, searching for items can be time consuming. In a futuristic supermarket, automatic text recognition system can recognize names on items along with their locations as a customer service. If the customer knows the location of an item, he or she need not go to that location but rather send a robot with text reading capability to bring the item to the counter to pay money and collect it.

Merchandise Movement in Industry: In the construction and transport industry, monitoring of merchandise movement can be automated if there is text recognition capability on ID imprints on merchandise. For instance, text recognition of dates and labels on wooden slabs enables computerized movement control and monitoring, thus dispensing with the time-consuming and labor-intensive process of manual reading and recording.

References

1. Sun Q-Y, Lu Y (2012) Text location in scene images using visual attention model. Int J Pattern Recogn Artif Intell 26(04):1–22
2. Jung K, Kim KI, Jain AK (2004) Text information extraction in images and video: a survey. Pattern Recogn 37:977–997
3. Chen D, Luttin J, Shearer K (2000) A survey of text detection and recognition in images and videos, IDIAP research report, pp 1–21
4. Zhang J, Kasturi R (2008) Extraction of text objects in video documents: recent progress. In: Proceedings of the eighth IAPR workshop on document analysis systems (DAS), pp 5–17
5. Doremann D, Liang J, Li H (2003) Progress in camera-based document image analysis. In: Proceedings of the seventh international conference on document analysis and recognition (ICDAR)
6. Chen D, Odobez JM (2005) Video text recognition using sequential Monte Carlo and error voting methods. Pattern Recogn Lett 1386–1403

7. Nagy G (2000) Twenty years of document image analysis. IEEE Trans Pattern Anal Mach Intel (PAMI) 38–62
8. Tang YY, Lee SW, Suen CY (1996) Automatic document processing: a survey. Pattern Recogn 1931–1952
9. Abele L, Wahl F, Scheri W (1981) Procedures for an automatic segmentation of text graphics and halftone regions in document, Scandinavian conference on image analysis, pp 177–182
10. Toyoda J, Noguchi Y, Nishmiura Y (1982) Study of extracting Japanese newspaper. Int Conf Pattern Recog 1113–1115
11. Wong IY, Casey RG, Wahl FM (1982) Document analysis system. IBM Res Dev 647–656
12. Jain AK, Chen Y (1994) Address block location using color and texture analysis, CVGIP. Image Underst 179–190
13. Jain AK, Bhattcharjee SK (1992) Address block location using Gabor filters. Pattern Recogn 1459–1477
14. Jain AK, Farrokhina F (1991) Unsupervised texture segmentation using Gabor filter. Pattern Recogn 1167–1186
15. Ohya J, Shio A, Akamatsu S (1994) Recognizing characters in scene images. IEEE Trans Pattern Anal Mach Intel (PAMI) 214–224
16. Zhong Y, Karu K, Jain AK (1995) Locating text in complex color images. Pattern Recogn 1523–1535
17. Kim HK (1996) Efficient automatic text location method and content-based indexing and structuring of video database. J Vis Commun Image Represent 7:336–344
18. Shim JC, Dorai C, Bolle R (1998) Automatic text extraction from video for content-based annotation and retrieval. In: Proceedings of international conference on pattern recognition (ICPR), vol 1, pp 618–620
19. Lienhart R, Stuber F (1996) Automatic text recognition in digital videos. In: Proceedings of SPIE, pp 180–188
20. Lienhart V, Effelsberg W (1998) Automatic text segmentation and text recognition for video indexing, Technical Report TR-98-009, PraktscheInformatik IV, University of Mannhein
21. Jain AK, Yu B (1998) Automatic text location in images and video frames. Pattern Recogn 31:2055–2076
22. Wu V, Manmatha R, Risean EM (1999) Text finder: an automatic system to detect and recognize text in images. IEEE Trans Pattern Anal Mach Intell (PAMI) 21:1224–1229
23. Wu V, Manmatha R, Risean EM (1997) Finding text in images. In: Proceedings of ACM international conference on digital libraries, pp 1–10
24. Mao W, Chung F, Lanm K, Siu W (2002) Hybird Chinese/English text detection in images and video frames. In: Proceedings of the international conference on pattern recognition (ICPR), vol 3, pp 1015–1018
25. Jeong KY, Jung K, Kim EY Kim JJ (1999) Neural network-based text location for news video indexing. In: Proceedings of the international conference on image processing (ICIP), pp 319–323
26. Jung K, Kim K, Kurata T, Kourogi M, Han J (2002) Text scanner with text detection technology on image sequence. In: Proceedings of the international conference on pattern recognition (ICPR), vol 3, pp 473–476
27. Kim KI, Jung J, Park SH, Kim HJ (2001) Support vector machine-based text detection in digital video. Pattern Recogn 34:527–529
28. Li H, Doermann D (2000) A video text detection system based on automated training. In: Proceedings of the international conference on pattern recognition (ICPR), pp 223–226
29. Li H, Doerman D, Kia O (2000) Automatic text detection and tracking in digital video. IEEE Trans Pattern Anal Mach Intell (PAMI) 9:147–156
30. Chen D, Shearer K, Bourlard H (2001) Text enhancement with asymmetric filter for video OCR. In: Proceedings of the international conference on image analysis and processing, pp 192–197
31. Shivakumara P, Phan TQ, Tan CL (2009) A robust wavelet transform based technique for video text detection. In: Proceedings of ICDAR, pp 1285–1289

32. Shivakumara P, Phan TQ, Tan CL (2010) New fourier-statistical features in RGB space for video text detection. IEEE Trans Circ Syst Video Technol (TCSVT) 20:1520–1532
33. Shivakumara P, Phan TQ, Tan CL(2010) New wavelet and color features for text detection in video. In: Proceedings of ICPR, pp 3996–3999
34. Shivakumara P, Dutta A, Tan CL, Pal U (2010) A new wavelet-median-moment based method for multi-oriented video text detection. In: Proceedings of DAS, pp 279–288
35. Shivakumara P, Phan TQ, Tan CL (2011) A laplacian approach to multi-oriented text detection in video. IEEE Trans Pattern Anal Mach Intell (TPAMI) 33:412–419
36. Shivakumara P, Huang W, Tan CL (2008) An efficient edge based technique for text detection in video frames. In: Proceedings of the international workshop on document analysis systems (DAS2008), pp 307–314
37. Shivakumara P, Huang W, Tan CL (2008) Efficient video text detection using edge features. In: Proceedings of the international conference on pattern recognition (ICPR08)
38. Shivakumara P, Phan TQ, Tan CL (2009) Video text detection based on filters and edge analysis. In: Proceedings of ICME, 2009, pp 514–517
39. Shivakumara P, Phan TQ, Tan CL (2009) A gradient difference based technique for video text detection. In: Proceedings of ICDAR, 2009, pp 156–160
40. Phan TQ, Shivakumara P, Tan CL (2009) A Laplacian method for video text detection. In: Proceedings of ICDAR, pp 66–70
41. Shivakumara P, Huang W, Trung PQ, Tan CL (2010) Accurate video text detection through classification of low and high contrast images. Pattern Recogn 43:2165–2185
42. Shivakumara P, Sreedhar RP, Phan TQ, Shijian L, Tan CL (2012) Multi-oriented video scene text detection through Bayesian classification and boundary growing. IEEE Trans Circ Syst Video Technol (TCSVT) 22:1227–1235
43. Sharma N, Shivakumara P, Pal U, Blumenstein M, Tan CL (2012) A new method for arbitrarily-oriented text detection in video. In: Proceedings of DAS, pp 74–78

Chapter 2
Video Preprocessing

Video text detection is one of the hot spots in pattern recognition, and a variety of approaches have been proposed for various real-life applications such as content-based retrieval, broadcast or game video analysis, license plate detection, and even address block location. However, in spite of such extensive studies, it is still not easy to design a general-purpose method [1]. This is because there are so many possibilities when extracting video texts that have variations in font style, size, color, orientation, and alignment or from a textured background with low contrast. Moreover, suppose the input of a text detection system is a sequence of video frames, the texts in the frames may or may not move, and the video itself can be in low resolution. These variations make the problem of automatic video text detection extremely difficult, and we thus need video preprocessing to reduce the complexity of the succeeding steps probably consisting of video text detection, localization, extraction, tracking, reconstruction, and recognition.

Figure 2.1 shows a few typical preprocessing stages in video text detection [2]. After inputting an original video frame (Fig. 2.1a), image segmentation techniques are employed to theoretically extract all the pixels belonging to text (Fig. 2.1b). Without knowing where and what the characters are, the aim of the segmentation step here is to initially divide the pixels of each frame from a video clip into two classes of regions which do not contain text and regions which potentially contain text. For other methods that consider video scene structures as scene contexts for text detection, a more general segmentation algorithm is potentially required to partition each video scene image into several meaningful parts such as street, building, and sky to reduce the searching space. After segmentation, each video frame can be considered to consist of homogeneous segments. By filtering the monochrome segments whose widths and heights are too large or too small to be instances of video characters (Fig. 2.1c), binarization and dilation are performed as shown in Fig. 2.1d. Sometimes motion analysis is also adopted to detect corresponding character candidate regions from consecutive frames since even stationary text in video may still move by some pixels around its original position from frame to

© Springer-Verlag London 2014
T. Lu et al., *Video Text Detection*, Advances in Computer Vision
and Pattern Recognition, DOI 10.1007/978-1-4471-6515-6_2

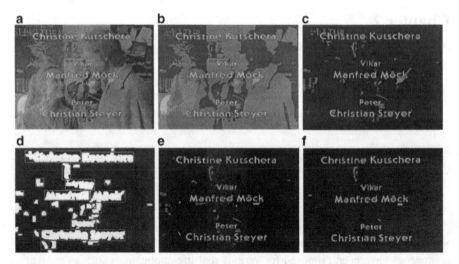

Fig. 2.1 Preprocessing stages for video text detection. (**a**) Original video frame, (**b**) image segmentation, (**c**) after size restriction, (**d**) after binarization and dilation, (**e**) after motion analysis, and (**f**) after contrast analysis and aspect ratio restriction [2]

frame (Fig. 2.1e). Moreover, to solve the problems like occlusion and arbitrary text directions, motion analysis is helpful by tracing text from temporal frames. Finally, image enhancement techniques such as contrast analysis and aspect ratio restriction (Fig. 2.1f) can be employed to obtain better preprocessing results for further video text detection or recognition. For example, the manually added graphics texts usually have a strong contrast between the character regions and their surrounding backgrounds for highlights and human reading. This property makes contrast analysis helpful to decide whether directly discarding a video segment or instead sending the segment for further video text detection and character recognition.

This chapter gives a brief overview of the abovementioned preprocessing techniques that are often used in video text detection. It is organized as follows. We first introduce some image preprocessing operators in Sect. 2.1. Sections 2.2 and 2.3 then discuss color-based and texture-based preprocessing techniques, respectively. Since image segmentation plays an important role in video text detection, we introduce several image segmentation approaches in Sect. 2.4. Next, Sect. 2.5 discusses motion analysis which is helpful to improve the efficiency or the accuracy of video text detection by tracing text from temporal frames. Finally, Sect. 2.6 concludes this chapter.

2.1   Preprocessing Operators

Image (or video frame) preprocessing is the term for operations on images (or video frames) at the lowest level of analysis. Generally, the aim of preprocessing operators for video text detection is an improvement of the image data by suppressing undesired degradations and simultaneously enhancing specific text relevant features. In this section, we will introduce several typical preprocessing operators that are either important for enhancing image features or helpful in suppressing information that is not relevant to video text detection.

2.1.1 Image Cropping and Local Operators

Image cropping is generally the first step after inputting a video frame. In this step, irrelevant parts in the image will be cropped such that further processing focuses on the regions of interest and thereby the computational cost is reduced.

Next, image preprocessing transformations are performed on the rest of the regions. The simplest kind of image preprocessing transformations is *local operator* [3], where the value of each output pixel only depends on that of its corresponding input pixel. Let x be the position of a pixel in an image and $f(x)$ be the value of the pixel; in the continuous domain, a local operator can be represented by

$$h(x) = g(f(x)) \tag{2.1}$$

where the function of g operates over some range, which can either be scalar or vector valued (e.g., for color images or 2D motion). The commonly used local operators are multiplication and addition with constants [4]:

$$g(x) = af(x) + b \tag{2.2}$$

where the two parameters of a and b can be respectively regarded as the gain and the bias parameters. Examples of local operators include *brightness adjustment* and *contrast enhancement* as shown in Fig. 2.2, where the brightness of every pixel in Fig. 2.2a is recalculated by $g(x) = x + 20$ in Fig. 2.2b, while the contrast is enhanced by $g(x) = x * 1.5$ in Fig. 2.2c.

Another commonly used operator is the linear blend operator, which is designed to *cross-dissolve two video frames*:

$$g(x) = (1 - \alpha) f_0(x) + \alpha f_1(x) \tag{2.3}$$

By varying α from 0 to 1, it can essentially be considered as an image morphing algorithm. To automatically determine the best balance between the brightness and the gain control, one approach is to average all the intensity values in a video frame, turn the result to middle gray, and finally expand the range to fill all the displayable values. We can visualize the color of the frame by plotting the histogram of each individual color channel as well as the luminance values [5]. Based on these distributions, relevant statistics such as the minimum, the maximum, and the average intensity values can be computed. Accordingly, histogram equalization can be performed to find an intensity mapping function such that the resulting histogram

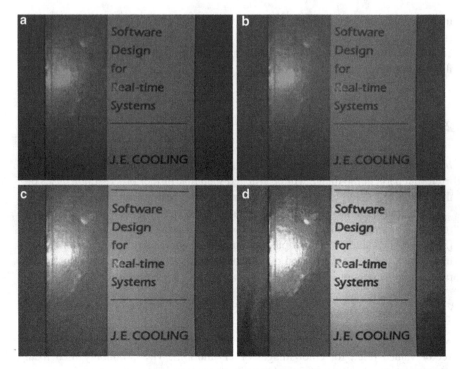

Fig. 2.2 Example local operators for image (video frame) preprocessing. (**a**) Original image, (**b**) the result by increasing the brightness on the original image $g(x) = x + 20$, (**c**) the result by increasing the contrast $g(x) = x * 1.5$, and (**d**) after histogram equalization

is flat. Figure 2.2d shows the result of applying *histogram equalization* on the original image in Fig. 2.2a. As we can see, the resulting image becomes relatively "flat" in the sense of the lacking of contrast.

2.1.2   Neighborhood Operators

Neighborhood operators are often designed to remove noises, sharpen image details, or accentuate image edges. The most commonly used neighborhood operator is *linear filter*, in which the value of an output pixel depends on a weighted sum of the input pixel values by

$$g(i, j) = \sum_{k,l} f(i - k, j - l) h(k, l) \qquad (2.4)$$

where $h(k, l)$ is called the weight kernel or the mask, k and l are two parameters for defining the range of neighbors.

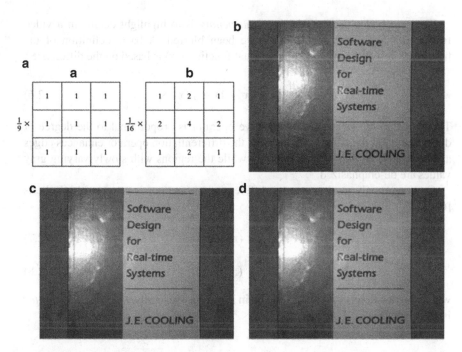

Fig. 2.3 Some example linear filters. (**a**) Two examples of average filters, (**b**) an example video frame with Gaussian noises, (**c**) the result after using the average filter with the second mask in (**a**), and (**d**) the result after using the median filter

The simplest linear filter used in video text detection is the *average filter*, which simply averages all the pixel values in a *K*K* window. It can be used for *noise reduction* or *image blurring* by filling the holes in lines or curves and thus remove unimportant details from an image. In Fig. 2.3, we show two example 3*3 average filters. The first filter *a* in Fig. 2.3a yields the standard average of the pixels under the mask

$$R = \frac{1}{9}\sum_{i=1}^{9} Z_i \qquad (2.5)$$

which is the average of the gray levels of the pixels in the 3*3 neighborhood. The second mask *b* in Fig. 2.3a yields a so-called weighted average, which assigns different importance weights to pixels by multiplying different coefficients. *Median filter* is another choice for smoothness, which selects the median value from the neighborhood as the output for each pixel. It can be used to filter certain types of random noises in video frame as well. Figure 2.3b gives an example video frame with Gaussian noises, and Fig. 2.3c shows the result after using the average filter with the mask *b* in Fig. 2.3a. The result after using the median filter is shown in Fig. 2.3d.

The principal objective of *image sharpening* is to highlight details in a video frame or enhance the details that have been blurred. A basic definition of the first-order derivative of a one-dimensional function $f(x)$ is based on the difference

$$\frac{\partial f}{\partial x} = f(x+1) - f(x) \tag{2.6}$$

Theoretically, the value of the derivative operator is proportional to the degree of discontinuity at the point x. In this way, the differentiation operator enhances edges and other discontinuities (e.g., noises), while the regions with slowly varying gray values are de-emphasized.

One commonly used first-order differentiation operator is proposed by Roberts [6] as

$$G_x = (z_9 - z_5) \tag{2.7}$$

$$G_y = (z_8 - z_6) \tag{2.8}$$

where the positions of pixels are shown in Fig. 2.4a. Generally, the *Roberts operator* is calculated by

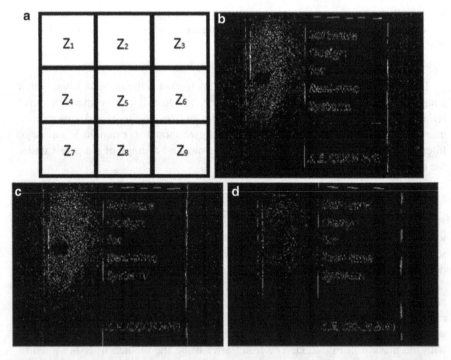

Fig. 2.4 Some filter examples. (**a**) One example table for demonstrating the filters, (**b**) the result example video frame (same with Fig. 2.3b) using Roberts filter, (**c**) the result using Sobel filter, and (**d**) the result using Laplacian filter

$$\nabla f \approx |z_9 - z_5| + |z_8 - z_6| \tag{2.9}$$

which is an approximation to the gradient.

Instead, another commonly used first-order *Sobel operator* [7] approximates the gradient by using absolute values at point z_5 with a 3*3 mask as follows:

$$\nabla f \approx |(z_7 + 2z_8 + z_9) - (z_1 + 2z_2 + z_3)|$$
$$+ |(z_3 + 2z_6 + z_9) - (z_1 + 2z_4 + z_7)| \tag{2.10}$$

where the idea behind is assigning a weight value to achieve smoothing and thereby giving more importance to the center point.

Following the similar idea of the differentiation operator, we can easily define the isotropic derivative operator in the second order by

$$\nabla^2 f = \frac{\partial^2 f}{\partial x^2} + \frac{\partial^2 f}{\partial y^2} \tag{2.11}$$

For image or video frame processing, it can be calculated as the difference between pixels by

$$\frac{\partial^2 f}{\partial x^2} = f(x+1) + f(x-1) - 2f(x) \tag{2.12}$$

which is called the *Laplacian filter*. We show the results filtered from Fig. 2.4 using Roberts, Sobel, and Laplacian operators in Fig. 2.4b–d, respectively.

2.1.3 Morphology Operators

The morphological operators [8] change the shape of an underlying object to facilitate further video text detection or optical character recognition. To perform such an operation, we often need first convert a colorful video frame into a binary image, which has only two elements of either a real foreground or a background complementary with respect to the other. It can be produced after thresholding as follows:

$$\theta(f, c) = \begin{cases} 1 & if\ f > c \\ 0 & else \end{cases} \tag{2.13}$$

We then convolve the binary image with a binary structuring element and accordingly select a binary output value. The structuring element can be any shape, from a simple 3*3 box filter to more complicated disc structures. Let f be the binary image after thresholding, s be the structuring element, S be the size of the structuring element (number of pixels), and $c = f * s$ be the integer-valued count of the number

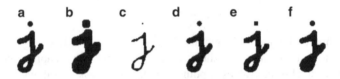

Fig. 2.5 Binary image morphology examples: (**a**) the original image f, (**b**) dilation, (**c**) erosion, (**d**) majority, (**e**) opening, (**f**) closing [4]

of $1s$ inside each structuring element as it is scanned over f; the standard operators for binary morphology can be represented as follows [4]:

1. **Dilation**: $dilate(f,s) = \theta(c, 1)$
2. **Erosion**: $erode(f,s) = \theta(c, S)$
3. **Majority**: $maj(f,s) = \theta(c, S/2)$
4. **Opening**: $open(f,s) = dilate(erode(f,s),s)$
5. **Closing**: $close(f,s) = erode(dilate(f,s),s)$

Figure 2.5b–f shows the results after using the five binary image morphology operators on the original character image f in Fig. 2.5a with a 3 * 3 structuring element s. As we can see from Fig. 2.5, the dilation operator grows (thickens) the character consisting of 1s, while the erosion operator shrinks (thins) it. The opening operator tends to smooth its contour and thus eliminate thin protrusions. The closing operator also tends to smooth contours but simultaneously strengthens thin gulfs and eliminates small holes by filling the gaps on the contour generally.

2.2 Color-Based Preprocessing

Gray or intensity plays an important role in video text analysis. For a binary video frame, it is relatively easy to cluster the pixels in the foreground into blocks which are adjacently linked together and thus segment them from the background for succeeding character recognition. However, for most video frames which can have several objects with different color or gray-level variations in illumination, color-based preprocessing techniques are necessary to reduce the complexity of succeeding video text detection and recognition.

A color image is built of several color channels, each of them indicating the value of the corresponding channel. For example, an RGB image consists of three primary color channels of red, green, and blue; an HSI model has three intuitive color characteristics as hue, saturation, and intensity; while a CMYK image has four independent channels of cyan, magenta, yellow, and black. These color representations are designed for specific devices and have no accurate definitions for a human observer. Therefore, color transformations are required to convert the representation of a color from one color space to another more intuitive one.

For video text detection task, the most common color transformation is the conversion from an RGB color model to a grayscale representation for performing other video preprocessing operators. For an RGB color, the lightness method calculates its grayscale value by

$$\text{gray} = \frac{\max(R, G, B) + \min(R, G, B)}{2} \qquad (2.14)$$

The average method simply averages the RGB values by

$$\text{gray} = \frac{R + G + B}{3} \qquad (2.15)$$

For better human perception, some methods give a weighted average on different RGB channels based on the theory that humans are more sensitive to green than other colors. For example, Hasan and Karam [9] present a morphological approach for text extraction. In their method, the RGB components of a color input image are combined to give

$$\text{gray} = 0.299R + 0.587G + 0.114B \qquad (2.16)$$

Sometimes RGB color needs to be converted to the HIS space for text analysis. The RGB to HSI transformation is

$$\begin{cases} H = \arctan\left(\frac{\beta}{\alpha}\right) \\ S = \sqrt{\alpha^2 + \beta^2} \\ I = (R + G + B)/3 \end{cases} \qquad (2.17)$$

with

$$\begin{cases} \alpha = R - \frac{1}{2}(G + B) \\ \beta = \frac{\sqrt{3}}{2}(G - B) \end{cases} \qquad (2.18)$$

Note that although color transformation is relatively simple and many researchers have adopted it to deal with color video frames, it still faces difficulties especially when the objects in the same video frame have similar grayscale values [1]. Figure 2.6 shows an example, where Fig. 2.6a is a color image and Fig. 2.6b is its corresponding grayscale image. Some text regions that are prominent in the color image become difficult to detect in the gray-level image after color transformation. To solve this problem, Shim et al. [10] use the homogeneity of intensity of text regions in images. Pixels with similar gray levels are merged into a group. After removing significantly large regions by regarding them as background, text regions are sharpened by performing a region boundary analysis based on the gray-level contrast.

Fig. 2.6 Difference between color image and its grayscale image for video text detection: (**a**) color image, (**b**) corresponding grayscale image [1]

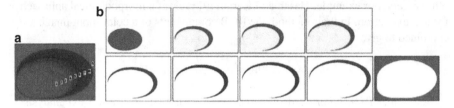

Fig. 2.7 A multicolored image and its element images: (**a**) an input color image, (**b**) nine element images [12]

Color clustering is another frequently adopted technique in video preprocessing. Kim [11] segments an image using color clustering by a color histogram in the RGB space. Non-text components, such as long horizontal lines and image boundaries, can be eliminated, potentially facilitating the tracking of horizontal text lines and text segments. Jain and Yu [12] apply bit dropping on a 24-bit color image to convert it to a 6-bit image and then quantize it by a color clustering algorithm. After the input image is decomposed into multiple foreground images, each foreground image goes through the same text localization stage. Figure 2.7 shows an example of the multi-valued image decomposition in their method.

Finally, other color-based preprocessing techniques like color reduction can also help enhance video frames for text analysis in some cases. For example, Zhong et al. [13] use color reduction to track the connected components (CCs) for text detection. They quantize the color space using the peaks in a color histogram in the RGB color space. This is based on the assumption that the text regions cluster together in this color space and occupy a significant portion of an image. Each text component goes through a filtering stage using heuristics, such as area, diameter, and spatial alignment.

2.3 Texture Analysis

Texture is an important visual clue for video analysis, and a number of texture features have been proposed in the past decades such as Gabor filters, wavelet, FFT, and spatial variance. These texture analysis techniques can potentially be helpful for video text detection by observing the fact that text regions in video frames generally have distinguished textural properties from their backgrounds. In this subsection, we prefer to introduce the situations of the recent research which are related to video text detection, rather than giving a more general introduction to texture analysis techniques.

Generally, along a horizontal scan line in a video frame, a text line consists of several interleaving groups of text pixels and background pixels. Accordingly, in [13], *spatial variances* along every horizontal line are used to distinguish text regions from the background. Another interesting observation on image text is that for a text line, the number of text-to-background and background-to-text transitions should be the same, and these transitions can be obtained by zero crossings of row gradient profiles. Figure 2.8 shows an example, where the left part of the row gradient profile related to a shrimp is irregular compared to the right representing gradients of the string of *that help you* [14]. Thereby, text lines can be found by extracting the rows having regularly alternate edges.

Based on the discussed observations, the *maximum gradient difference* (MGD) text feature for text detection is presented [14]. MGD is defined for any one pixel, as the difference between the max and the min values within a local 1*N window of the gradient image which can be obtained by any gradient extractor. Specifically, MGD is defined as follows:

$$Max(x, y) = \max_{\forall t \in [-\frac{N}{2}, \frac{N}{2}]} g(x, y - t) \tag{2.19}$$

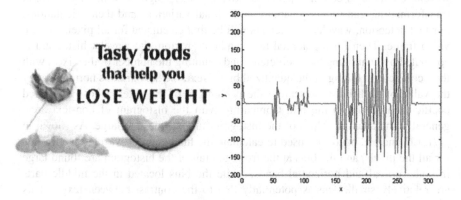

Fig. 2.8 An example image and its gradient profile of the horizontal scan line $x = 80$ [14]

$$Min(x, y) = \min_{\forall t \in [-N/2, N/2]} g(x, y - t) \tag{2.20}$$

$$MGD(x, y) = Max(x, y) - Min(x, y) \tag{2.21}$$

Typically, pixels of text regions have large MGD values, while background regions have small MGD values. The computed MGD values will be helpful to search for potential text regions. For example, Shivakumara et al. [15] use k-means on the computed MGD values to classify pixels into two types of texts that have a higher cluster mean and non-texts that have a relatively lower cluster mean.

Intensity variations also play a useful role in text detection. If we scan horizontal texts row by row, the scan lines of text regions and background regions will be different in their distributions of intensity. Pixels in text regions manifest that the distribution of their intensities are separated with grayscale values of stroke pixels and between-strokes pixels having relatively high contrast, while those of regions below and above text are uniform in intensities within a specific domain. Thereby, the mean and the deviation of grayscale values of potential text segments can be used to merge neighboring top and bottom text lines to form candidate text regions by performing bottom-up and top-down scanning. Sometimes the intensities of raw pixels that make up the textural pattern can be directly fed to a classifier, e.g., the SVM due to its capability of handling high dimensional data. Kim et al. [16] further set a mask to use the intensities of a subset of the raw pixels as the feature vector and accordingly propose a classification-based algorithm for text detection using a sparse representation with discriminative dictionaries.

Wavelet transform techniques first compute texture features through various descriptors and then a classifier will be used to discriminate text and non-text or further respectively cluster them into text and non-text regions by measuring the Euclidian distances between the texture features. Histograms of wavelet coefficients are popular to capture the texture properties in detecting texts. As known, 1-D wavelet coefficients can effectively identify the sharp signals, while 2-D wavelet transformations can properly capture both signal variations and their orientations. For text detection, wavelet coefficients will be first calculated for all pixels in each video frame. Then for a potential text candidate region, the wavelet histogram is computed by quantizing the coefficients and counting the number of the pixels with their coefficients falling in the quantized bins. Next, the histogram is normalized by the value of each bin representing the percentage of the pixels whose quantized coefficient is equal to the bin. Comparing with the histogram of non-text area, generally, the average values of the histogram in text lines are large. As shown in [17], LH and HL bands are used to calculate the histogram of wavelet coefficients for all the pixels, and the bins at the front and tail of the histogram are found large in both vertical and horizontal bands, while the bins located in the middle parts are relatively small. This is potentially due to the contrast between text and its background.

Rather than histograms, the statistical features of wavelet coefficients are also employed to capture the texture property of text in video frames. Such statistical features typically include energy, entropy, inertia, local homogeneity, mean, and the second-order (μ_2) and the third-order (μ_3) central moments of wavelet coefficients shown as follows:

$$energy = \sum_{i,j} W^2(i,j) \qquad (2.22)$$

$$entropy = \sum_{i,j} W(i,j) \log W(i,j) \qquad (2.23)$$

$$inertia = \sum_{i,j} (i-j)^2 W(i,j) \qquad (2.24)$$

$$Homogeneity = \sum_{i,j} \frac{1}{1+(i-j)^2} W(i,j) \qquad (2.25)$$

$$mean = \frac{1}{N^2} \sum_{i,j} W(i,j) \qquad (2.26)$$

$$\mu_2 = \frac{1}{N^2} \sum_{i,j} (W(i,j) - mean)^2 \qquad (2.27)$$

$$\mu_3 = \frac{1}{N^2} \sum_{i,j} (W(i,j) - mean)^3 \qquad (2.28)$$

where $w(i,j)$ is a wavelet coefficient at position (i,j) of the window with the size $N \times N$. Shivakumara et al. [18] use 2-D Haar wavelet decomposition to directly detect video texts based on three high-frequency sub-band images of LH, HL, and HH. After computing features for pixels, k-means algorithm is applied to classify the feature vectors into two clusters of background and text candidates. In [19], the entropy, μ_2, and μ_3 are also used to define the texture feature for text detection. More methods which adopt different wavelets features can be found by referring to [20–22].

Gray-level co-occurrence matrix (GLCM) is another kind of texture feature which is computed over a small square window with size $N*N$ centered at the pixel (x, y). GLCM is a tabulation M encoding how often different combinations of pixel values (gray levels) occur in a frame. Specifically, $M(i, j)$ counts the number of two pixels having particular (co-occurring) gray values of i and j. The distance of these two pixels is d along a given direction θ. When divided by the total number of neighboring pixels along (d, θ) a video frame, the matrix becomes the estimate of the joint probability $p_{(d,\theta)}(i,j)$ of the two pixels. Figure 2.9 shows an example of the construction of the gray-level co-occurrence matrix for $d = 1$, $\theta = \{0°, 180°\}$, and $\theta = \{90°, 270°\}$ [52].

Correlation, *entropy*, and *contrast* of the gray-level co-occurrence matrix are further used in [19] to represent image texture. Correlation is used to model the similarity among the rows or the columns in the matrix, entropy essentially indicates the complexity of image texture by measuring the randomness of the matrix, while

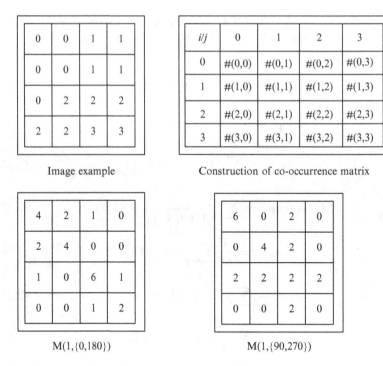

Image example   Construction of co-occurrence matrix

M(1,{0,180})   M(1,{90,270})

Fig. 2.9 The construction of the co-occurrence matrix [52]

the contrast encodes the variation of pixels in a local region which can be regarded as the intensity of the texture intuitively. The mentioned features are computed as follows:

$$correlation = \frac{\sum_{i=1}^{N}\sum_{j=1}^{N}(i \cdot j)\, P_d\,(i, j) - \mu_x \mu_y}{\sigma_x \sigma_y} \qquad (2.29)$$

$$entropy = -\sum_{i=1}^{N}\sum_{j=1}^{N} P_d\,(i, j)\log P_d\,(i, j) \qquad (2.30)$$

$$contrast = \sum_{n=0}^{n=1} n^2 \sum_{i=1}^{N}\sum_{j=1}^{N} P_d\,(i, j),\, |i - j| = n \qquad (2.31)$$

where $P_d(i,j)$ is the gray-level co-occurrence matrix with the offset d along any direction. μ_x, σ_x, μ_y, and σ_y are the means and standard variances of $P_x(i)$ and $P_y(j)$, respectively. Hanif and Prevost [23] further use marginal probabilities of the joint distribution $p_{(d,\theta)}(i,j)$ to include texture information, shape, and spatial relationship between the pixels to discriminate text and non-text.

Gabor filter is also used to model texture in text detection. A 2-D Gabor filter is essentially a Gaussian kernel modulated by a sinusoidal carrier wave, as defined below, which gives different responses for different positions in a window centered at (x, y)

$$g(x, y; \rho, \theta, \varphi, \sigma, \gamma) = \exp\left(-\frac{x'^2 + y^2 y'^2}{2\sigma^2}\right) \cos\left(2\pi \frac{x'}{\rho} + \varphi\right)$$

$$x' = x \cos\theta + y \sin\theta, \ y' = -x \sin\theta + y \cos\theta \qquad (2.32)$$

Given a proper window, the Gabor filter response is obtained by the convolution with a Gabor filter. Yi and Tian [24] define a suitability measurement to analyze the confidence of Gabor filters in describing stroke components and the suitability of Gabor filters. The k-means algorithm is applied to cluster the descriptive Gabor filters to form clustering centers defined as Stroke Gabor Words (SGWs), which provide a universal description of stroke components. When testing natural scene images, heuristic layout analysis is also applied to search for text candidates.

Qian et al. [25] put forward the DCT coefficients in text detection and localization. The DCT coefficients from an 8×8 image block $f(x, y)$ are expressed as

$$AC_{uv} = \frac{1}{8} C_u C_v \sum_{x=0}^{7} \sum_{y=0}^{7} f(x, y) \cos\frac{(2x + 1)\pi\mu}{16} \times \cos\frac{(2y + 1)\pi v}{16}$$

$$C_u, C_v = \begin{cases} \frac{1}{\sqrt{2}} & u, v = 0 \\ 1 & \text{others} \end{cases} \qquad (2.33)$$

Three horizontal AC coefficients, three vertical AC coefficients, and one diagonal AC coefficient from an 8×8 block are finally selected to capture the horizontal, vertical, and diagonal textures. These AC coefficients are used to represent the texture intensity of the 8×8 block approximately by

$$I(i, j) = \sum_{u=1}^{3} |AC_{u0}(i, j)| + \sum_{v=1}^{3} |AC_{0v}(i, j)| + |AC_{11}(i, j)| \qquad (2.34)$$

Generally, texts have sufficient contrast to the background. Thereby, a region-based smooth filter F is further adopted to distinguish the text blocks from the background:

$$F = \frac{1}{16} \begin{bmatrix} 1 & 2 & 1 \\ 2 & 4 & 2 \\ 1 & 2 & 1 \end{bmatrix} \qquad (2.35)$$

Except for the mentioned usages, the limitations of texture-based transformations for video text preprocessing potentially include its big computational complexity due to the need of scanning of every video frame at several scales and the lack of precision due to the inherent fact that only small (or sufficiently scaled down) text exhibits the properties required by a video text detection algorithm. Additionally, texture-based preprocessing is typically unable to help detect sufficiently slanted texts.

2.4   Image Segmentation

A lot of techniques have been developed to perceive images, which in general
consist of three layers of the so-called Image Engineering (IE): processing (low
layer), analysis (middle layer), and understanding (high layer), as shown in Fig. 2.10
[26]. As the first step of IE, image segmentation greatly affects the subsequent
tasks of video frame analysis including video text detection. Note that in the video
case, every video frame is factorized and treated as an individual image in the
segmentation step as introduced.

The objective of segmentation is to partition an image into separated regions
which ideally correspond to interested objects (e.g., video texts) and accordingly
obtain a more meaningful representation of the image. There are some general rules
to be followed for the regions resulted from segmentation as [27]:

1. They should be uniform and homogeneous with respect to specific characteristics.
2. Their interiors should be simple enough and without too many small holes.
3. Adjacent regions should have significantly different values with respect to the
   characteristics on which they are uniform.
4. Boundaries of every segment should be simple, not ragged, and must be spatially
   accurate.

Theoretically, each image can be segmented into multiple separated regions using
two strategies, namely, *bottom-up segmentation* and *top-down segmentation*. For the
former, pixels are partitioned into regions if they have similar low-level features,
in which image semantics are seldom considered. Super pixels are sometimes
generated for the following analysis. For the latter, pixels are partitioned into regions
by following strong semantics of the image in the tasks like object recognition and
content understanding. We here mainly discuss the bottom-up algorithms which are
considered as a step of video preprocessing without any predefined knowledge or
semantics.

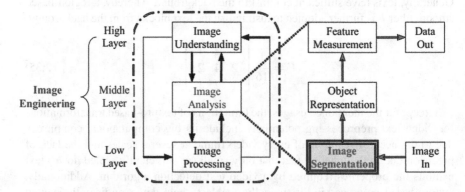

Fig. 2.10 The role of image segmentation [26]

Generally, the simplest way of bottom-up segmentation is using a proper threshold to *transform a grayscale image to a binary one*. The critical issue of this method is how to select such a proper threshold since spatial information is ignored and blurred region boundaries will bring havocs. *Histogram-based methods* are another simple way of bottom-up segmentation since they only require one pass through the pixels and therefore are efficient. In these methods, a histogram is first computed from all the pixels in the image, and then peaks and valleys in the histogram are detected and used to locate the clusters in the image for segmentation [28]. In some cases like for a monochrome image, the value between two histogram peaks can be used as the threshold of binarization, where the background can be defined by the maximum part of the histogram. Note that binarization of complex backgrounds through a single threshold value obtained from the histogram will potentially lead to a loss of object information against the background, e.g., the texts in Fig. 2.11a, b are lost after binarization using Otsu's method [29].

Comparatively, *edge-based methods* make use of edge operators to produce an "edginess" value at each pixel [30] to obtain edges. Then the regions within connected edges are considered as different segments since they lack continuity with other adjacent regions. Edge detection operators are also studied and implemented to find edges in images, and Fig. 2.12 gives some edge detection results using the Sobel operator. Generally, edges are useful to provide aids for other image segmentation algorithms especially in the refinement of segmentation results.

Image segmentation can be formulated as a graph partitioning and optimization problem. It transforms an image into a weighted indirect graph $G = (V, E)$, where the vertex set V represents image points in the feature space and the edge set E

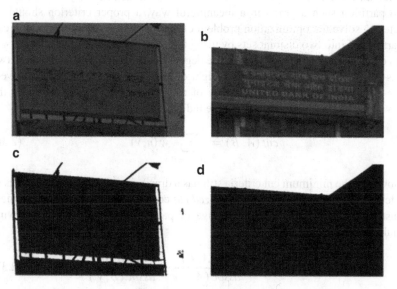

Fig. 2.11 Image binarization by a histogram: (**a**) and (**b**) are two scene image examples, (**c**) and (**d**) respectively illustrate their binarization results using Otsu's method [29]

Fig. 2.12 Edge detection examples with the Canny operator on the second row and Sobel operator on the last row

represents point connectivity. There in general exists a weight $w(i, j)$ for each edge to measure the similarity of vertex i and vertex j. Then the vertices are expected to be partitioned into disjoint sets of $V_1, V_2 \ldots V_k$, where the similarity between the vertices in the same set V_i is relatively high by a specific measure, while that between the vertices across different sets V_i and V_j will be relatively low.

To partition such a graph in a meaningful way, a proper criterion should be selected to solve the optimization problem effectively and efficiently. A graph can be partitioned into two disjoint sets by using the edge cut technique which removes edges connecting two different parts. The degree of dissimilarity between these two pieces can be computed as the total weight of the edges that have been removed. In *the minimum cut* criteria, the quality of a bipartition can be measured by the following equation where a smaller value indicates a better partition:

$$cut\,(A, B) = \sum_{u \in A, v \in B} w\,(u, v) \tag{2.36}$$

However, the minimum cut criteria still has a drawback of obtaining small sets of isolated nodes in the graph. The *normalized cut* criteria [34] make an improvement against it and introduce the size leverage of partition vertices by the following formulation:

$$Ncut\,(A, B) = \frac{cut\,(A, B)}{assoc\,(A, V)} + \frac{cut\,(A, B)}{assoc\,(B, V)} \tag{2.37}$$

$$assoc\,(A, V) = \sum_{u \in A, v \in V} W\,(u, v) \tag{2.38}$$

Against the former cut criteria, the normalized cut considers association within a group, and isolated points will no longer have a small cut value to avoid bias partitions. Formally, let x be a $|V|$ dimension indicating vector with $x_i = 1$ if v_i is partitioned into segment A, and -1 otherwise, W is a $|V| \times |V|$ matrix with $W_{ij} = -w(i,j)$ representing the distance between vertex i and j, and D is a $|V| \times |V|$ diagonal matrix with $d_i = \sum_j W(i,j)$. Then let

$$k = \frac{\sum_{x_i > 0} d_i}{\sum_i d_i}, \quad b = \frac{k}{1-k}, \quad y = (1+x) - b(1-x) \qquad (2.39)$$

Finally, the image segmentation problem based on *normalized cut* criteria can be formulized as an optimization problem [34]:

$$\min_x Ncut(x) = \min_y \frac{y^T(D-W)y}{y^T D y}$$
$$s.t. \ y^T D1 = 0 \qquad (2.40)$$

which can be solved according to the theory of *generalized eigenvalue system*. Although there exists a major stumbling block that an exact solution to minimize the normalized cut is an NP-complete problem, approximate discrete solutions x can be achieved efficiently from y. Some examples of normalized cut are shown in Fig. 2.13.

Graph-based segmentation [33] is an efficient approach by performing clustering in the feature space. Such a method works directly on the data points in the feature

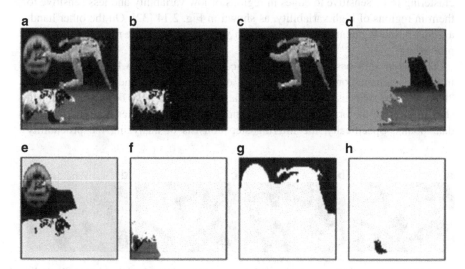

Fig. 2.13 Examples of normalized cut for image segmentation. (**a**) original image, (**b–h**) the segmented regions [34]

space, without a filtering processing step. The key to the success of these methods is using an adaptive threshold scheme. Formally, let $G = (V, E)$ represent the image and a weighting system w_E associating with edges. The final segmentation results $S = \{V_1, V_2, \ldots, V_r\}$ can be achieved from the following algorithm:

1. Sort $E = (e_1, e_2, \ldots, e_{|E|})$ according to $w_E = (w_1, w_2, \ldots w_{|E|})$.
2. Initial $S^0 = \{\{v_1\}, \{v_2\}, \ldots, \{v_{|V|}\}\}$, where each cluster contains exactly one vertex.
3. For $t = 1, 2, \ldots, |E|$

   (a) $e_t = (v_i, v_j)$. $V^{t-1}(v_i)$ is the cluster containing v_i on the iteration t-1, and $l_i = max\ mst(V^{t-1}(v_i))$ is the longest edge in the minimum spanning tree of $V^{t-1}(v_i)$. Likewise for l_j.
   (b) Merge $V^{t-1}(v_i)$ and $V^{t-1}(v_j)$ if

$$W_{e_t} < \min\left\{l_i + \frac{k}{|V^{t-1}(v_i)|}, l_j + \frac{k}{|V^{t-1}(v_j)|}\right\} \tag{2.41}$$

   where k is a predefined empirical parameter.

4. $S = S^{|E|}$.

Specifically, during the clustering procedure, a minimum spanning tree of the data points is first generated, from which any length of edges within a data-dependent threshold indicates a merging process, in contrast to the mean shift algorithms which use a fixed threshold. The connected components are merged into clusters for segmentation. The merging criteria allows efficient graph-based clustering to be sensitive to edges in regions of low variability and less sensitive to them in regions of high variability, as shown in Fig. 2.14 [32]. On the other hand, a graph-based segmentation algorithm can well generate image regions for further processing.

The mean shift-based method introduced in [31] has also been widely used in image segmentation recently. It is one of the techniques under the heading of "feature space analysis." The mean shift method comprises two basic steps: a mean shift filtering of the original image data and a subsequent clustering of the filtered data points. Specifically, the filtering step consists of analyzing the probability

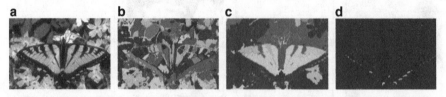

Fig. 2.14 Examples of efficient graph-based image segmentation: (**a**) original image, (**b–d**) the results of different granularities. Note that from fine to coarse, no granularity can generate a complete butterfly [32]

Fig. 2.15 Examples of mean shift segmentation: (**a**) original image, (**b–g**) the results with different granularities [31]

density function (pdf) of the image data in the feature space, then finding the modes of the underlying pdf in a sphere or window and associating with them any points in their basin of attraction. After mean shift filtering, every data point in the feature space will be replaced by its corresponding mode. Then clustering is described as a simple postprocessing step, in which the modes that are less than a specific kernel radius apart are grouped together and their basins of attraction are accordingly merged. This suggests using single linkage clustering, which effectively converts the filtered points into segmentation. Actually, the quantity of the sphere or windows decides the granularities during segmentation and Fig. 2.15 illustrates some examples. It can be found that a mean shift algorithm is quite sensitive to the mentioned window parameters, and a slight variation of the parameters will cause a large change in the granularity of the segmentation, as shown in Fig. 2.15b–g, which changes from over-segmentation to under-segmentation. This issue is a major stumbling block with respect to using mean shift segmentation as a reliable preprocessing step for other algorithms [32].

2.5 Motion Analysis

Motion analysis has been investigated in many video applications especially for object tracking or object recognition. It studies methods in which two or more video frames from an image sequence are processed. As a preprocessing technique, motion vector analysis from temporal frames is believed helpful for video text detection. It produces time-dependent information about the motions of both the foreground objects and their backgrounds to provide hints for identifying texts from consecutive video frames. Moreover, it potentially plays a key role in detecting and tracking video texts from multiple directions or with occlusions. For example, Palma et al. [35] present an automatic text extraction solution for digital video based on motion analysis. In their motion analysis module, the correlation between frames is exploited to improve the results of video text detection. The major goals of motion analysis are to refine the text detection in terms of removing false alarms in individual frames, interpolating the location of accidentally missed text characters and words in individual frames, and temporally localizing the beginning and end of each word as well as its spatial location within each frame. Their method proposed for motion analysis is based on the comparison of regions in successive frames and includes five typical steps:

1. **Text Tracking**: This step is responsible for tracking the already detected text along the fames that constitute each text sequence targeting the formation of temporally related chains of characters. Each character chain here represents the same character during its existence in the video sequence and consists in a collection of similar regions, occurring in several contiguous frames. Every time a character region is detected for the first time, a position is stored and a signature is computed for that character region by using the features of luminance, size, and shape. Each frame contributes with one region classified as a character for the construction of a character chain.

2. **Text Integration**: This step groups the character chains in order to form words based on the spatial and temporal analysis of each character chain. Three temporal elements are adopted: (a) temporary coexistence, (b) duration, and (c) motion. The chains not included in words at this phase are considered as noise and are discarded.

3. **Character Recovery**: Video temporal redundancy is explored to complete the words with missing characters as least for some frames, e.g., due to noise or too textured background. In order to complete the words, they are extended to the size of their biggest chain of characters, and the characters missing in the chains are recovered by means of temporal interpolation with motion compensation. Thus, by using temporal redundancy, the text detection for each frame is improved by completing the words with missing characters for some frames.

4. **Elimination of Overlapped Words**: It is important to improve the performance for scene text. Usually, overlapping of words occurs when false words are detected, e.g., due to shadows or three-dimensional text. Every time two or more words overlap, more precisely their bounding boxes overlap at least for one frame; the words with the smaller areas are discarded.

5. **Text Rotation**: This step performs the rotation of the text to the horizontal position in order to be recognized OCR systems.

Figure 2.16 shows the benefit of motion analysis for the extraction of text from video sequences. The result of extracting text from a single frame is shown in Fig. 2.16b, while Fig. 2.16c shows the result of extracting text for the same frame but exploiting the temporal redundancy by motion analysis in the context of a video sequence. In [47], motion analysis is adopted to capture continuous changes between adjacent video frames, and then the dynamic attention algorithm is used to detect video caption blocks to search for video text candidates.

Fig. 2.16 Examples of the benefits of motion analysis for video text extraction: (**a**) original video frame, (**b**) text detection from a single video frame, and (**c**) better text detection for the same frame but using temporal redundancy for recovering lost characters [35]

Optical flow is the most common technique used in motion analysis [36–40] by exploiting two constraints from video frames: brightness constancy and spatial smoothness. The brightness constancy constraint is derived from the observation that surfaces usually persist over time, and hence, the intensity value of a small region in video remains the same despite its position changes [41, 42]. Using the brightness constancy, gradient methods can be used to analyze the derivatives of video intensity values to compute optical flows. As a supplement, the spatial smoothness constraint comes from the observation that neighboring pixels generally belong to the same surface and thus have nearly the same image motion characteristic.

Regardless of the difference between the two main types of methods, the majority are based on the following three stages in computing optical flows:

1. Preliminary processing using appropriate filters in order to obtain the desired signal structure and improve the signal-to-noise ratio
2. Calculating basic measurements such as partial derivatives after a certain time period or local correlation areas
3. Integrating the measurements in order to calculate a two-dimensional optical flow

As a representative approach, the Horn-Schunck (HS) method uses global constraint of smoothness to express a brightness variation in certain areas of the frames in a video sequence. HS is a specially defined framework to lay out the smoothness of the flow field, which can be described as follows [46]:

1. Calculate optical flows between two adjacent frames (after registration as needed).
2. For each pixel in the 2-D optical flow data, perform PCA for a local mask, and two eigenvalues are assigned to the central pixel.
3. Apply the Otsu's thresholding to the eigenvalues of all the pixels.

Let $I(x,y,t)$ denote the brightness of a pixel at position (x, y) and the tth frame; the image constraint at $I(x,y,t)$ with Taylor series can be expressed by

$$\frac{\partial I}{\partial x}\partial x + \frac{\partial I}{\partial y}\partial y + \frac{\partial I}{\partial t}\partial t = 0 \tag{2.42}$$

which results in

$$I_x u + I_y v + I_t = 0 \qquad (2.43)$$

where $u = \partial x/\partial t$ and $v = \partial y/\partial t$ are the x and y components of the velocity or optical flow of $I(x,y,t)$, respectively. $I_x = \partial I/\partial x$, $I_y = \partial I/\partial y$, and $I_t = \partial I/\partial t$ are the derivatives of the image at (x,y,t) in the corresponding directions. A constrained minimization problem can then be formulated to calculate optical follow vector (u^{k+1}, v^{k+1}) for the $(k+1)$th frame by

$$u^{k+1} - \overline{u}^k = I_x \cdot \frac{I_x \overline{u}^k + I_y \overline{v}^k + I_t}{\alpha^2 + I_x^2 + I_y^2} \qquad (2.44)$$

$$v^{k+1} - \overline{v}^k = I_y \cdot \frac{I_x \overline{u}^k + I_y \overline{v}^k + I_t}{\alpha^2 + I_x^2 + I_y^2} \qquad (2.45)$$

where $\overline{u}^k$ and $\overline{v}^k$ are the estimated local average optical flow velocities and α is a weighting factor. Based on the norm of an optical flow, one can determine if the motion exists or not, while the direction of this vector provides the motion orientation.

Next, two optical flow images can be constructed by pixel optical flow vector (u, v). A mask of size $n*n$ slides through these u and v images. At location (i, j), a two-dimensional data matrix $\mathbf{X}$ can be constructed, which includes all the 2-D vectors covered by the mask. The covariance matrix is calculated as

$$\sum = \overline{X}^T \overline{X} \qquad (2.46)$$

where $\overline{X}$ is the optical flow matrix after mean removal. After eigendecomposition, two eigenvalues (λ_1, λ_2) are assigned to the central pixel of the mask and motion detection will be accomplished by analyzing or thresholding the eigenvalues. Since λ_1 is the major flow component and λ_2 is the minor flow component, it may be more efficient to consider (λ_1, λ_2) than the values in the original (u, v) space. Note that although only λ_1 is intuitively needed to be considered because it corresponds to the major flow component while λ_2 corresponds to the minor flow component or even turbulence, in practice λ_2 is often considered as well since pixels inside object boundaries usually have quite large λ_2 but not λ_1,. Thus, thresholding may need to be taken on the λ_2 histogram determined by using the Ostu's method [29], and a pixel is claimed to have motion if either λ_1 or λ_2 is above the corresponding thresholds.

Figure 2.17a shows the framework of the HS algorithm with a 3*3 mask and resulting 2*9 data matrices [44]. In Fig. 2.17b, two video frames are input, and the result after using the HS optical flow method is shown in Fig. 2.17c. The final result is given in Fig. 2.17d after Kalman filtering.

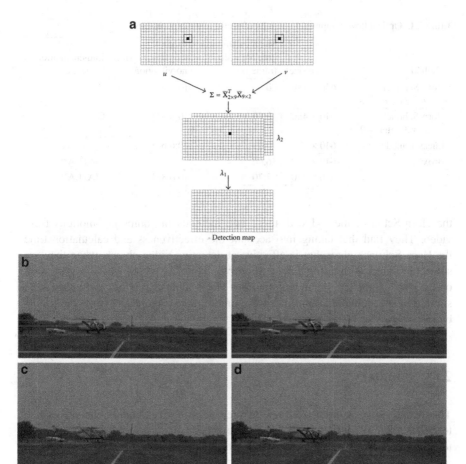

Fig. 2.17 The framework of the HS algorithm. (**a**) The framework of optical flow computation, (**b**) two input frames from video, (**c**) the result after using the HS optical flow method, and (**d**) the final result after Kalman filtering [44]

There are two other classic optical flow algorithms, namely, the Lucas-Kanade method [45] and the Brox method [36]. The Lucas-Kanade method assumes that the flow is essentially constant in a local neighborhood of the pixel. Thus, the goal of the Lucas-Kanade method is to minimize the sum of squared error between two video frames. Since the pixel values are essentially unrelated to its coordinates, the Lucas-Kanade algorithm assumes that a current estimate of vector p is known and then iteratively solves for increments to the parameters Δp for optimization. The Brox method relies on the brightness and gradient constancy assumptions, using the information of video frame intensities and the gradients to find correspondences. With respect to the Horn-Schunck method, it is more robust to the presence of outliers and can cope with constant brightness changes. Głowacz et al. [43] compare

Table 2.1 Optical flow computation: results of preliminary experiments [43]

Method	Image size	Mean calculation time for a single frame (s)	Range (for frames with no vibration)	Implementation language
Horn-Schunck $\alpha = 31, iter = 8$	640×480	0.09	[0;2.67]	C
Horn-Schunck $\alpha = 33, iter = 9$	640×480	0.10	[0;3.36]	C
Lucas-Kanade $\tau = 32$	640×480	0.09	[0;6.64]	C
Brox	640×480	36.00	–	MATLAB
	320×240	7.70	[0;0.88]	MATLAB

the Horn-Schunck method with these two methods in computing motions from video. They find that taking into account the effectiveness and calculation time the Horn-Schunck algorithm is effective at detecting video objects when they are subject to binarization using a fixed threshold. Table 2.1 presents basic information on the tests conducted. It can be found that Horn-Schunck and Lucas-Kanade have similar mean calculation time costs for a single frame. Figure 2.18 gives the results by respectively using the three optical flow computation methods.

2.6   Summary

This chapter gives a brief overview of preprocessing techniques related to video text detection. We introduce image preprocessing operators and color-based and texture-based preprocessing techniques which are most frequently used in video analysis. Since image segmentation potentially helps reduce the searching space and more important, provides contextual hints in complex video scenes for video graphics text and scene text detection, we then give a brief introduction on automatic segmentation technique. Finally, considering the necessity of temporal redundancy analysis in detecting texts from video sequences, we introduce how to compute motions from video frames and how video text detection benefits from motionanalysis.

Most of the introduced preprocessing operators and methods have been realized by MATLAB or OpenCV (Open Source Computer Vision Library), so readers can make use of these open sources for practice. A more systematical and detailed introduction to the discussed techniques may be found in the references for image processing and machine vision in [48–51].

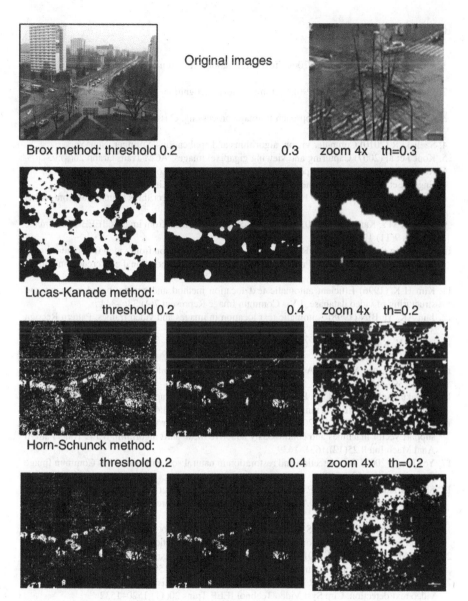

Fig. 2.18 Effects of the optical flow binarization calculated using three methods [43]

References

1. Jung K, In Kim K, Jain AK (2004) Text information extraction in images and video: a survey. Pattern Recog 37(5):977–997
2. Lienhart RW, Stuber F (1996) Automatic text recognition in digital videos. Proc SPIE 2666(3):180–188
3. Crane R (1996) Simplified approach to image processing: classical and modern techniques in C. Prentice Hall PTR. 317
4. Szeliski R (2010) Computer vision: algorithms and applications. Springer, New York
5. Kopf J et al (2007) Capturing and viewing gigapixel images. ACM Trans Graph 26(3):93
6. Roberts LG (1963) Machine perception of three-dimensional solids, DTIC Document
7. Engel K et al (2006) Real-time volume graphics: AK Peters, Limited
8. Ritter GX, Wilson JN (1996) Handbook of computer vision algorithms in image algebra, vol 1. Citeseer
9. Hasan YMY, Karam LJ (2000) Morphological text extraction from images. IEEE Trans Image Process 9(11):1978–1983
10. Jae-Chang S, Dorai C, Bolle R (1998) Automatic text extraction from video for content-based annotation and retrieval. In: Proceedings of the fourteenth international conference on pattern recognition, 1998
11. Kim H-K (1996) Efficient automatic text location method and content-based indexing and structuring of video database. J Vis Commun Image Represent 7(4):336–344
12. Jain AK, Yu BIN (1998) Automatic text location in images and video frames. Pattern Recogn 31(12):2055–2076
13. Zhong Y, Karu K, Jain AK (1995) Locating text in complex color images. Pattern Recogn 28(10):1523–1535
14. Wong EK, Chen M (2003) A new robust algorithm for video text extraction. Pattern Recogn 36(6):1397–1406
15. Shivakumara P, Trung Quy P, Tan CL (2011) A laplacian approach to multi-oriented text detection in video. IEEE Trans Pattern Anal Mach Intell 33(2):412–419
16. Kim KI, Jung K, Kim JH (2003) Texture-based approach for text detection in images using support vector machines and continuously adaptive mean shift algorithm. IEEE Trans Pattern Anal Mach Intell 25(12):1631–1639
17. Ye Q et al (2007) Text detection and restoration in natural scene images. J Vis Commun Image Represent 18(6):504–513
18. Shivakumara P, Trung Quy P, Tan CL (2009) A robust wavelet transform based technique for video text detection. In: ICDAR '09. 10th international conference on document analysis and recognition, 2009
19. Zhong J, Jian W, Yu-Ting S (2009) Text detection in video frames using hybrid features. In: International conference on machine learning and cybernetics, 2009
20. Zhao M, Li S, Kwok J (2010) Text detection in images using sparse representation with discriminative dictionaries. Image Vis Comput 28(12):1590–1599
21. Shivakumara P, Trung Quy P, Tan CL (2010) New Fourier-statistical features in RGB space for video text detection. Circ Syst Video Technol IEEE Trans 20(11):1520–1532
22. Rongrong J et al (2008) Directional correlation analysis of local Haar binary pattern for text detection. In: IEEE international conference on multimedia and expo, 2008
23. Hanif SM, Prevost L (2007) Text detection in natural scene images using spatial histograms. In: 2nd workshop on camera based document analysis and recognition, Curitiba
24. Chucai Y, YingLi T (2011) Text detection in natural scene images by Stroke Gabor Words. In: International conference on document analysis and recognition (ICDAR), 2011
25. Qian X et al (2007) Text detection, localization, and tracking in compressed video. Signal Process Image Commun 22(9):752–768
26. ZHANG YJ (2002) Image engineering and related publications. Int J Image Graph 02(03):441–452

27. Haralick RM, Shapiro LG (1985) Image segmentation techniques. Comp Vis Graph Image Process 29(1):100–132
28. Shapiro LG, Stockman GC (2001) Computer vision. Prentice-Hall, New Jersey, pp 279–325
29. Otsu N (1975) A threshold selection method from gray-level histograms. Automatica 11(285–296):23–27
30. Saraf Y (2006) Algorithms for image segmentation, Birla Institute of Technology and Science
31. Comaniciu D, Meer P (2002) Mean shift: a robust approach toward feature space analysis. Pattern Anal Mach Intell IEEE Trans on 24(5):603–619
32. Pantofaru C, Hebert M (2005) A comparison of image segmentation algorithms. Robotics Institute, p 336
33. Felzenszwalb P, Huttenlocher D (2004) Efficient graph-based image segmentation. Int J Comp Vis 59(2):167–181
34. Shi J, Malik J (2000) Normalized cuts and image segmentation. Pattern Anal Mach Intell IEEE Trans 22(8):888–905
35. Palma D, Ascenso J, Pereira F (2004) Automatic text extraction in digital video based on motion analysis. In: Campilho A, Kamel M (eds) Image analysis and recognition. Springer, Berlin, pp 588–596
36. Brox T et al (2004) High accuracy optical flow estimation based on a theory for warping. In: Pajdla T, Matas J (eds) Computer vision – ECCV 2004. Springer, Berlin, pp 25–36
37. Beauchemin SS, Barron JL (1995) The computation of optical flow. ACM Comput Surv 27(3):433–466
38. Anandan P (1989) A computational framework and an algorithm for the measurement of visual motion. Int J Comp Vis 2(3):283–310
39. Weickert J, Schnörr C (2001) A theoretical framework for convex regularizers in PDE-based computation of image motion. Int J Comp Vis 45(3):245–264
40. Mémin E, Pérez P (2002) Hierarchical estimation and segmentation of dense motion fields. Int J Comp Vis 46(2):129–155
41. Sun D et al (2008) Learning optical flow. In: Forsyth D, Torr P, Zisserman A (eds) Computer vision – ECCV 2008. Springer, Berlin, pp 83–97
42. Black MJ, Anandan P (1996) The robust estimation of multiple motions: parametric and piecewise-smooth flow fields. Comp Vis Image Underst 63(1):75–104
43. Głowacz A, Mikrut Z, Pawlik P (2012) Video detection algorithm using an optical flow calculation method. In: Dziech A, Czyżewski A (eds) Multimedia communications, services and security. Springer, Berlin, pp 118–129
44. Horn BKP, Schunck BG (1981) Determining optical flow. Artif Intell 17(1–3):185–203
45. Lucas BD, Kanade T (1981) An iterative image registration technique with an application to stereo vision. In: IJCAI
46. Kui L et al (2010) Optical flow and principal component analysis-based motion detection in outdoor videos. EURASIP J Adv Signal Proc
47. Zhao Y et al (2011) Real-time video caption detection. In: Proceedings of the ninth IAPR international workshop on graphics recognition
48. Gonzalez RC, Woods RE, Eddins SL Digital image processing using matlab. Prentice Hall
49. Nixon MS, Aguado AS Feature extraction & image processing for computer vision, 3rd edn. Academic
50. Forsyth DA, Ponce J Computer vision: a modern approach, 2nd edn. Prentice Hall Press
51. Petrou M, Petrou C Image processing: the fundamentals. Wiley
52. Haralick RM, Shanmugam K (1973) Its'Hak Dinstein. Textual features for image classification. IEEE Trans Syst Man Cybern 3(6):610–621

Chapter 3
Video Caption Detection

Generally, video contains two types of text. The first type pertains to caption text. Texts of this type are edited texts or graphics texts artificially superimposed into the video and are relevant to the content of the video. The second type belongs to scene text, which is naturally existing text, usually embedded in objects in the video. Since caption text is edited according to content of video, it is useful in several applications especially for indexing and retrieving based on semantics. In the same way, scene text is as equally important as caption text as it is useful in identifying exciting events in sports video and understanding scenes to study the environment. This chapter concerns the first type of text. The state-of-the-art methods for detection of caption text will be presented.

3.1 Introduction to Video Caption Detection

An important aspect of caption text is that it represents meta-information, which is intentionally inserted by the video producers according to well-accepted conventions. Good examples of caption text are anchor's name, location, and event in the TV news. Video text is a separate channel of information that is not always conveyed as closed-captioned, auditory, or transcript data. This text can be manually recorded during video production or automatically detected from archived video material. Therefore, video text on the frames can be used for video annotations, indexing, semantic video analysis, and search. For example, the origin of a broadcast is indicated by a graphics station logo in the right-hand top or bottom of the screen. Such station logos can be automatically recognized and used as annotation. Anchor/correspondent names and locations in a news program are often displayed on the screen and can be recognized by extracting text showing in the bottom one-third of the video frame. Musician names and music group names, talk show hosts and guests, and other TV personalities are also introduced and identified in

© Springer-Verlag London 2014
T. Lu et al., *Video Text Detection*, Advances in Computer Vision
and Pattern Recognition, DOI 10.1007/978-1-4471-6515-6_3

a similar fashion. So, by detecting text box and recognizing the text, video can be indexed based on TV personality or a location. This information can then be used for retrieving news clips based on proper names or locations [1–5].

Video text is also useful in performing text analysis and categorizing text into different classes such as video topics, person appearances, sports scores, etc. The spatial designator of the text region containing the character block can provide clues about the category of the text such as image caption, channel number, sports score, etc. Hence, text semantics and text location within the frame are valuable cues for automatic video categorization. The location and size of the text in commercials can be used in conjunction with other features for reliable commercial detection. Tracking text movement helps in finding scrolling, static, of flying video text. For example, the presence of scrolling text often signals the beginning or the ending of programs. This can help in finding program boundaries. The subtitle in a video can be analyzed to extract the transcript, index, and query video streams. Text detection can also be used along with the shot detection algorithm to extract important frames (key frames) and generate a visual table of contents that is more meaningful for consumers [1–5].

An interesting application of video text detection is recognition of the ticker that runs during games, talk shows, and news. This ticker could convey weather updates or stock market figures. In this manner, additional information can be extracted and retrieved for future use. This information can be viewed as something coming from completely different channel from the broadcast program itself, as it is unrelated to the program in view [1–5].

The field of video text detection research actually started with the detection of caption text in the early development of the field. This is mainly because caption text is generally easier to handle than the other type of text, namely, the scene text which will be discussed in the next chapter, as scene text presents a different set of challenges. As caption texts are manually added into the video, prominent colors are often chosen to enhance visibility and readability. In some situations, texts appear in uniform background such as in the case of movie credits at the end of the movie. Moreover, because the texts are created by some word editor or graphics generator, the text characters are well defined with sharp edges. These characteristics of caption text therefore are amenable to detection by virtue of the discernible contrast between the text and its background. Because of the contrast, detection of edges and gradients is one of the most common methods for caption text detection. Text comes in a linear grouping of characters with each character comprising of strokes linked together in some ways. Thus intuitively, connected component analysis provides a way for caption text detection. Moreover, looking at each text character as a whole, there is some relative degree of regular spatial arrangement of strokes and edges in comparison with the background. This offers yet another promising way for capturing text detection through texture analysis. Finally, machines can be trained by using some of the above features obtained from edges, contrasts, connectivity, and texture to construct feature vectors for different kinds of machine learning classifiers.

In the following sections, text detection methods reported in the literature can be broadly divided into two main categories of methods, namely, (1) feature-based methods which include edge, texture, connected component, and frequency domain-based methods and (2) machine learning-based methods which include support vector machine, neural network, and Bayesian classifier-based methods. Various methods in these categories in details in subsequent sections will be discussed.

3.2 Feature-Based Methods

Feature-based methods can be further divided into edge, texture, and connected component-based methods. Generally, the feature-based methods work on the basis that features of text pixel have high values than features of non-text pixels because a text pixel is defined as a pixel that has a higher contrast compared to its background.

3.2.1 Edge-Based Methods

Visually, it is apparent that text in video or any image contains rich information of vertical and horizontal edges, especially for English texts. This clue leads researchers to explore edge-based methods for text detection in video. Besides, near edge or on edge, there will be high sharpness, and transitions from black to white and white to black are observed that give some kind of regular pattern due to uniform spacing between characters and words. Therefore, this is the basis for most of the edge-based methods for text detection in video.

Among the several textual properties in the image, edge-based methods focus on the high contrast between the text and the background. The edges of the text boundary are identified and merged, and then several heuristics are used to filter out the non-text regions. Usually, an edge filter (e.g., Canny operator) is used for edge detection, and a smoothing operator or a morphological operator is used for the merging stage.

Smith and Kanade [6] apply a 3×3 horizontal differential filter to the input image and perform thresholding to find vertical edges. After a smoothing operation that is used to eliminate small edges, adjacent edges are connected and a bounding box is computed. Then heuristics including aspect ratio, fill factor, and size of each bounding box are applied to filter out non-text regions. Finally, the intensity histogram of each cluster is examined to find clusters that have similar texture and shape characteristics.

Hasan and Karam [2] present morphological approach for text extraction using RGB color models. Although this approach is simple and many researchers have adopted it to deal with color images, it has difficulties in dealing with objects that have similar grayscale values, yet different colors in the color space. After the color conversion, the edges are identified using morphological gradient operator.

The resulting edge image is then thresholded to obtain a binary edge image. Adaptive thresholding is performed for each candidate region in the intensity image, which is less sensitive to illumination conditions and reflections. Edges that are spatially close are grouped by dilation to form candidate regions, while small components are removed by erosion. Non-text components are filtered out using size, thickness, aspect ratio, and gray-level homogeneity. The method is insensitive to skew and text orientation and curved text strings can also be extracted. Chen et al. [7] use the Canny operator to detect edges in the image. They propose using one edge point in a small window in the estimation of scale and orientation to reduce the computational complexity. The edges of the text are then enhanced using this scale information. Morphological dilation is performed to connect the edges into clusters. Some heuristics knowledge such as the horizontal-vertical aspect ratio and height is used to filter out non-text clusters. The text localization is applied to the enhanced image.

Shivakumara et al. [8–10] present a method based on edge filters, including averaging, median, and their combination with the help of Canny edge and Sobel edge maps of the input image to segment the text region. The method uses vertical and horizontal bars to identify text candidates in the segmented text region. This method is fast, but it gives lots of false alarms due to heuristics proposed in the method.

Shivakumara et al. [11] propose another method based on gradient difference to identify the text candidates with the help of k-means clustering to overcome the problem of the previous method. In the same way, a Laplacian-based method [12] is also proposed to enhance text pixel information based on maximum gradient difference which considers high positive and negative gradient values to classify the low text contrast text pixels. k-means clustering algorithm on the enhanced image and the heuristics helps to improve the text detection accuracy. The combination of edge information and texture features are also proposed at the block level to classify high-contrast images and low-contrast images such that the proposed feature can classify text regions accurately [13].

In the following, we will describe in greater details a method that uses edges and filters [8].

3.2.1.1   Text Detection Using Edges and Filters

First, this method proposes rules using arithmetic mean filter and median filters to classify text blocks in the video image. Then the method proposes a vertical and horizontal bar concept to detect actual text from the text candidates. The whole 256×256-sized image is divided into equal 64×64-sized blocks as shown in Figs. 3.1 and 3.2, respectively. The block size is chosen to be 64×64 because the block is expected to have at least two words.

In order to derive rules to classify a given block, the method uses arithmetic mean filter (AF) and median filter (MF). These filters are well-known filters to remove noise in the image. However, these filters are used here to define rules for identifying

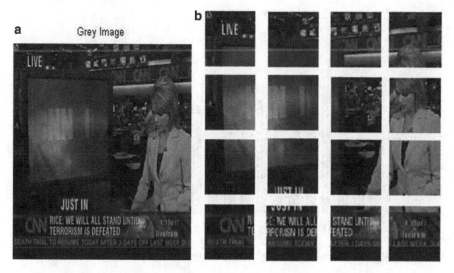

Fig. 3.1 Dividing an image into blocks. (**a**) Grayscale image, (**b**) blocks of the image

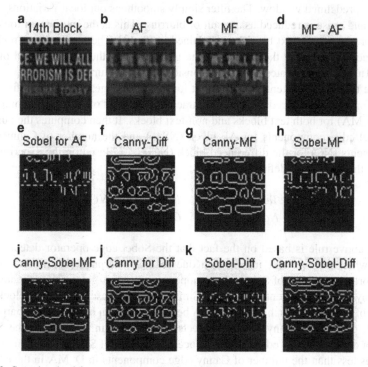

Fig. 3.2 Steps involved for candidate text block selection

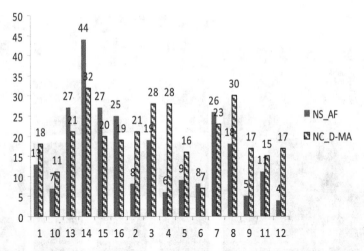

Fig. 3.3 Illustration of rule 1 for text block classifications

blocks containing text. The arithmetic mean filter computes the average intensity within a predefined window. The filter simply smoothens out local variations in the image, and noise is reduced as a result of blurring. This is the motivation to derive rules for identifying text blocks as explained in [8, 13]. The median filter replaces the value of a pixel by the median of the gray levels in the neighborhood of that pixel. This filter eliminates noise with considerably less blurring.

Note that the AF attenuates noise but it blurs the image. The method finds the blur information produced by AF, by subtracting the output of AF from the output of MF (D_MA) for both text blocks and non-text blocks. It then computes the number of Sobel edge components for AF block (NS_{AF}) and the number of Canny edge components (NC) for the differenced block (NC_{D_MA}). Based on the experimental results, the first rule is defined as follows:

$$R1 = \begin{cases} Text\ Block, & if\ NS_{AF} > NC_{D\_MA} \\ NonText\ Block, & Otherwise \end{cases} \tag{3.1}$$

The above rule is based on the fact that the Sobel edge operator detects more edges when there is text information due to high sharpness in the text block. Therefore, the number of Sobel edge components in AF is greater than the number of Canny edge components in D_MA. Similarly, in the case of non-text block, the degree of blurring is much less in D_MA because the given block has no sharpness. In such cases, the Canny detector detects some edges in D_MA but the Sobel detector does not detect edges in AF. Hence, the number of Sobel edge components in AF is less than the number of Canny edge components in D_MA in the case of non-text block. This is clearly illustrated in Fig. 3.3, where the NS_{AF} is greater than the NC_{D_MA} for the text blocks 13, 14, 15, and 16 and the NS_{AF} is less than the

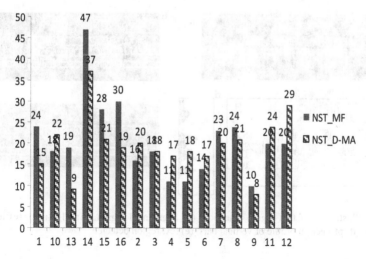

Fig. 3.4 Illustrations of rule 2 for text block classification

NC_{D_MA} for the non-text blocks 2, 3, 4, 5, 8, 9, 11, and 12 by referring to Fig. 3.1. However, R1 fails to classify blocks 1 and 10 as text blocks because of the less text in the blocks. Similarly, R1 fails to classify blocks 6 and 7 as non-text blocks because of the high-contrast objects in the blocks.

To deal with the above failure cases, another rule is derived by extracting strong edges using Canny edge block and Sobel edge block. A block with weak edges (WE) is obtained by subtracting the Sobel edge block from Canny edge block, and then subtraction of the number of weak edges (NWE) from the number of Canny edges (NC) gives the number of strong edges (NST). The same procedure is applied on MF block and D_MA block to obtain strong edges. The rule for deciding text block is defined as follows. If the number of strong edges in the MF block (NST_{MF}) is greater than the number of strong edges in D_MA block (NST_{D_MA}), then it is a text block otherwise it is a non-text block, i.e.,

$$R2 = \begin{cases} Text\ Block, & if\ NST_{MF} > NST_{D\_MA} \\ NonText\ Block, & Otherwise \end{cases} \quad (3.2)$$

This is true because the Sobel detector detects more edges when there is text information. Therefore, the method gets fewer weak edges in case of text block. Hence, the number of strong edges in MF block is greater than the number of strong edges in D_MA block. On the contrary, weak edges are fewer than Canny edges for non-text bock. This is illustrated in Fig. 3.4 where R2 classifies blocks 1, 13, 14, 15, and 16 by referring to Fig. 3.1 as the text blocks, and it fails to classify block 10 as text block since block 10 has little text information. Similarly, R2 classifies blocks 2, 3, 4, 5, 6, 11, and 12 as non-text blocks, and it fails to classify blocks 7, 8, and 9 as non-text blocks because these blocks have high-contrast objects.

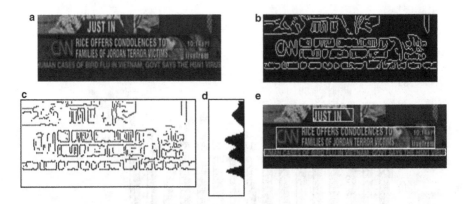

Fig. 3.5 Illustration of text region detection. (**a**) Segmented region, (**b**) edge map, (**c**) feature selection, (**d**) projection profile of vertical bars, (**e**) text region detected

The method analyzes each text block identified by the above rules to identify the candidate text block using the combination of filters and edges. Then the candidate text block is used to grow along the text region direction in Sobel edge image of the input image to obtain a complete text region with the help of the rules. For each text region, the method proposes vertical and horizontal bar concept [8] to detect text lines in video image as shown in Fig. 3.5 where (a) is the text region, (b) is the edge map, and (c) is the results of vertical and horizontal bars marked by blue color. The projection profile of the vertical and horizontal bars is analyzed to find exact text lines based on the fact that text lines are separated by the spacing between them as shown in Fig. 3.5d and final text detection results can be seen in Fig. 3.5e where text lines are enclosed by rectangular boxes.

3.2.1.2 Summary

Edge-based methods are fast since most of the methods use edge information as candidate information for detecting text lines in video image. However, features extracted based on edge pattern such as vertical and horizontal bars may be overlapped with the features in the background due to the complexity of the background. Therefore, generally, edge-based methods are sensitive to background and thus give more false positives. In addition, the methods work well for horizontal text detection but not multi-oriented text detection due to the limitation of the projection profile analysis.

3.2.2 Texture-Based Methods

Text in video can be treated as a special texture appearance. To extract such observation, texture-based methods are proposed. Texture-based methods use the observation that texts in mages have distinct properties that distinguish them from the background. Techniques based on Gabor filters, wavelet, FFT, spatial variance, etc., can be used to detect the textual properties of a text region in an image.

Zhong et al. [2] use the local spatial variations in a grayscale image to locate text regions with a high variance. They utilize a horizontal window of size 1×21 to compute the spatial variances for pixels in a local neighborhood. Then the horizontal edges in the image are identified using Canny edge detector, and the small edge components are merged into longer lines. From this edge image, edges with opposite directions are paired into the lower and upper boundaries of text lines. However, this approach can only detect horizontal components with a large variation compared to the background.

A similar method has been applied to vehicle license plate localization by Park et al. [14]. In this case the horizontal variance of the text is also used for license plate localization. Two time delay neural networks are used as horizontal and vertical filters. Each neural network receives HSI color values for small window of an image as input and decides whether or not the window contains a license plate number. After combing two filtered images, bounding boxes for license plates are located based on projection profile analysis.

In contrast, Wu et al. [15] segment the input image using a multi-scale texture segmentation scheme. Potential text regions are detected based on nine second-order Gaussian derivatives. A nonlinear transformation is applied to each filtered image. The local energy estimates, computed at each pixel using the output of the nonlinear transformation, are then clustered using k-means algorithm. The process is referred to as texture segmentation. Next, chip generation stage is initiated based on stroke information. These texture segmentation and chip generation stages are performed at multiple scales to detect text with a wide range of sizes and then mapped back onto the original image. Although insensitive to the image resolution due to its multi-scale and texture discrimination approach, this method tends to miss very small texts.

Sin et al. [16] use frequency features such as the number of edge pixels in horizontal and vertical directions and Fourier spectrum to detect text regions in real scene images. Based on the assumption that many text regions are on rectangular background, rectangular search is then performed by detecting edges, followed by the Hough transform. However, it is not clear how these three stages are merged to generate the final result.

Mao et al. [17] propose a texture-based text localization method using wavelet transform. Haar wavelet decomposition is used to define local energy variations in the image at several scales. Binary image, which is acquired after thresholding the local energy variations, is analyzed by connected component-based filtering using geometrical attributes such as size and aspect ratio. All the text regions, which are detected at several scales, are merged to give the final result.

Since the utilization of texture information for text localization is also sensitive to the character font size and style, it is difficult to manually generate a texture filter set for each possible situation. Therefore, to alleviate the burden of manually designing texture filters, several learning-based methods have been proposed for the automatic generation of a filter set.

Jain and Jeong et al. [18] use a learning-based texture discrimination method for text information extraction in complex color images, where a neural network is employed to train a set of texture discrimination masks that minimize the classification error for the two texture classes: text regions and non-text regions. The textual properties of the text regions are analyzed using the R, G, and B color bands. The input image is scanned by the neural network, which receives the color values from the neighborhood of a given pixel as input.

Kim et al. [19] use support vector machines (SVMs) for analyzing the textual properties of text in images. After texture classification using an SVM, a profile analysis is performed to extract text lines.

A learning-based method is also employed by Li et al. [20] for localizing and tracking text in video, where a small window is applied to scan the input image. Each window is then classified as either text or non-text using a neural network after extracting feature vectors. The mean value and the second- and the third-order central moments of the decomposed sub-band images, computed using wavelets, are used as the features. The neural network is operated on a pyramid of the input image with multiple resolutions.

A major problem with the traditional texture-based approach is its computational complexity in the texture classification stage, which accounts for most of the processing time. In particular, texture-based filtering methods require an exhaustive scan of the input image to detect and localize text regions. This makes the convolution operation computationally expensive. To tackle this problem, Jung et al. [21] adopt a mean shift algorithm as a mechanism for automatically selecting regions of interest (ROIs), thereby avoiding a time-consuming texture analysis of the entire image. By embedding a texture analyzer into the mean shift, ROIs related to possible text regions are first selected based on a coarse level of classification. Only those pixels within the ROI are then classified at a finer level, which significantly reduces the processing time when text size does not dominate the image size.

The above methods all focus on graphics and caption texts. Shivakumara et al. [22–24] have developed a host of methods which have the extended ability on scene text in addition to the caption text. Essentially, their methods explore the generic properties of video text regardless of whether they are caption or scene texts. Their method reported in [22] is based on wavelet and statistical features to detect text in video irrespective of the type of text, where the statistical features are extracted from each wavelet sub-bands followed by a k-means clustering algorithm to classify text region and non-text region. Though the method is expensive, it has the extended capability on scene text detection. In another method [23], statistical features are extracted using Fourier transform in RGB space to detect text in video. The method demonstrates that the use of color for statistical features improves text detection accuracy as the combination of color and wavelet sub-bands enhances low-contrast text. To further extend to detection of multi-oriented text, yet another method [24] uses the combination of wavelet and median moments to extract features. To tackle the problem of multi-oriented text, a boundary growing method based on nearest neighbor criteria has been proposed. In the same way, another combination of Fourier and Laplacian [25] is proposed to increase the contrast of the text pixels followed by a maximum difference operation to widen the gap between text and non-text pixels. In the following, we will give more details on this texture-based method to show the use of texture features in text detection.

3.2.2.1   Text Detection Using Texture Features

This method proposes texture features for text detection and extract from different directions of edges because edge is a distinctive characteristic which can be used to find possible text areas. Text is mainly composed of strokes in horizontal, vertical, up-right, and up-left directions. For the gray image as shown in Fig. 3.6a, the method uses a Sobel operator to get four directional edge maps which represent the edge density and edge strength in these four directions. Figure 3.6b–e shows the edge maps of the image in four directions, and in Fig. 3.6f, the average edge map is shown. As text has weak and irregular texture property to some extent, the method treats text as a special texture. The method employs statistical features in the edge map to capture the texture property. More specifically, the features which include mean, standard deviation, energy, entropy, inertia, and local homogeneity of edge maps are computed. First, a sliding window of size $w \times h$ ($w = 16$ and $h = 8$) pixels is moved over each edge map. For each window position and for each edge map, the features are computed using the formula as follows:

$$\mu = \frac{1}{wh}\sum_{i=1}^{w}\sum_{j=1}^{h} E(i,j) \tag{3.3}$$

$$\sigma = \sqrt{\frac{1}{wh}\sum_{i=1}^{w}\sum_{j=1}^{h}[E(i,j) - \mu]^2} \tag{3.4}$$

$$E = \sum_{i,j} E^2(i,j) \tag{3.5}$$

$$Et = \sum_{i,j} E(i,j) . \log E(i,j) \tag{3.6}$$

$$I = \sum_{i,j}(i-j)^2 E(i,j) \tag{3.7}$$

$$Hm = \sum_{i,j}\frac{1}{1+(i-j)^2}E(i,j) \tag{3.8}$$

Here, $E(i,j)$ is the edge map, at pixel position (i,j) in the window of size $w \times h$. After feature computation, the method obtains 24 features, which are the 6 features mentioned above multiplied by four edge maps. These features need to be normalized in the range from 0 to 1, which form the feature vector representation

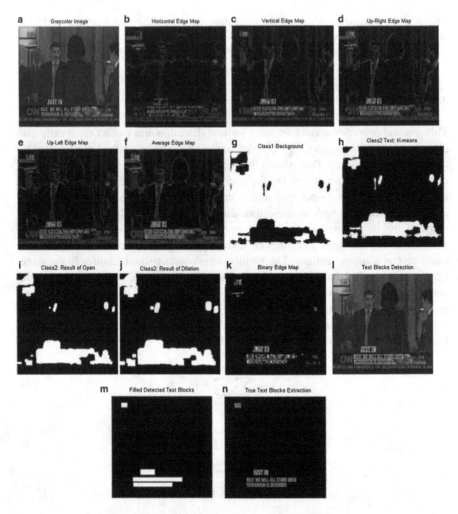

Fig. 3.6 Steps involved in the method for text detection. (**a**) Given image, (**b**) horizontal edge map, (**c**) vertical edge map, (**d**) up-right edge map, (**e**) up-left edge map, (**f**) average edge map, (**g**) background separation, (**h**) foreground separation, (**i**) result of opening, (**j**) result of dilation, (**k**) generated binary edge map, (**l**) detection results, (**m**) clearly visible, (**n**) text blocks extracted

for each pixel. Then k-means algorithm is applied to classify the feature vector into two clusters: background and text candidates. Area of the text candidates is used for classifying background and text. The sample output of the k-means algorithm is shown by separating the background and the text as shown in Fig. 3.6g, h, respectively. After this step, the method gets the initial text candidates which are binary. The method uses morphological operations such as opening and dilation, as shown in Fig. 3.6i, j, respectively, to get connected components and to discard too small objects as background. The position of every connected component of the text candidates is projected on the average edge map to get the corresponding edge map of the text candidates. Every edge map of the text candidates is binarized as shown in Fig. 3.6k by a threshold value. The sample detection result is shown in Fig. 3.6l. The detected text blocks are filled by the white color to make visible in Fig. 3.6m, and the true text blocks are extracted as shown in Fig. 3.6n.

3.2.2.2 False-Positives Filtering

In order to minimize false positives, the method introduces new features such as straightness and cursiveness, in addition to the height and width of the text block. The straightness of a connected component is defined as follows. If the centroid of a component falls on the component itself, then the component is considered as a straight component otherwise it is considered as a cursive component. Figure 3.7 shows sample edge blocks corresponding to text blocks detected by the method, and Fig. 3.8a shows edge characteristics for block 1 in Fig. 3.7. It is observed that the number of blank columns between the edge components in the block is more compared to non-text blocks and the number of straight edge components in the text block is more than the number of cursive edge components. Therefore, based on these observations, the method proposes new features to define straightness and cursiveness of the edge components as follows. Let $X = \{x_1, x_2, \ldots, x_n\}$ and $Y = \{y_1, y_2, \ldots, y_n\}$ be the sets of x and y coordinates, respectively, of the pixels belonging to a connected component of a binary edge map. The centroid of the component is (C_x, C_y) defined as $C_x = \frac{1}{n}\sum_{i=1}^{n} x_i$ and $C_y = \frac{1}{n}\sum_{i=1}^{n} y_i$, where n is the

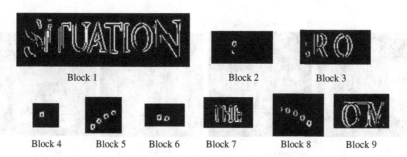

Block 1   Block 2   Block 3

Block 4   Block 5   Block 6   Block 7   Block 8   Block 9

Fig. 3.7 Sample edge blocks

Fig. 3.8 Observations to derive heuristics for eliminating false positives: Edges that are satisfying (Cent_Comp=1) for block 1 in Fig. 3.7

number of pixels in the component. With this, the straightness of the component is defined as

$$Cent\_Comp = \begin{cases} 1, & if\ (C_x \in X) \cap (C_y \in Y) \\ 0, & Otherwise \end{cases} \tag{3.9}$$

If $(Cent\_Comp = 1)$, then the component is considered as a straight component else it is a cursive component. Sample edges that are satisfying $(Cent\_Comp = 1)$ are shown in Fig. 3.8a. The method finds the number of space (N_S) between the components in the detected block. The method also computes height (H), width (W), aspect ratio (A_R), and density (A_HW) which is the sum of pixels in the detected text block divided by the area $(H * W)$ of the text block. As the density of edge pixels is higher when the text is present in the text block, this density measure is used in false-positive elimination:

$(i)\ ((H < 6) \vee (W <= 5) \vee (A < 24) \vee (H > 70))$,
$(ii)\ ((A\_HW > 0.3) \wedge (N\_S = 0) \wedge (N\_CT = 0))$.

N_CT is the number of components that satisfy $(Cent\_Comp = 1)$. Threshold (i) aims to eliminate the bocks whose height, width, and area are too small. In addition, it also eliminates the blocks whose height is too high. Threshold (ii) aims to eliminate the blocks whose density is low, number of blank columns is zero, and number of straight edge components is zero. To test the robustness of the proposed thresholds, the method is tested on different frames with different types of text. Figure 3.9 shows a few sample results on different frames such as low-contrast frame (Fig. 3.9a), high-contrast frame (Fig. 3.9c), and complex background frame (Fig. 3.9e) for eliminating false positives using the above two conditions.

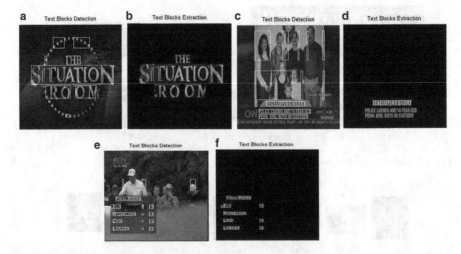

Fig. 3.9 False positives removed with the above heuristics. (**a**) Text detection, (**b**) text extraction, (**c**) text detection, (**d**) text, (**e**) text detection, (**f**) text

3.2.2.3   Summary

The method described in this section is good for complex background as it extracts texture features by combining edge direction and texture features. However, the method requires more processing time compared to edge-based and corner-based methods because of expensive computations involved in textures and large number of features. The method considers only horizontal text lines for text detection.

3.2.3   Connected Component-Based Methods

Connected component-based methods use a bottom-up approach by grouping small components into successively larger components until all regions are identified in the image. A geometrical analysis is needed to merge the text components using spatial arrangement of the components so as to filter out non-text components and mark the boundaries of the text regions.

Ohya et al. [26] present a four-stage method: (1) binarization based on local thresholding, (2) tentative character component detection using gray-level difference, (3) character recognition for calculating the similarities between the character candidates and the standard patterns stored in a database, and (4) relaxation operation to update the similarities. They are able to extract and recognize characters, including multi-segment characters, under varying illuminating conditions, sizes, positions, and fonts when dealing with scene text images, such as freight train, signboard, etc. However, binary segmentation is inappropriate for video frames, which can have several objects with different gray levels and high levels of noise and variations in illumination. Furthermore, this approach places several restrictions related to text alignment, such as upright characters with no touching, as well as the color of the text (monochrome).

Lee and Kankanhalli [27] apply a connected component-based method to the detection and recognition of text on cargo containers, which may suffer from uneven lighting conditions and variable characters' size. Edge information is used for coarse search prior to the connected component generation. The difference between adjacent pixels is used to determine the boundaries of potential characters after quantizing the input image. Local threshold values are then selected for each text candidate, based on pixels on the boundaries. These potential characters are used to generate connected components with the same gray level. Thereafter, several heuristics are used to filter out non-text components based on aspect ratio, contrast histogram, and run-length measurement. Despite their claims that the method could be effectively used in other domains, experimental results were only presented for cargo container images.

Zong et al. [28] use a connected component-based method using color reduction. They quantize the color space using the peak in a color histogram in the RGB color space. This is based on an assumption that text regions tend to cluster together in this color space and occupy a significant portion of the image. Each text component goes through a filtering stage using heuristics, such as area, diameter, and spatial alignment.

Kim [29] segments the image using color clustering in a color histogram in the RGB space. Non-text components, such as long horizontal line and image boundaries, are eliminated. Then, horizontal text lines and text segments are extracted based on iterative projection analysis. In the postprocessing stage, these text segments are merged based on certain heuristics. Since several threshold values need to be determined empirically, this approach is not suitable as a general-purpose text localizer.

Lienhart et al. [30] regard text regions as connected components with the same or similar color and size and apply motion analysis to enhance the text extraction results for video sequence. The input image is segmented based on the monochromatic nature of the text component using a split-and-merge algorithm. After dilation, motion information and contrast analysis are used to enhance the extracted results. A block-matching algorithm using the mean absolute difference criterion is employed to estimate the motion. Their primary focus is on caption text, such as pre-title sequences, credit titles, and closing sequences, which exhibit a higher contrast with the background. This makes it easy to use the contrast difference between the boundary of the detected components and their background in filtering stage.

Jain and Yu [31] apply a connected component-based method after preprocessing, which includes bit dropping, color clustering, multi-valued image decomposition, and foreground image generation. A 24-bit color image is bit dropped to a 6-bit image and then quantized by a color clustering algorithm. After the input image is decomposed into multiple foreground images, each foreground image goes through the same text localization stage. Connected components are generated in parallel for the entire foreground image using a block adjacency graph. The localized text components in the individual foreground images are then merged into one output image. The algorithm extracts only horizontal and vertical text and not skewed text. The authors point out that their algorithm may not work well when the color histogram is sparse.

Due to their relatively simple implementation, connected component-based methods are widely used. Nearly all connected component-based methods have four processing stages: (1) preprocessing, such as color clustering and noise reduction, (2) connected component generation, (3) filtering out non-text components, and (4) component grouping. A connected component-based method could segment a character into multiple connected components, especially in cases of polychrome text strings and low-resolution and noisy video images. Further, the performance of the connected component-based method is severely affected by component grouping, such as a projection profile analysis of text line selection. In addition, several threshold values are needed to filter out the non-text components, and these threshold values are dependent on the image/video database. We will now give details of a connected component-based method using Laplacian operation [32].

3.2.3.1 Text Detection Using Laplacian and Connected Component Analysis

This method is quite popular compared to edge-based, corner-based, and texture-based methods. In this method, initially the low video image is enhanced by performing Laplacian operation on the input image. Then connected component analysis is done for detecting text in video.

3.2.3.2 Text Candidate Detection

Since Laplacian is a second-order derivative, it gives high positive and negative peaks where there is text pixel due to high contrast at or near text [32]. This clue leads to the use of a maximum Laplacian difference operation to include high negative values which represent text pixels. The maximum Laplacian difference is the difference between max and min Laplacian values of the sliding window. The size of the sliding window is 1×11 based on the general width of a typical text stroke. This operation gives a high value if there is a high negative Laplacian value. As a result, the method gives high values for text and low values for non-text. Therefore, k-means with $k = 2$ clustering algorithm is employed on maximum difference matrix to obtain clusters that contain text information. This can be seen in Fig. 3.10 where (a) and (c) are the input frames and (b) and (d) are the respective outputs of k-means clustering algorithm. Figure 3.10 shows that this method is able to detect the presence of both horizontal and non-horizontal text.

Then the method presents skeletonization and connected component analysis to detect text line in video image.

3.2.3.3 Connected Component Classification

Traditionally, rectangular bounding boxes are used for displaying the detected horizontal text. However, they are not suitable for non-horizontal text because

Fig. 3.10 The method is able to identify the candidate text regions for both horizontal and non-horizontal text. (**a**) Horizontal text image, (**b**) text clusters, (**c**) non-horizontal text image, (**d**) text clusters

Fig. 3.11 Skeleton of a
connected component.
(**a**) Connected component,
(**b**) Skeleton

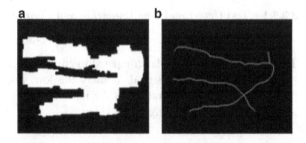

they do not fit the shape of the characters closely and contain many unnecessary background pixels. Therefore, this method proposes to use connected components (CCs) for displaying purposes.

There are two types of CCs: *simple* and *complex*. A simple CC is either a text string or a false positive. On the other hand, a complex CC contains multiple text strings which are connected to each other and to false positives in the background. The segmentation step will be described in detail in the next section. This section explains how to classify every CC as either simple or complex. Skeleton is a well-defined concept in digital image processing to represent the structure of a region (Fig. 3.11a). The intersection points (or junction points) of a skeleton show the locations where the subcomponents of different orientations are connected to each other (Fig. 3.11b), and thus, the rule for CC classification is defined based on the number of intersection points:

$$N\_Inter\sec tion = |Inter\sec tion\,(Skeleton\,(c_i))|$$
$$Type\,(c_i) = \begin{cases} Simple & \text{if } N\_Inter\sec tion = 0 \\ Complex & \text{otherwise} \end{cases} \qquad (3.10)$$

$\{c_i\}$ is the set of CCs in the text cluster returned by the previous step. Skeleton(.) returns the result of skeletonization (including pruning of short spurs). Intersection(.) returns the set of intersection points.

At the end of this step, simple CCs are retained while complex CCs are sent for segmentation.

3.2.3.4   Connected Component Segmentation

In order to output only the text part of a complex CC, there is a need to segment or split it into multiple simple CCs based on the intersection points. For example, in Fig. 3.12a, point A shows the location where the second and third text lines of Fig. 3.12c connect to each other. By segmenting the complex CC from B to A, it is possible to get back the second text line.

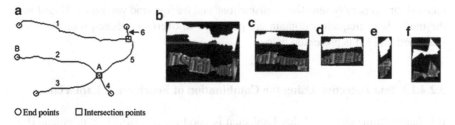

O End points   □ Intersection points

Fig. 3.12 Skeleton segments of Fig. 3.10d and their corresponding subcomponents. For each subcomponent, the corresponding pixels from the input image are also shown. (**a**) Skeleton segments, (**b**) *1*, (**c**) *2*, (**d**) *3*, (**e**) *4*, (**f**) *5*

BA is called a skeleton segment, which is defined as a continuous path from an intersection point to either an end point or another intersection point. In addition, the path should not include any other point in the middle. For each skeleton segment, the method extracts the corresponding subcomponent from the complex CC. Figure 3.12b–f shows the subcomponents of the six skeleton segments in Fig. 3.12a. Note that the subcomponent of segment 1 has already covered segment 6, and thus, there is no separate subcomponent for segment 6. The first four subcomponents are classified as text, while the last subcomponent is classified as false positive (rules based on number of end points and intersection points). In Fig. 3.12, the connected text lines are successfully separated from each other, although some characters are missed due to low contrast.

3.2.3.5   Summary

The method's focus is on text orientation because traditional methods only consider horizontal text. The Laplacian operation is performed on input video image to obtain text cluster results. The method then employs skeletonization to segment a complex CC into constituent parts and thus separate connected text strings from each other. However, the main problem of this kind of method is that the method performance depends on preprocessing step and it must preserve the shape of the text lines. Sometimes, this may not be possible because of disconnection and low resolution of the video.

3.2.4   Frequency Domain Methods

It is observed from the literature on text detection in spatial domain that the methods do not give consistent results for the different datasets because spatial domain-based methods are generally sensitive to distortions and background variations. Therefore, the methods in frequency domain are proposed to overcome these problems. One such method [33] is presented below.

3.2.4.1 Text Detection Using the Combination of Fourier and Laplacian

It is learnt from Sect. 3.2.4 that Laplacian is good for text detection in video. The same method is explored in Fourier domain to make it even more robust. Thus, a combination of Fourier and Laplacian is used here to increase the low contrast of the text in video. This is because video texts usually have very low contrast against complex local backgrounds; it is important to preprocess the input image to highlight the difference between text and non-text regions. Thus, the method proposes a two-step process called Fourier-Laplacian filtering to smooth out noise in the image and to detect candidate text regions.

The first step uses an ideal low-pass filter in the frequency domain to smooth out noise. The rationale is that the high-frequency components of the Fourier transform contain information about noise and thus should be cut off.

The second step follows the work reported in [32], which uses the Laplacian mask in the spatial domain to detect candidate text regions. After the image is filtered, text regions have many positive and negative peaks of large magnitudes. The reverse is true for non-text regions, which makes it possible to differentiate between text and non-text regions (Fig. 3.13c). To combine this step with the previous step, the method uses the Laplacian operator in the frequency domain (instead of the spatial domain):

$$\nabla^2 f(x, y) = \frac{\partial^2 f(x, y)}{\partial x^2} + \frac{\partial^2 f(x, y)}{\partial y^2}$$

$$\Im\left[\frac{\partial^2 f(x, y)}{\partial x^2} + \frac{\partial^2 f(x, y)}{\partial y^2}\right] = -\left(u^2 + v^2\right) F(u, v) \tag{3.11}$$

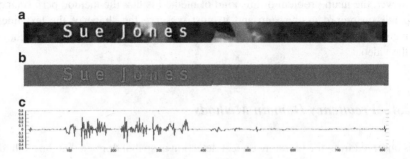

Fig. 3.13 Profiles of text and non-text regions in the Laplacian-filtered image. In (c), the x-axis shows the column numbers while the y-axis shows the pixel values. (a) Input, (b) Laplacian filtered, (c) profile of the middle row of (b)

The combined Fourier-Laplacian filtering is as follows:

$$
\begin{aligned}
F(u, v) &= \Im[f(x, y)] \\
G(u, v) &= H_2(u, v)\,[H_1(u, v)\,F(u, v)] \\
H_1(u, v) &= \begin{cases} 1 & \text{if } D(u, v) \le D_0 \\ 0 & \text{otherwise} \end{cases} \\
H_2(u, v) &= -(u^2 + v^2) \\
g(x, y) &= \Im^{-1}[G(u, v)]
\end{aligned}
\tag{3.12}
$$

$f(x, y)$ and $g(x, y)$ are the original image (converted to grayscale) and the filtered image. $H_1(u, v)$ is the ideal low-pass filter, while $H_2(u, v)$ is the Laplacian operator. $D(u, v)$ is defined as the distance from (u, v) to the origin of the Fourier transform, and D_0 is the cutoff distance.

Figure 3.14 compares the effects of Fourier-Laplacian filtering and Laplacian filtering alone. Images (b) and (c) are the absolute images of $g(x, y)$, and the pixel values are normalized to the range [0, 1]. In these images, bright pixels correspond

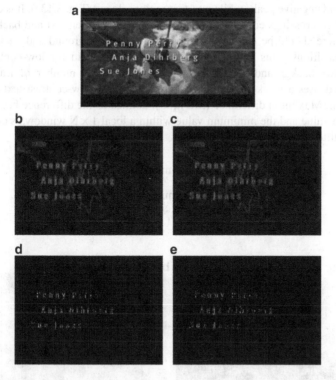

Fig. 3.14 Fourier-Laplacian filtering produces a clearer separation between text and non-text than Laplacian filtering. (**a**) Input, (**b**) Fourier-Laplacian-filtered, (**c**) Laplacian-filtered, (**d**) Binarized, (**e**) Binarized

to text pixels, while dark pixels correspond to non-text pixels. It is observed that image (b) is brighter than image (c), which means that Fourier-Laplacian filtering produces a clearer separation between text and non-text than Laplacian filtering. In order to show the difference in brightness more clearly, the method binarizes (b) and (c) with a fixed threshold of 0.5, i.e., a pixel is considered as a bright pixel if its grayscale value is greater than 0.5. Again, image (d) contains more white pixels than image (e). Thus, Fourier-Laplacian filtering is better than Laplacian filtering alone. The advantage of the former over the latter is that the ideal low-pass filter helps to smooth noise in video images and reduce the problem of noise sensitivity of the Laplacian operator.

The Fourier-Laplacian filter is similar to the Laplacian of Gaussian (LoG) because both filters consist of a smoothing filter and the Laplacian filter. The difference is that the former employs an ideal low-pass filter.

While the later makes use of the Gaussian filter. The ideal low-pass filter is chosen because it has simpler parameters than the (spatial) LoG, which makes it easier to tune and generalize better to different datasets.

Figure 3.15 shows a sample result of Fourier-Laplacian filtering for non-horizontal text. For both horizontal and non-horizontal text, text regions have many positive and negative peaks while non-text regions do not (Fig. 3.13c). It is observed that the zero crossings correspond to the transitions between text and background. Ideally, there should be the same number of text-to-background and background-to-text transitions. This condition, however, does not hold for low-contrast text on complex background. Thus, instead of counting the number of transitions, the method uses a weaker condition to ensure that the low-contrast texts are not missed out. Maximum difference (MD) [33], defined as the difference between the maximum value and the minimum value within a local $1 \times N$ window, is computed from the filtered image:

$$
\begin{aligned}
Max(x, y) &= \max_{\forall t \in [-N/2, N/2]} g(x, y - t) \\
Min(x, y) &= \min_{\forall t \in [-N/2, N/2]} g(x, y - t) \\
MD(x, y) &= Max(x, y) - Min(x, y)
\end{aligned}
\tag{3.13}
$$

Fig. 3.15 Result of Fourier-Laplacian filtering for non-horizontal text. (**a**) Input, (**b**) Fourier-Laplacian filtered

Note that (x, y) in the above notation represents a pixel on row x and column y. The MD map is obtained by moving the window over the image (Fig. 3.15b).

Text regions have larger MD values than non-text regions because of the larger magnitudes of the positive and negative peaks. The method uses k-means to classify all pixels into two clusters, text and non-text, based on the Euclidean distance of MD values. Let the two clusters returned by k-means be C_1 (cluster mean M_1) and C_2 (cluster mean M_2). Since the cluster order varies for different runs, the following rule to identify the text cluster:

$$Text\_Cluster = \begin{cases} C_1 & \text{if } M_1 > M_2 \\ C_2 & \text{otherwise} \end{cases} \qquad (3.14)$$

This clustering step can also be thought of as binarizing the MD map. k-means is chosen for simplicity, and it does not require any threshold values. The morphological operation *opening* is used to remove small artifacts.

The end result of this step, the text cluster, plays an important role in the method because if it misses low-contrast text lines, the subsequent steps will not be able to recover those lines. The method employs three main techniques. First, because video images are noisy due to compression, an ideal low-pass filter is used to smooth out noise. Second, the Laplacian operator is a second-order derivative operator which gives stronger response to fine detail than first-order derivative operators and thus ensures that low-contrast text lines are not missed out. Its disadvantage of noise sensitivity is largely reduced because the image has been smoothed. Finally, the method employs the maximum difference (instead of the normal difference between corresponding positive and negative peaks) to further increase the gap between text and non-text. Final text detection results of the method can be seen in Fig. 3.16.

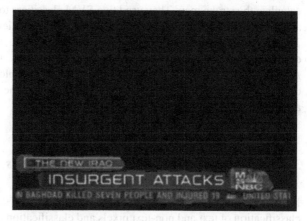

Fig. 3.16 Final text detection results of the method

3.2.4.2   Summary

This section describes a method that is able to handle both graphics text and scene text of any orientation. The Laplacian in the frequency domain helps to identify the candidate text regions, while the skeleton-based connected components analysis serves to segment a complex CC into constituent parts and separate connected text strings from each other.

3.3   Machine Learning-Based Methods

Machine learning-based methods are used for text block verification and to improve text detection accuracy by removing false positives. Since video contains low-resolution and complex background, it is hard to prevent false positives with any feature extraction. In order to improve precision by removing false positives, the extracted features are feed to different classifier to classify text and non-text blocks correctly. There are three popular classifiers used for text detection in this field that are as follows.

3.3.1   Support Vector Machine-Based Methods

Support vector machine has the ability to convert nonlinear problem to linear problem, and it also can solve the problem of multidimensional feature problem. Jung et al. described stroke filter to identify text candidates, and then SVM is used for verification of the candidate text. Based on verification score and color distribution, the text line refinement is done. Li et al. [34] used stroke filter to calculate the stroke map. They used two SVM classifiers to obtain rough text region and to verify the candidate text lines. Localization is achieved by projection profile. The second SVM is used to verify localized text lines. A hybrid system for text detection based on edges, local binary pattern operator, and SVM is proposed by Anthimpoulos et al. [35]. After the detection of text block using the edge map, dilation, opening, projection profile analysis, and machine learning step using SVM are introduced for refinements.

3.3.2   Neural Network Model-Based Methods

It is known that neural network classifier is good for solving complex problems like classification of text and non-text pixels and classification of text block and non-text blocks. Several methods have used NN for classifying text and non-text pixels as well as removing false positives. Zhang and Sun [36] used a pulse-couple neural network edge-based method for locating text. The work uses NN in the frequency domain for solving text localization problem. Due to the problem of deciding weights and number of hidden layers, NN work is not popular for text detection. Therefore, there are hardly any methods using NN for text detection. However, the use of Bayesian classifier is shown as an effective method for classification of text and non-text pixel among other classifiers.

3.3.3 Bayes Classification-Based Methods

As discussed in the above sections, classifier performance depends on the number of samples for training and the parameters for tuning. Therefore, classifier-based methods restrict the ability to detect text in different scripts though they remove false positives and improve the accuracy. However, a Bayesian classifier reported in [37] has been shown to work without a priori knowledge of the input data and it learns automatically the conditional probability and a priori probabilities. This method is described in greater details below.

3.3.3.1 Text Detection Using Bayesian Classifier

The method involves four major steps. In the first step, it calculates the product of Laplacian and Sobel operations on the input image to enhance the text details. This is called the Laplacian-Sobel Product (LSP) process. The Bayesian classifier is used for classifying true text pixels based on three probable matrices as described in the second step. The three probable matrices are obtained on the basis of LSP such that high-contrast pixels in LSP are classified as text pixels (HLSP), k-means with $k = 2$ of maximum gradient difference of HLSP (K-MGD-HLSP), and k-means of LSP (KLSP). Here MGD is the difference between max and min values of a sliding window over HLSP. Text candidates are obtained by intersecting the output of Bayesian with the Canny map of the input image. The boundary growing method based on a nearest neighbor concept is described in the third step. The fourth step provides geometrical properties of text blocks to eliminate false positives.

3.3.3.2 Text Enhancement

It is noticed that text regions typically have a large number of discontinuities from text-to-background regions and background to text. Thus, this property gives a strong indication of the presence of text. In this section, the method tries to exploit this property by using Laplacian and Sobel masks and combining the results as follows. The method uses a 3×3 mask to obtain fine enhanced details of text pixels. The Laplacian operation is a second-order derivative and is used to detect discontinuities in four directions: horizontal, vertical, up-left, and up-right

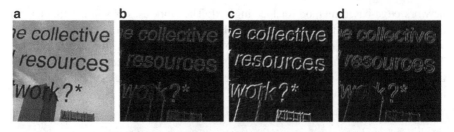

Fig. 3.17 Laplacian-Sobel Product process. (**a**) Input, (**b**) Laplacian, (**c**) Sobel, (**d**) LSP

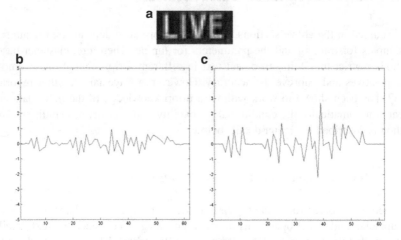

Fig. 3.18 High positive and negative values. (**a**) Text sample, (**b**) Laplacian for (**a**), (**c**) LSP for (**a**)

for the image in Fig. 3.17a. As a result, it enhances details of both low- and high-contrast pixels in the image as shown in Fig. 3.17b. However, this operation produces more noisy pixels than the Sobel operation [37]. This noise may be the cause for poor performance of the text detection. On the other hand, it is known that Sobel mask operation is a first-order derivative, and hence, it produces fine details at discontinuities in horizontal and vertical directions [37]. This results in an enhancement at high-contrast text pixels but no enhancement at low-contrast text pixels as shown in Fig. 3.17c for the image shown in Fig. 3.17a. Thus, the method uses a new operation called Laplacian-Sobel Product (LSP) to preserve details at both high- and low-contrast text pixels while reducing noise in relatively flat areas as shown in Fig. 3.17d. LSP is the product of the results of Laplacian and Sobel operations in order to obtain fine details at text pixel areas in the image. This is clearly illustrated in Fig. 3.18 where (a) is a sample text image, (b) is a graph of Laplacian values along the middle scan line in (a), and (c) is a graph of LSP values along the same middle scan line in (a). It can be noticed from Fig. 3.18b and c the high positive and negative peaks for LSP compared to the Laplacian results alone. This is evident that LSP enhances details at text pixels.

Further, in order to show that LSP is better than Laplacian alone in terms of quantitative measures, experiments are conducted using only Laplacian and LSP for horizontal text detection. The experimental results will be presented in the experimental section.

3.3.3.3 Bayesian Classifier for True Text Pixel Classification

Classification of exact text and non-text pixel is an important step in text detection as it affects the performance of the text detection methods. Therefore, the method considers this as a two-class classification problem using a Bayesian classifier method for classifying text and non-text pixels accurately. To estimate the posterior probability of the Bayesian classifier, the method needs to have a priori and conditional probabilities. The method estimates conditional probabilities based on three probable text matrices that are (1) HLSP (P_1), (2) K-MGD-HLSP (P_2), and (3) KLSP (P_3), for which, the LSP is the basis as it is described in the previous section. The method chooses 100 sample images randomly from the database to produce the three probable text matrices.

Pixel values in LSP show that there are text pixels that have high positive and negative values as it is seen in Fig. 3.18c. The method derives three probable matrices by keeping these values. HLSP performs classification of text pixels whose magnitudes are greater than 0.5 in the normalized LSP as shown in Fig. 3.19a. HLSP gives high-contrast pixels in LSP, but it may lose low-contrast text pixels that have negative values.

K-MGD-LSP is the classification of high-contrast text pixels by applying k-means with $K = 2$ on MGD of HLSP, where MGD is the difference between the max and min gradient values in a sliding window over HLSP as shown in Fig. 3.19b. K-MGD-HLSP gives high-contrast and low-contrast pixels since it involves MGD and it helps in selecting pixels which have high negative and positive values in LSP. In this case, there are less chances of losing text pixels.

KLSP is the classification of probable text pixels by k-means on LSP as shown in Fig. 3.19c. This may include both text and non-text pixels as it does not care about negative and positive values of pixels in LSP. In this way, the method computes three probable text matrices to estimate posterior probability. Note that the three

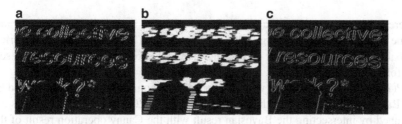

Fig. 3.19 Three probable matrices. (**a**) HLSP (P1), (**b**) K-MGD-HLSP (P2), (**c**) KLSP (P3)

Fig. 3.20 Posterior probability estimation and text candidates: (**a**) TPM, (**b**) NTPM, (**c**) Bayesian result, (**d**) text candidates

probable text matrices P_1, P_2, and P_3 each represent a binary decision on every text pixel. Collectively, the method uses the average of the binary decisions to estimate the conditional text probability matrix (TPM) as shown in Fig. 3.20a. By the same token, the method finds three probable non-text matrices N_1, N_2, and N_3 based on the same processes above using the same sample images, representing each a binary decision on every pixel's likelihood of being a non-text. Similarly, the method uses their collective decisions to estimate the conditional non-text probability matrix (NTPM) as shown in Fig. 3.20b.

More specifically, the conditional text probability matrix (TPM) is defined as follows where T represents the text class:

$$P\left(f\left(x,y\right)\big|T\right) = \frac{P_1\left(f\left(x,y\right)\right) + P_2\left(f\left(x,y\right)\right) + P_3\left(f\left(x,y\right)\right)}{3} \qquad (3.15)$$

Similarly, the conditional non-text probability matrix (NTPM) is defined as follows where NT represents the non-text class:

$$P\left(f\left(x,y\right)\big|NT\right) = \frac{N_1\left(f\left(x,y\right)\right) + N_2\left(f\left(x,y\right)\right) + N_3\left(f\left(x,y\right)\right)}{3} \qquad (3.16)$$

Now the above conditional probabilities are used to estimate a posterior probability matrix (PPM). Bayesian classifier formula for each pixel $f(x,y)$ is given by

$$P\left(T\big|f\left(x,y\right)\right) = \frac{P\left(f\left(x,y\right)\big|T\right)P(T)}{P\left(f\left(x,y\right)\big|T\right)P(T) + P\left(f\left(x,y\right)\big|NT\right)P(NT)} \qquad (3.17)$$

where $P(T|f(x,y))$ is the probability that a pixel $f(x,y)$ in the resultant output frame of the Bayesian classifier in Fig. 3.20c is a text pixel. $P(T)$ and $P(NT)$ are the a priori probabilities calculated based on text and non-text pixels in LSP. The method sets the following decision:

$P(T|f(x,y)) \geq 0.5 \rightarrow BC(x,y) = 1$, where BC is the resultant matrix produced by the Bayesian classifier algorithm as shown in Fig. 3.20c. Then text candidates are obtained by intersecting the Bayesian result with the Canny operation result of the original image as shown in Fig. 3.20d.

3.3.3.4 Boundary Growing Method for Traversing Multi-oriented Text

The main problem of multi-oriented text detection is traversing the text pixels detected by the Bayesian classifier along the text direction to fix a closed bounding box. This is because the complex background in video makes traversing only text pixels more challenging and interesting. Unlike conventional projection profile used by other text detection methods for horizontal text, the method introduces a new idea of boundary growing method (BGM) based on the nearest neighbor concept. The basis for this method is that text lines in the image always appear with characters and words in regular spacing in one direction. The method scans a text candidate image (Fig. 3.20d) from the top-left pixel to the bottom-right pixel. When the method finds a component during scanning, it fixes a bounding box for that component and it allows the bounding box to grow until it reaches a pixel of the component where an adjacent bounding box is formed. This process will continue till the end of the text line. The end of the text line is determined empirically based on the spacing between characters, words, and lines. Figure 3.21 illustrates the boundary growing procedure for the first text lines shown in Fig. 3.20d, where (a)–(f) show the process of growing bounding boxes along the text direction. This process may give false positives as shown in Fig. 3.21g because this process sometimes covers background information. The method uses a few heuristics such as aspect ratio of the bounding box and edge ratio to eliminate false positives. Some false positives nevertheless may still remain as shown in Fig. 3.21h after the elimination process. Finally, the method uses few heuristics to eliminate such false positives.

3.3.3.5 Summary

The method presented in this section shows that Bayesian classifier is useful for text detection and is better than other classifier-based methods. The combination

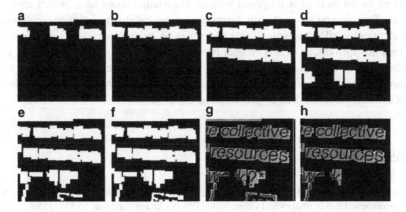

Fig. 3.21 Boundary growing method

of Laplacian and Sobel is worth to enhance low-contrast text in video as it considers advantage of both Laplacian and Sobel. Three probable text matrices and three probable non-text matrices are derived based on clustering and the result of enhancement method. To traverse the multi-oriented text, the method proposes a boundary growing method based on the nearest neighbor concept.

3.4 Summary

This chapter focuses on caption text detection in video using different methods, namely, feature-based methods (which include edge-based, texture-based, connected component analysis-based, time domain-based methods) and machine learning-based methods (which include Bayesian classifier-based methods). Edge-based methods generally rely on high contrast of text pixels. Therefore, the developed methods are good for text detection in video containing plane background and high-contrast texts. However, though the methods are fast, they produce more false positives when there is a complex background. Texture-based methods explore texture property of text information to detect text in video. However, the methods are computationally expensive compared to other methods because of high computations for texture computation. In addition, these methods are sensitive to fonts, font sizes, etc. Therefore, simple connected component-based methods are proposed to speed up text detection process. These methods work well when texts have uniform color and have similar geometrical properties. These constraints are not valid for scene text detection in video. Hence, though these methods are simple and fast, the methods do not achieve good accuracy for all kinds of text detection. The machine learning-based methods are developed by keeping high false positives in mind to improve method's accuracy. These methods are good when they get a large number of samples for training. Therefore, these methods restrict the ability of detection of different script text lines. To overcome this problem, Bayesian classifier-based method is proposed without knowledge about ideal information of dataset. This method automatically learns a priori probability to estimate conditional probabilities. While the focus of this chapter is on caption text detection, some of the methods introduced in this chapter have the capability to detect scene text. For instance, the Fourier and Laplacian methods are powerful enough to capture text features not only in caption texts but also in natural scenes. More specific methods for scene text detection will be presented in Chap. 4.

References

1. Dimitrova N, Agnihotri L, Dorai C, Bolle R (2000) MPEG-7 video text description scheme for superimposed text in images and video. Signal Process Image Commun 16:137–155
2. Jung K, Kim KI, Jain AK (2004) Text information extraction in images and video: a survey. Pattern Recognit 37:977–997

3. Chen D, Luttin J, Shearer K (2000) A survey of text detection and recognition in images and videos, IDIAP research report, pp 1–21
4. Zhang J, Kasturi R (2008) Extraction of text objects in video documents: recent progress. In: Proceedings of the eighth IAPR workshop on document analysis systems (DAS), pp 5–17
5. Doermann D, Liang J, Li H (2003) Progress in camera-based document image analysis. In: Proceedings of the seventh international conference on document analysis and recognition (ICDAR)
6. Smith MA, Kanade T (1995) Video skimming for quick browsing based on audio and image characterization, Technical report CMU-CS-95-186. Mellon University, Pittsburgh
7. Chen D, Shearer K, Bourlard H (2001) Text enhancement with asymmetric filter for video OCR. In: Proceedings of the international conference on image analysis and processing, pp 192–197
8. Shivakumara P, Huang W, Tan CL (2008) An efficient edge based technique for text detection in video frames. In: Proceedings of the international workshop on document analysis systems (DAS 2008), pp 307–314
9. Shivakumara P, Huang W, Tan CL (2008) Efficient video text detection using edge features. In: Proceedings of the international conference on pattern recognition (ICPR08)
10. Shivakumara P, Phan TQ, Tan CL (2009) Video text detection based on filters and edge analysis. In: Proceedings of the ICME 2009, pp 514–517
11. Shivakumara P, Phan TQ, Tan CL (2009) A gradient difference based technique for video text detection. In: Proceedings of the ICDAR 2009, pp 156–160
12. Phan TQ, Shivakumara P, Tan CL (2009) A Laplacian method for video text detection. In: Proceedings of the ICDAR, pp 66–70
13. Shivakumara P, Huang W, Trung PQ, Tan CL (2010) Accurate video text detection through classification of low and high contrast images. Pattern Recognit 43:2165–2185
14. Park SH, Kim KI, Jung K, Kim HJ (1999) Locating car license plates using neural networks. IEEE Electron Lett 35:1475–1477
15. Wu V, Manmatha R, Risean EM (1999) TextFinder: an automatic system to detect and recognize text in images. IEEE Trans Pattern Anal Mach Intell (PAMI) 21:1224–1229
16. Sin B, Kim S, Cho B (2002) Locating characters in scene images using frequency features. Proc Int Conf Pattern Recognit (ICPR) 3:489–492
17. Mao W, Chung F, Lanm K, Siu W (2002) Hybrid Chinese/English text detection in images and video frames. Proc Int Conf Pattern Recognit (ICPR) 3:1015–1018
18. Jain AK, Zhong Y (1996) Page segmentation using texture analysis. Pattern Recognit 29: 743–770
19. Kim KI, Jung J, Park SH, Kim HJ (2001) Support vector machine-based text detection in digital video. Pattern Recognit 34:527–529
20. Li H, Doermann D (2000) A video text detection system based on automated training. Proc Int Conf Pattern Recognit (ICPR) 223
21. Jung K (2001) Neural network-based text location in color images. Pattern Recognit Lett 22:1503–1515
22. Shivakumara P, Phan TQ, Tan CL (2009) A robust wavelet transform based technique for video text detection. In: Proceedings of the ICDAR, pp 1285–1289
23. Shivakumara P, Dutta A, Tan CL, Pal U (2010) A new wavelet-median-moment based method for multi-oriented video text detection. In: Proceedings of the DAS, pp 279–288
24. Shivakumara P, Phan TQ, Tan CL (2010) New Fourier-Statistical Features in RGB space for video text detection. IEEE Trans Circ Syst Video Technol (TCSVT) 20:1520–1532
25. Shivakumara P, Phan TQ, Tan CL (2011) A Laplacian approach to multi-oriented text detection in video. IEEE Trans Pattern Anal Mach Intell (TPAMI) 33:412–419
26. Ohya, Shio A, Akamatsu S (1994) Recognizing characters in scene images. IEEE Trans Pattern Anal Mach Intell (PAMI) 16:214–224
27. Lee CM, Kankanhalli A (1995) Automatic extraction of characters in complex images. Int J Pattern Recognit Artif Intell (IJPRAI) 9:67–82

28. Zhong Y, Karu K, Jain AK (1995) Locating text in complex color images. Pattern Recognit 28:1523–1535
29. Kim HK (1996) Efficient automatic text location method and content-based indexing and structuring of video database. J Vis Commun Image Represent 7:336–344
30. Lienhart R, Stuber F (1996) Automatic text recognition in digital videos. In: Proceedings of the SPIE, pp 180–188
31. Jain AK, Yu B (1998) Automatic text location in images and video frames. Pattern Recognit 31:2055–2076
32. Phan TQ, Shivakumara P, Tan CL (2010) A skeleton-based method for multi-oriented text detection. In: Ninth IAPR international workshop on document analysis and systems (DAS10), pp 271–278
33. Shivakumara P, Phan TQ, Tan CL (2011) A Laplacian approach to multi-oriented text detection in video. IEEE Trans PAMI 33(2):412–419
34. Li X, Wang W, Jiang S, Huang Q, Gao W (2008) Fast effective text detection. In: Proceedings of the international conference on image processing (ICIP), pp 969–972
35. Anthimopoulus M, Gatos B, Pratikakis I (2008) A hybrid system for text detection in video frames. International Conf Doc Anal Syst (DAS) 1:286–292
36. Zhang X, Sun F (2011) Pulse coupled neural network edge based algorithm for image text locating. Tsinghua Sci Technol 16:22–30
37. Shivakumara P, Sreedhar RP, Phan TQ, Shijian L, Tan CL (2012) Multi-oriented video scene text detection through Bayesian classification and boundary growing. IEEE Trans CSVT 22:1227–1235

Chapter 4
Text Detection from Video Scenes

Text in video contains valuable information and is exploited in many content-based video applications. There mainly exist two kinds of text occurrences in videos, namely, graphics and scene text. Graphics text is artificially added in order to describe the video content, while scene text is textual content captured by a camera as a necessary part of a video scene, e.g., the name of a restaurant or road signs. Scene text potentially benefits developing useful video applications such as video information retrieval, mobile-based scene classification, and video object recognition. However, scene text detection has not been systematically explored even people have developed a lot of optical character recognition (OCR) techniques in the past decades. For example, the problem of visual content understanding has been one of the most challenging goals in the computer vision and pattern recognition community, which has manifested in various forms of visual segmentation, object detection, object recognition, and image classification, or the addressing of all these tasks. To explain a typical street scene like the Google Street View in Fig. 4.1, popular visual understanding methods detect and identify objects such as car, person, tree, road, and sky from the scene image successfully. However, regions containing text tends to be ignored [2].

Essentially, viewers easily fixate on text when shown scene images both containing text and other visual objects. The computer vision community has now shown a huge interest in this problem of scene text detection from video or image in the recent years, and understanding scene text is becoming more important than ever, especially with the rapid growth of camera- or video-based mobile applications and devices today.

On the other hand, text from video or image natural scenes is extremely challenging to detect and recognize. Traditional OCR is considered as one of the most successful applications, but the performance of OCR drastically drops when applied to such natural scenes containing both text and various scene objects [1]. There are several reasons for this. First, the variety of color, font, size, and orientation of scene text bring difficulties of OCR techniques (see Fig. 4.2a, where

© Springer-Verlag London 2014

T. Lu et al., *Video Text Detection*, Advances in Computer Vision
and Pattern Recognition, DOI 10.1007/978-1-4471-6515-6_4

Fig. 4.1 A typical street scene image taken from Google Street Map. The scene contains signboards with text on the building and windows. Scene objects such as cars, buildings, garbage can, tree, and regions of road and sky together describe an outdoor scene

scene texts have a large variety of appearances, with issues such as very different fonts, shadows, low resolution, and occlusions). Second, scene images exhibit wide range of unknown imaging conditions which in general add sensitivity to noises, shadows, occlusion, lights, motion blur, and resolution. Third, the inputs of most of the OCR engines are well-segmented texts which have been distinguished from background pixels. Unfortunately, the segmentation of scene text is much harder for natural scene images. Finally, there exists less overall structure with high variability both in geometry and visual appearance in scene images, and there are generally far less texts in scenes [3]. Figure 4.2b shows the OCR results on the original scene images. It can be seen that standard off-the-shelf OCR techniques perform very poorly on such scene images.

This chapter gives an introduction to the current progress on scene text detection especially in the past several years. It starts from discussing the visual saliency of scene texts in Sect. 4.1 to describe the characteristics of text in natural scene images. Then, the recent developments of scene text detection from video or image are discussed in Sect. 4.2, roughly being categorized into bottom-up, top-down, statistic and learning, temporal or motion analysis, and hybrid approaches. Next, scene character recognition methods are introduced in Sect. 4.3. Section 4.4 shows typical scene text datasets, and finally Sect. 4.5 concludes this chapter.

4.1   Visual Saliency of Scene Texts

Although detection of scene text is a complex problem for computers, humans can easily distinguish scene texts from their complex backgrounds in the same scene without difficulties. It is probably due to the ability of humans to simultaneously process multiple channels of scene context and then focus the attention on scene texts. We thereby first explore the salient visual characteristics of scene texts before introducing the details of text detection methods, especially focusing on imitating

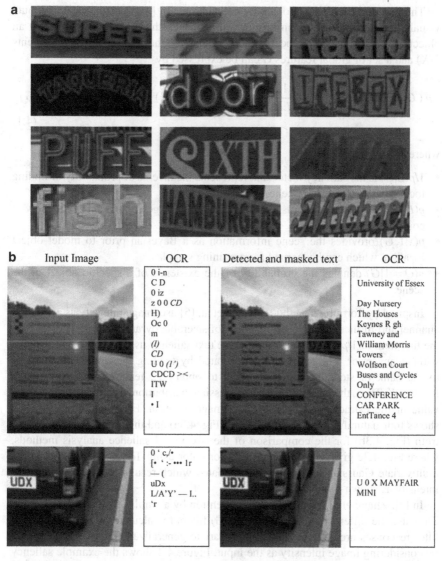

Fig. 4.2 Scene text variations and OCR results on natural scene images: (**a**) scene texts have a large variety of appearances, with issues such as very different fonts, shadows, low resolution, and occlusions, and (**b**) columns from left to right: original image, OCR output on the original image, text segmentation mask (superimposed of gray-level versions of original images), OCR output on the masks [3]

human perceptions through visual saliency models. We introduce several typical saliency representations, namely, probability-based maps (*Torralba's saliency map*, *Zhang's fast saliency map*), graph-based maps (*Harel's graph-based saliency map*, *Itti's saliency map*), and curvature-based maps (*Karaoglu's curvature saliency map* and *Shivakumara's gradient vector flow*).

The first approach uses probability calculations. In [4], Torralba et al. compute visual attention by a Bayesian framework, in which the probability of finding an object $p(O = 1, X | L, G)$ at a location $X = (x, y)$ given the set of local measurements $L(X)$ and a set of global features G can be expressed by

$$p(O = 1, X | L, G) = \frac{1}{p(L|G)} p(L|O = 1, X, G) p(x|1, G) p(O = 1|G)$$

(4.1)

where

- $1/p(L|G)$ is the saliency factor that represents the inverse of probability of finding local measurements in a scene.
- $p(L|O = 1, X, G)$ represents the knowledge of target appearance and how it contributes to the object.
- $p(x|1, G)$ provides the scene information as a Bayesian prior to model object location, which can be learned from training samples.
- $p(O = 1|G)$ denotes the probability of the existence of a specific object in the scene.

Inspired by Torralba's method, Shahab et al. [5] use image intensity as a separate channel and further compute the response of steerable pyramid filters. They choose the first item of $1/p(L|G)$ to calculate scene text saliency using local image features without any prior. The features are generated by feeding the raw RGB channels to the bank of steerable pyramid filters to obtain 72 features for every image location X. Then, they use multivariate Gaussian distribution to estimate the saliency value of the extracted features at each image location. For illustration, Fig. 4.3 shows four natural scene text images (see Fig. 4.3a) and the corresponding ground truth (Fig. 4.3b) for the comparison of the two visual salience analysis methods, where Fig. 4.3c gives the saliency maps for color using Torralba's method, and a multivariate Gaussian distribution is estimated which results in saliency maps for intensity as shown in Fig. 4.3d.

In [7], Zhang et al. compute human attention by a similar Bayesian framework. They use the difference of Gaussian (DoG) filters to calculate local saliency. The filter responses are estimated by a multivariate generalized Gaussian distribution by considering image intensity as the input. Figure 4.4 shows the example saliency maps from Fig. 4.3a using Zhang's model.

The second approach uses graph-based computations. In [6], Harel et al. propose a graph-based saliency (GBVS) model to ultimately highlight a handful of "significant" locations, composed of the following three stages:

1. *Extraction*: Extract feature vectors at locations over the scene image.
2. *Activation*: Form an "activation map" (or maps) using the feature vectors.
3. *Normalization/Combination*: Normalize the maps into a single map.

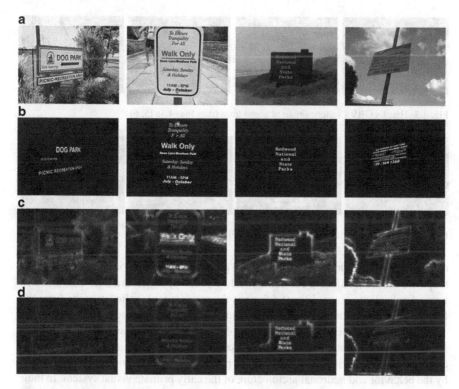

Fig. 4.3 Example scene text images and the corresponding Torralba's saliency maps: (**a**) the original scene text images, (**b**) the ground truth texts, (**c**) Torralba's saliency map of scene texts (Color), and (**d**) Torralba's saliency map of scene texts (intensity) [5]

Fig. 4.4 Zhang's fast saliency map of scene texts from Fig. 4.3a [5, 7]

Specifically, during the first stage, they extract the features of color, intensity, and orientation from scene images. In the second stage, Markov chains over various image maps are defined, and the equilibrium distribution over map locations is used to calculate the activation map and saliency maps. Then, they construct a fully connected directed graph joining all the nodes of the feature map and assign weight to the edges proportional to the dissimilarity between the nodes and their spatial closeness. A Markov process on such a graph is defined to estimate the equilibrium distribution of such a chain. Accordingly, the result of this stage is an activation map

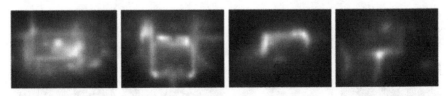

Fig. 4.5 Harel's GBVS saliency map of scene texts from Fig. 4.3a [5, 6]

Fig. 4.6 Itti's saliency map of scene texts from Fig. 4.3a [5, 8]

or conspicuity map derived from pairwise contrast. In the final stage, the activation maps are normalized using the same Markov process, which are later combined to give a final saliency map. Figure 4.5 gives the result sample saliency maps from the four outdoor scene images in Fig. 4.3a using Harel's GBVS model.

To break down the complex problem of scene representation and scene content understanding by rapidly selecting conspicuous locations to be analyzed in detail in a computational efficient way, Itti et al. [8] present a visual attention system, inspired by the behavior and neuronal architecture of the early primate visual system. In their method, multi-scale image features of color, intensity, and orientation are combined into a single topographical saliency map. A dynamic neural network then selects attended locations in order of decreasing saliency.

In Itti's model, visual input is first decomposed into a set of topographic feature maps. They use a dyadic Gaussian pyramid to progressively subsample the image from scale 0 (1:1) to scale 8 (1:256) in 8 octaves. Altogether 12 color maps are generated using specialized double opponent colors such as red-green and blue-yellow. Moreover, they use Gabor filters tuned to 0, 45, 90, and 135° and calculate the response of these filters on intensity values. After subsampling from the filter response, 24 orientation maps will be obtained using the center-surround operation. Next, different spatial locations then compete for saliency within each map, such that only locations which locally stand out from their surround can persist. Finally, all feature maps are fed into a master "saliency map" by topographically computing local conspicuity over the entire visual scene. Essentially, such a map is believed to be located in the posterior parietal cortex and consequently represents a complete account for bottom-up saliency without any top-down guidance to shift attention. Figure 4.6 gives the results of Itti's saliency model on the scene texts from Fig. 4.3a.

These saliency maps are effective to reveal various salient regions in scenes but potentially play different roles in revealing scene text regions. In [5], Shahab et al. evaluate the performances of the introduced saliency models for detecting scene texts. They select the scenery image dataset in [9] as the benchmark and compare

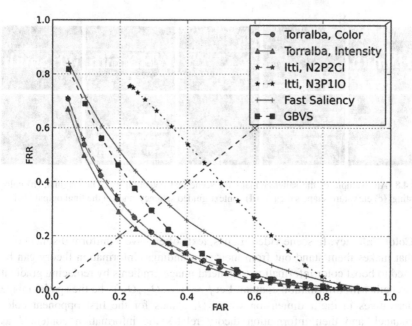

Fig. 4.7 ROC curves in scene text detection using different saliency models [5]

the salient pixels with the ground truth of scene texts. The comparison of different saliency models is shown in Fig. 4.7. They find that Torralba's saliency map using the intensity channel clearly performs the best with equal error rate of 0.23, and the performance of Itti's best parameter combination (N2P2CI) is comparable to that of Torralba's saliency maps obtained by using the color information. According to Fig. 4.7, Zhang's fast saliency model is less suitable for scene text detection, potentially due to the fact that it is very sensitive to slight variations of intensity. The worst performing Itti's parameter combination (N3P1IO) is given for reference in their evaluations.

In the curvature-based approach, curvature saliency also shows its potential use in distinguishing scene texts from the background by gathering text distribution statistics due to its robustness to imaging conditions. Karaoglu et al. [10] propose scene text detection based on curvature saliency cues to prevent an exhaustive spatial and scale search over all possible regions. They focus on curvature and color saliencies for scene text detection, where curvature saliency and color saliency are respectively computed as follows:

- **Curvature Saliency**. The curvature saliency defined by $D = \sqrt{f_{I,xx}^2 + f_{I,xy}^2 + f_{I,yy}^2}$ is employed, where $f_{I,xx}^2$ and $f_{I,yy}^2$ stand for the second-order derivatives of the intensity image $f_I(x, y)$ in the x and y dimensions, respectively. Due to the contrast between text and its background, text regions strongly respond to curvature saliency (see Fig. 4.8c).

Fig. 4.8 An example of the saliency maps for scene text detection. (**a**) The original, (**b**) color boosting, (**c**) curvature shape saliency, (**d**) context-guided saliency, and (**e**) the final output [10]

- **Color Saliency**. In scene video frames, texts often have a uniform distinct color that makes them stand out from their surroundings. Information theory can be used to boost color information to general image gradients by replacing gradient strength with information content. Let $f_x = (O_{1x}, O_{2x}, O_{3x})^T$ be the spatial image derivatives in the x dimension where O_1 stands for the first opponent color channel, and then information theory relates the information content I as $I(f_x) = -\log(p(f_x))$, where $p(f_x)$ is the probability of the spatial derivative. The saliency of text color transitions can then be enhanced by integrating color boosting (see Fig. 4.8b).

Accordingly, the curvature and color boosting maps are individually reconstructed and normalized to a fixed range [0, 1] to make a linear combination and feature integration possible. The saliency maps are converted into binary images by setting saliency values greater than zero to 1 and keep all others at 0 to extract connected components on the saliency maps. Note that predefined priors on text regions and non-text regions of spatial occurrence probability (see Fig. 4.8c) help avoid an exhaustive search for character detection. The binary and filtered saliency map is further processed to fill the holes within regions and enlarged with morphological dilation. The final returned saliency maps are scene text detection output. Since the method does not rely on heuristics nor on a learning phase, it can detect a priori unseen text styles at any orientation and scale.

In [27], Shivakumara et al. explore gradient vector flow (GVF) [28] for identifying dominant text pixels using the Sobel edge map of an input image in video. The GVF is a vector that minimizes the energy functional by

$$\varepsilon = \iint \mu \left(u_x^2 + u_y^2 + v_x^2 + v_y^2 \right) + |\nabla f|^2 \left| g - \nabla f^2 \right| dx dy \qquad (4.2)$$

where $g(x, y) = (u(x, y), v(x, y))$ is the GVF field and $f(x, y)$ is the edge map of the input video image. Sobel provides fine details for text and fewer details for non-text, while Canny gives lots of erratic edges for background. The GVF is extension

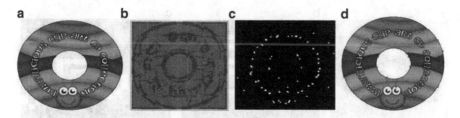

Fig. 4.9 Dominant point selection based on GVF. (**a**) Original video frame, (**b**) GVF for (**a**), (**c**) dominant text pixels, and (**d**) dominant pixels extracted from the input video frame [27]

of gradient which extends the gradient map farther away from the edges and into homogeneous regions using computational diffusion process. This results in the inherent competition of the diffusion process which will create vectors that point into boundary concavities. GVF is believed to help propagate gradient information of magnitude and direction into homogeneous regions, helping detect multiple forces at corner points of object contours. This cue allows using multiple forces at corner points of edge components in the Sobel edge map of an input video frame to identify them as dominant pixels. Accordingly, the dominant pixels will remove most of the background information to simplify the problem of text detection along multiple orientations. Figure 4.9a shows an input image, and Fig. 4.9b is the GVF for all the pixels in Fig. 4.9a. It is observed from Fig. 4.9b that dense forces at corners of contours and at curve boundaries of text components are more cursive than non-text components in general. The dominant text pixels are shown in Fig. 4.9c by removing almost all non-text components and Fig. 4.9d by overlaying on the input video frame, respectively.

To further illustrate how GVF information helps in selecting dominant text pixels, a single character "a" is chosen in Fig. 4.10a. After getting the Sobel edge map shown in Fig. 4.10b, GVF arrows on the Sobel edge map are shown in Fig. 4.10c. It can be seen that all the GVF arrows are pointing toward the inner contour of the character image "a." It is because of the low contrast in the background and the high contrast at the inner boundary of the character image "a." Thus, from Fig. 4.10d, they observe that corner points and cursive text pixels on the contour attract more GVF arrows compared to non-corner points and non-text pixels. The overall area shows that a greater number of GVF forces are pointing toward that text pixel.

Based on these observations, they first extract edge components corresponding to dominant pixels in the Sobel edge map, which called text candidates (TC) of the text lines. Then, two grouping schemes are proposed. The first finds the nearest neighbors based on geometrical properties of TC to group broken segments into word patches. The second is based on the direction and the size of the candidate TC to enable arbitrarily oriented text line detection in video frame.

Theoretically, visual text saliency computation helps search for specific regions from complex scenes in a reduced space to improve the efficiency, especially for detecting text from video. It thereby can be considered as a preprocessing step

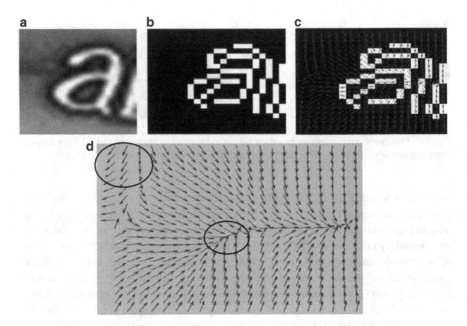

Fig. 4.10 Magnified GVF for corner and non-corner pixels marked by oval shape. (**a**) A character from video, (**b**) the Sobel edge map of (**a**), (**c**) GVF overlaid on the Sobel edge map, and (**d**) GVF for the character in (**a**) [27]

adopted in the early stage of a scene text detection algorithm to search for text region candidates or used as a kind of visual feature to facilitate distinguishing scene text candidates from their complex backgrounds.

4.2 Natural Scene Text Detection Methods

As introduced at the beginning of this chapter, the computer vision and recognition pattern community has shown a great interest in scene text detection especially in the recent years with the rapid growth of camera-based or video-based applications and mobile devices. A lot of state-of-the-art methods have been proposed; however, most of them can only handle this problem under particular conditions due to the complexity of natural scenes. To be brief, we introduce the recent methods on scene text detection by roughly categorizing them into five classes, namely, *bottom-up, top-down, statistic and learning, temporal or motion analysis*, and *hybrid* approaches.

4.2.1 Bottom-Up Approach

A bottom-up approach is most crucial for scene text detection, which actually concentrates the focus of most researchers in the past years by improving the state-of-the-art algorithms from the classic document analysis research community. Now, it integrates information of pixels to detect texts across a wide range of scales in scene videos or images.

The existing bottom-up methods generally first group image pixels that belong to the same character by analyzing color homogeneity or tracking stroke width after extracting edge features. Then, the detected characters are grouped to form text lines according to color, size, and other geometrical characteristics. Connected component-based methods [11, 12] can be considered as a typical bottom-up approach to detect texts from scene images, which extract character candidates from scenes by the classic connected component analysis followed by grouping character candidates into text. Additional checks may be performed to remove false positives during the detection.

The nearly constant stroke width has been proved to be a useful feature in bottom-up methods for separating text from other scene elements, which can be utilized to recover regions that are likely to contain text. Epshtein et al. [3] leverage this fact in their work by measuring the width variance because text tends to maintain a nearly fixed stroke width. They show that a local image operator combined with geometric reasoning can be used to recover text reliably (see their framework in Fig. 4.11). Essentially, their main idea is showing how to compute the stroke width for each pixel. Using the logical and flexible geometric reasoning, places with similar stroke width can be grouped together into bigger components that are likely to be scene words in their method. Figure 4.11c shows that the operator output can be utilized to separate text from other high-frequency content of a scene.

Epstein's method differs from other approaches in that it does not look for a separating feature per pixel. Instead, they collect enough information to enable smart grouping of pixels, for example, a pixel gradient is considered important only if it has a corresponding opposing gradient. Such geometric verification of a stroke greatly reduces the amount of detected pixels by forcing the co-occurrence of potentially matched pairs in a small region. Another potential advantage is that they do not use any language-specific filtering mechanisms or statistics within a slide window, which allows the method to detect multilingual texts from scene images.

The definition of the stroke width transform (SWT) is the basis of their method to group pixels into letter candidates. SWT computes per pixel the width of the most likely stroke containing the pixel. The output of the SWT is an image of size equal to the size of the input image where each element contains the width of the stroke associated with the pixel. Accordingly, a stroke is defined to be a contiguous part of an image that forms a band of a nearly constant width, as shown in Fig. 4.12a.

Fig. 4.11 The overview of scene text detection using stroke width: **a** original image with gray values, **b** an array containing likely stroke widths for each pixel converted from (**a**), **c** width variance in each component, and **d** the detected text [3]

The SWT of each element is initialized to ∞. To recover strokes without knowing the actual width, they first compute edges using the Canny detector. After that, a gradient direction d_p of each edge pixel p is considered (Fig. 4.12b). If p lies on a stroke boundary, then d_p must be roughly perpendicular to the orientation of the stroke. They follow the ray $r = p + n \cdot d_p, n > 0$ until another edge pixel q is found. Consider the gradient direction d_q at pixel q. If d_q is roughly opposite to $d_p(d_q = -d_p \pm \pi/6)$, each element s of the SWT output image corresponding to the

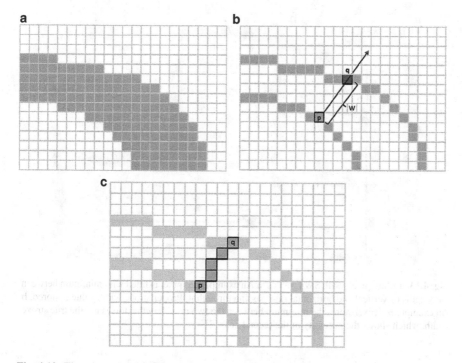

Fig. 4.12 The process of SWT computation. **a** A typical stroke, where the pixels on it are darker than the background pixels, **b** p is a pixel on the boundary of the stroke. Searching in the direction of the gradient at p leads to finding q, which is the corresponding pixel on the other side of the stroke, and **c** each pixel along the ray is assigned by the minimum of its current value and the found width of the stroke [3]

pixels along the segment $[p, q]$ is assigned the width $\left\| \overrightarrow{p - q} \right\|$ unless it already has a lower value (Fig. 4.13a). Otherwise, the ray will be discarded if the matching pixel q is not found, or if d_q is not opposite to d_p.

Figure 4.13b shows that the SWT values will not be true stroke widths after the first pass described above in more complex situations with corners. Accordingly, they pass along each non-discarded rag again, compute median SWT value m of all its pixels, and then set all the pixels of the ray with SWT values above m to be equal to m.

Edge-based bottom-up methods employ color quantization and region growing to group neighboring pixels during text detection. However, connected components may not preserve the full shape of the characters due to low contrast or color bleeding of the text lines. Moreover, most methods address the detection of horizontal text but not multi-oriented text since extension to multi-oriented text is no trivial matter. This is because most of the non-horizontal text lines are much more difficult to track due to varying lighting and complex transformations. In [13], Shivakumara et al. propose a robust Laplacian approach to detect multi-oriented

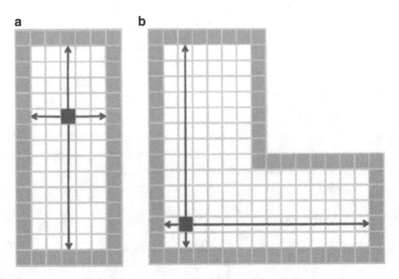

Fig. 4.13 Filling pixels with SWT values. **a** An example red pixel is filled with minimum between the lengths of vertical and horizontal rays passing through it. Proper stroke width value is stored. **b** An example *red* pixel stores the minimum between the two rays' lengths; this is not the true stroke width, which shows the necessity of the second pass [3]

scene texts in video. It consists of four stages: *text region identification, connected component classification, connected component segmentation*, and *false-positive elimination*.

During text region identification, they use the Fourier-Laplacian transformations. Since video text can have a very low contrast against complex backgrounds, it is necessary to process the input image to highlight the difference between text and non-text regions. A two-step process called Fourier-Laplacian filtering to smooth noise is processed. The first step uses an ideal low-pass filter in the frequency domain to smooth noise based on the fact that the high-frequency components of the Fourier transform contain information about noise and thus should be cut off. Then, the second step uses the Laplacian mask in the spatial domain to detect candidate video text regions that have many positive and negative peaks of large magnitudes. To combine the two steps, they use the Laplacian operator in the frequency domain instead of the spatial domain:

$$\nabla^2 f(x, y) = \frac{\partial^2 f(x, y)}{\partial x^2} + \frac{\partial^2 f(x, y)}{\partial y^2}$$

$$\Im\left[\frac{\partial^2 f(x, y)}{\partial x^2} + \frac{\partial^2 f(x, y)}{\partial y^2}\right] = -\left(u^2 + v^2\right) F(u, v) \qquad (4.3)$$

The combined Fourier-Laplacian filtering is:

$$F(u, v) = \Im[f(x, y)]$$
$$G(u, v) = H_2(u, v)[H_1(u, v) F(u, v)]$$
$$H_1(u, v) = \begin{cases} 1 & \text{if } D(u, v) \leq D_0 \\ 0 & \text{otherwise} \end{cases}$$
$$H_2(u, v) = -(u^2 + v^2)$$
$$g(x, y) = \Im^{-1}[G(u, v)] \tag{4.4}$$

where $f(x, y)$ and $g(x, y)$ are the original grayscale image and the filtered image, $H_1(u, v)$ is the ideal low-pass filter, while $H_2(u, v)$ is the Laplacian operator. $D(u, v)$ is defined as the distance from (u, v) to the origin of the Fourier transform and D_0 is the cutoff distance.

The remaining stages after obtaining the result of Fourier-Laplacian filtering for non-horizontal text are as follows:

- Connected component classification by using skeletonization. Since connected component analysis is not good enough to handle the problems of video characters in this step, other operators like the ring radius transform (RRT) [14] can be used to further improve the recognition rate by reconstructing character contours.
- Connected component segmentation based on edge density.
- False-positive elimination from the set of connected components $\{b_i\}$ using two features, namely, *the straightness* comes from the observation that text strings appear on a straight line while false positives can have irregular shapes, and *the edge density* defined by

$$e_i = Sobel(b_i)$$
$$Edge\_Density(b_i) = \frac{Edge\_Length(e_i)}{CC\_Area(b_i)} \tag{4.5}$$

where $Sobel(.)$ returns the binary Sobel edge map, e_i contains edge information only for the white pixels of b_i, $Edge\_Length(.)$ is the total length of all edges in the edge map, $CC\_Area(.)$ is the area of the CC, and $Edge\_Length(.)$ and $CC\_Area(.)$ can be computed by counting the number of edge pixels and white pixels, respectively.

Figure 4.14 shows several scene text detection examples after these stages. Note that multi-oriented text of different font sizes can be successfully detected using the Laplacian-based bottom-up method.

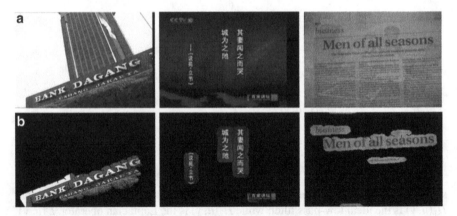

Fig. 4.14 Detecting multi-orientation scene texts using connected components. **a** Input scene images and **b** the detected blocks from the images in (**a**) [13]

For bottom-up video text detection, another main cause of failure to achieve good text detection rate and low false alarm rate is the reliance on a fixed threshold by assuming that text has a high contrast over the background. In order to accurately detect boundary of the text lines in video images, Shivakumara et al. [15] further explore an idea of classifying low-contrast and high-contrast video images. In their work, high contrast refers to sharpness, while low contrast refers to dim intensity values in video images. They present heuristic rules based on text stroke analysis to collectively classify low-contrast and high-contrast video images and then implement an edge and texture feature-based method to show the need for an adaptive threshold based on the video image contrast. Based on these, an automated means for determining the adaptive threshold with the view to achieve better detection rate, low false-positive rate, and low inaccurate boundary rate are used to avoid a fixed threshold in detecting texts.

There are still other challenges in detecting scene texts using the bottom-up approach. For example, there always exist text-like components which are hardly distinguishable from texts, making a bottom-up method not always able to detect correct scene texts. We need to consider other cues inside scenes to avoid such difficulties in bottom-up methods, such as extracting the maximally stable extremal regions (MSERs) by the strategy of minimizing regularized variations [51] and using part-based tree-structured character detection [52] rather than using the conventional sliding window character detection strategy.

4.2.2 Top-Down Approach

Context theoretically plays an important role in disambiguating characters, which can be considered as a top-down approach to model visual context in natural scenes

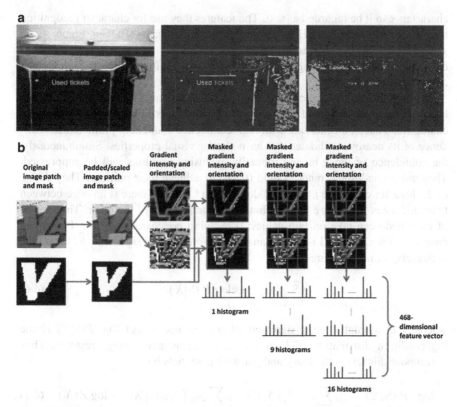

Fig. 4.15 Candidate character detection and feature extraction. (**a**) The leftmost image is the original input, the center image shows bright-center-dark-surround segments where different colors indicate different segments after using SWT, and the rightmost image contains dark-center-bright-surround segments. (**b**) Extracting hierarchical HOG features from a candidate character, where gradient is signed and each histogram is an 18-dimensional vector [16]

to facilitate text detection. Pan et al. [16] categorize two types of contexts for scene text detection: *linguistic context* and *visual context*. The former resorts to a language model to eliminate invalid character sequences and correspondingly leave text candidates. The latter utilizes visual information from other parts of a scene to help determine whether a visual-like character is indeed text.

In [16], they first initialize character candidates from the segments obtained by SWT. Figure 4.15a shows an example of this step, where SWT estimates the stroke width at each pixel location, and pixels with similar stroke widths are grouped together to form segments which are considered character candidates. Note that the center image contains brighter segments surrounded by darker regions, while the rightmost image contains darker segments surrounded by brighter regions. Next, instead of applying binary classification to identify characters, they perform multiclass character recognition on each candidate by a multiclass random forest classifier. During this process, only when a candidate resembles one of the learned characters can it be regarded as text. The features they use for character recognition are three-level hierarchical Histogram of Oriented Gradients (HOGs). Figure 4.15b shows their feature extraction process. As a result of this step, every character candidate is assigned a recognition confidence as the initial detection score named characterness.

During modeling visual context, their intuition is that if two nearby candidates have similar color, size, and stroke width, then it is more likely that they are both characters. That is, a candidate with high confidence could help promote the confidence of its nearby candidates that have similar visual properties. Simultaneously, the confidence of those having mutually exclusive positions will be suppressed. They use a conditional random field (CRF) to achieve their purpose. They define each character candidate i to be a node n_i in the CRF, and there is an edge between two candidates if they are both within the influence field of the other. The state S_i of each node can take on two values: 0 meaning noncharacter, while 1 meaning character. Then, the goal is to find an optimal joint state assignment, $\widehat{S}$, for all the nodes, given image features X:

$$\widehat{S} = \arg\max_{S} \log P\,(S|X) \tag{4.6}$$

where S is a joint state assignment of all the nodes and $\log\ P(S|X)$ is the log condition distribution of joint state assignment given image features. They decompose this term into unary and pairwise potentials by

$$\log\ \ P\,(S|X) = \eta_u \sum_i \omega_i\,(S_i\,|\,X_i) + \eta_P \sum_{i,j} \phi_{ij}\,\left(S_i, S_j\,|\,X_{ij}\right) - \log Z(X) \tag{4.7}$$

where $\omega_i(S_i|X_i)$ is the unary potential for candidate i, $\phi_{ij}(S_i, S_j|X_{ij})$ is the pairwise potential for candidates i and j, and $Z(X)$ is the partition function. η_u and η_P, respectively, denote the two weights for the unary and pairwise potentials, which are determined by maximizing the detection F measure on the ICDAR training dataset.

In their model, the unary potential for node i is defined by

$$\omega_i\,(S_i\,|\,X_i) = \begin{cases} 1 - c_i & \text{if } S_i = 0 \\ c_i & \text{if } S_i = 1 \end{cases} \tag{4.8}$$

For two bounding boxes of two candidates, they define three kinds of pairwise relationships, namely, *compatible*, *irrelevant*, and *repulsive*, to derive the pairwise potential. The relationships between the bounding boxes of two candidates are calculated by a similarity score V_S:

$$V_S = \exp\left\{-\lambda_S\left(\frac{\left\|\overline{g}_i - \overline{g}_j\right\|^2}{2\sigma_C^2} + \frac{\max\left(0, r_0 - r_{ij}\right)^2}{2\sigma_S^2} + \frac{\left(w_i - w_j\right)^2}{2\sigma_W^2}\right)\right\} \tag{4.9}$$

and a repulsion score V_R:

$$V_R = 1 - \min \left(1, \frac{\left\| x_i - x_j \right\|}{\max \left(D_i, D_j \right)} \right)^{\lambda_R} \tag{4.10}$$

where $\overline{g}_i$ and $\overline{g}_j$ are the average colors of two candidates i and j, r_0 is the lower limit of the height ratio that does not incur penalty, and w_i and w_j are their stroke widths. λ_S, σ_C, σ_S, and σ_W control the sensitivity of the similarity score. X_i and X_j are the center coordinates of the two boundary boxes, D_i and D_j are the half diagonals of the two bounding boxes, λ_R controls the sensitivity of the repulsion score, and r_{ij} is the relative height ratio of the two candidates, calculated by

$$r_{ij} = \frac{\min \left(h_i, h_j \right)}{\max \left(h_i, h_j \right)} \tag{4.11}$$

Figure 4.16 shows their results by using visual context to enhance true detections and suppress false detections, in which they use the color statistics from already detected texts to recover the missing text strokes as failure cases of the SWT algorithm.

Fig. 4.16 Using visual context to enhance true detections and simultaneously suppress false detections. The original images are shown in the leftmost column. The center column shows the detection score for individual character candidates separately (*brighter red* indicates higher characterless). The rightmost column displays the refined characterless after CRF inference that incorporates scene contextual information [16]

Fig. 4.17 Character/noncharacter classifier in [17]: (**a**) character, (**b**) noncharacter, (**c**) Armenian script, (**d**) Russian script, and (**e**) Kannada script [17]

Other top-down information like linguistic context can also be adapted to improve the recognition rate of video texts. Neumann and Matas [17] present a general method for text localization and recognition by resorting to a language model to eliminate invalid character sequences. Armenian, Russian, and Kannada language models are considered in their method (see Fig. 4.17).

Ideally, there should be more types of scene contexts that can be considered to predict text regions or narrow the detections and thus integrated into scene text detection algorithms. We believe such top-down information has the ability to provide very useful hints other than the bottom-up cues to facilitate more accurate video text detection in the future.

4.2.3   Statistical and Machine Learning Approach

Statistical algorithms in general scan the image at different scales using a sliding widow and classify image areas as text or non-text statistic features, e.g., density and distribution. Then, machine learning classifiers are adopted to train the extracted samples and test new input scene text image based on the learned model parameters.

In [18], Yildirim et al. propose a structural and statistical approach that attempts to detect and recognize scene text in a unified manner by searching for words directly, without reducing the image into text regions or individual characters. They first replace binary features in multiclass Hough forests [19], which is an efficient method to compute the generalized Hough transform for multiple types of objects by adopting random forests, with cross-scale binary features to achieve better recognition rates as follows:

$$f = \begin{cases} 1 \text{ if } P^{l_1}(x_1) > P^{l_2}(x_2) + \tau \\ 0 \text{ otherwise} \end{cases} \tag{4.12}$$

where f is the binary feature, P^l is image patch P in lth representation type, $\mathbf{x}_1$ and $\mathbf{x}_2$ are patch coordinates, and τ is an offset value. In their method, each representation corresponds to a blurred version of the image processed with averaging filters with different kernel sizes. Therefore, every feature effectively compares the mean values of two randomly positioned rectangles with random dimensions. Figure 4.18 shows a representation of a cross-scale feature on an image patch.

Then, they use 24×24 pixel images and densely sample them with 8×8 pixel patches in the training step. After recursively splitting the image patches using a cross-scale binary feature selected by minimizing metric functions in [19], leaf nodes are declared, and the number of image patches for each class label and relative patch position is stored for testing as a Hough vote. Next, in the testing step, the trained multiclass Hough forests transform a test image into a likelihood map for each text character by computing and accumulating Hough votes of each test image patch. An example for the letter "a" in the Hough vote image is illustrated in Fig. 4.19. Altogether 62 characters of digits, capitals and small letters and downsize images of ten different scales are trained and detected.

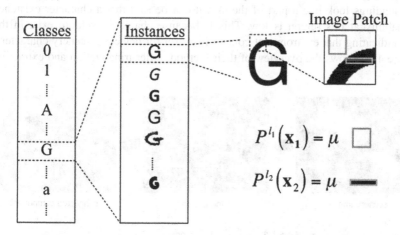

Fig. 4.18 Representation of a cross-scale binary feature, μ denotes the average pixel value for a given rectangular region [18]

Fig. 4.19 Generalized Hough transform for character "a" by using Hough forests [18]

Finally, during the recognition step, since letters may resemble each other either locally or globally (e.g., the letter "W" can be confused with two successive "V"s or "U"s and vice versa), they use a pictorial structure model to produce lexicon priors with the help of an English word list. A word will be recognized when the following function is locally minimized in the image:

$$w = \arg\min_{n, \forall c_i} \left(-\sum_{i=1}^{n} V(L_i) + \sum_{i=1}^{n-1} C(L_i + L_{i+1}) \right) \qquad (4.13)$$

where w is the recognized word, L_i is the coordinate quadruplet (scale, character, 2-D position), V is the likelihood value of having that character at that scale and position, and C is the cost function for two adjacent letters. In this way, the search space is reduced to robustly recognize the actual word.

Yasuhiro et al. [20] further integrate environmental context, which is expected to regulate the probability of character existence at a specific region in a scenery image as discussed in Sect. 4.2.2, into the random forest vote framework. Consider a small region or connected component in a scenery image. If the region and its surroundings look like a part of the sky, it can be said that a character existence probability at this region is low. This is because characters seldom exist in the sky, indicating that environment context is useful for detecting scenery characters. Figure 4.20 shows the overview of their method. After trinarization and extracting

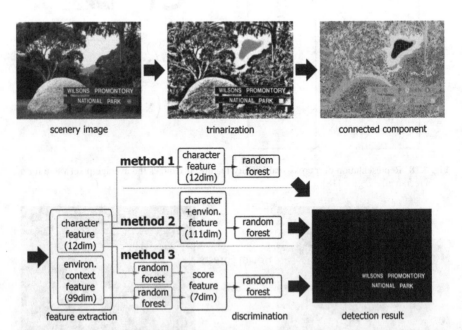

Fig. 4.20 Overview of the method in [20]. Method 1: only using the 12 character features, method 2: using the 12 character features and the 99 environmental features, and method 3: additionally the likelihoods of scene component categories are calculated and used as score features [20]

connected components (CCs) from the original scene image, scene character detection is formulated as a character/noncharacter discrimination problem at each CC. For this purpose, they extract 12 different character features such as the ratio between areas of the CC and the entire image, the number of holes, mean of stroke width and edge contrast, and 99 environmental context features for each CC. Among the environmental context features, 84 are texton features [21], based on 21 responses from 9 Gaussian filters, 4 Laplacian of Gaussian filter, and 8 Gaussian derivative filters. For each response, the mean, standard derivation, Kurtosis, and skewness within the CC are calculated. The remaining 15 features are employed to represent non-texture characteristics of environmental context, including 12 color features, 2 positional features, and 1 area feature. Next, different combinations of the features are trained and tested by random forest, which is an ensemble of K classifiers.

Figure 4.21 shows some scene text detection results using their machine learning method. In Fig. 4.21a, method 1 produces many false detections around the sky and green regions. After using environmental context, those false detections decrease drastically. Figure 4.21b is a visualization of the score feature of Fig. 4.21a. The false detections by method 1 are found in the sky region, and the region has high sky feature values. This fact indicates that the high sky score feature values could suppress the false detection and thus environmental context is useful to improve character detection performance.

To help blind and visually impaired subjects walking through city scenes, Chen and Yuille [22] collect a dataset of city images taken partly by blind volunteers and partly by normally sighted viewers. They manually label and extract the text regions and perform statistical analysis of the text regions to determine which image features are available indicators of text and have low entropy. They obtain weak classifiers by using joint probabilities for feature response *on* and *off* text. Formally, a good feature $f(I)$ will determine two probability distributions $P(\vec{f}(I)|\text{text})$ and $P(\vec{f}(I)|\text{non} - \text{text})$. A weak classifier by using the

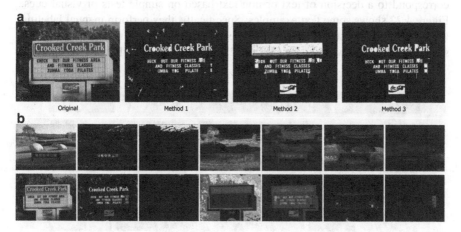

Fig. 4.21 Detection results: (**a**) results for comparisons and (**b**) visualization of scene feature value: original image, character, sky, *green*, sign, ground, building [20]

log-likelihood can then be obtained. This is made easier if tests are found for which $P(\vec{f}(I)|\text{text})$ is strongly peaked at a place where $P(\vec{f}(I)|\text{non}-\text{text})$ is small. These weak classifiers are further used as the input to an AdaBoost machine learning model to train a strong classifier:

$$H_{\text{Ada}}(I) = \text{sign}\left(\sum_{t=1}^{T}\alpha_t h_t(I)\right) \tag{4.14}$$

where AdaBoost algorithm learns a "strong classifier" $H_{\text{Ada}}(I)$ by combining a set of T "weak classifiers" $\{h_t(\mathbf{I})\}$ using a set of weights $\{\alpha_t\}$. Finally, an adaptive binarization and extension method is applied to those regions selected by the cascade classifier to obtain scene texts.

In their algorithm, the most important component is a strong classifier which is trained by the AdaBoost learning algorithm on labeled data. AdaBoost requires specifying a set of features from which to build the strong classifier. Therefore, they select the feature set guided by the principle of *informative features*, including:

- Features that have lower entropy by designing block patterns, that is, the features which compute properties averaged within these regions will typically have low entropy because the fluctuations will be averaged out.
- Histograms of the intensity, gradient direction, and intensity gradient, and particularly, these joint histograms are considered useful tests for distinguishing between text and non-text regions.
- Features based on performing edge detection and intensity gradient thresholding. These features count for the number of extended edges in the image, and also considered properties with low entropy since there will typically be a fixed number of long edges whatever the letters in the text region.

They calculate joint probability distributions of these feature responses *on* and *off* text to obtain weak classifiers as log-likelihood ratio tests. The weak classifiers correspond to a decision of text or non-text based on simple tests of visual cues. Figure 4.22 shows some text examples. Specifically, they perform manual labeling for the training dataset and divide each text window into several overlapping text segments with fixed width-to-height ratio 2:1, resulting in a number of text segments

Fig. 4.22 Text example used for getting positive examples for training AdaBoost [22]

which are used as positive examples. The negative examples are obtained by a bootstrap process [23]. Finally, the strong classifier is applied to subregions of the image at multiple scale and outputs text candidate regions. Averagely, there are 2~5 false positives in images of 2,048 × 1,536 pixels.

Similarly, Lee et al. [24] extract six different classes of texture features and use Modest AdaBoost [25] with multi-scale sequential search to detect text in natural scenes. Specifically, they first use the following six types of feature sets for the CART weak classifier, namely:

- Variance and expectation of X-Y derivatives
- Local energy of Gabor filter
- Statistical texture measure of image histogram
- Measurement of variance of wavelet coefficient
- Edge detection and edge interval calculation
- Connected component analysis

Next, they use Modest AdaBoost which modifies Gentle AdaBoost with an inverted distribution and is found to perform superior to Gentle and Real AdaBoost in detecting scene texts. Their overall scheme is shown in Fig. 4.23, essentially

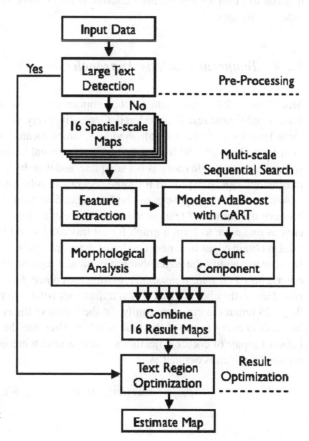

Fig. 4.23 Design of the overall scheme using Modest AdaBoost to detect scene text [24]

composed of three phases: (1) preprocessing of the dataset before learning to resize images containing extremely large text, (2) multi-scale sequential search by increasing the size of spatial scale linearly from 64×48 (width $\times$ height) to $1,024 \times 768$ pixels, and (3) linear combination of the resulting maps at 16 spatial scales with equal weights into a single $1,024 \times 768$ map, and text region optimization by maximizing the expected text region through constructing a rectangular region based on min and max positions of original region.

In order to detect multi-oriented text in video frames, [26] proposes a Bayesian classifier without assuming a priori probability about the input frame but estimating it based on probable matrices. Text candidates are obtained by intersecting the output of their Bayesian classifier with the Canny edge map of the originally input video frame. Finally, a boundary growing method is introduced to traverse the multi-oriented scene text lines.

Statistical approach has now been applied in the recent research of scene text detection from videos or images. However, its main shortcoming attributed to this category is the high computational complexity since a sliding window is required to scan the entire image, requiring thousands of calls to the classifier per image. It makes developing of real-time text detection systems relatively difficult. Moreover, it needs to build a large training dataset to cover more situations of scene text in videos or images.

4.2.4   Temporal Analysis Approach

Much less work has been done for the temporal or motion analysis of video text, and usually only static text is considered. Generally, every video text line has to remain for at least $1\sim2$ s to be readable in videos, which means a single text line will exist in at least about $25\sim50$ frames that have tiny visual variations. The detection and recognition in a single frame is not adequate, and thereby a giant amount of temporal information can be exploited for more accurate or robust video text detection.

Wu et al. [49] propose a method for text detection by estimating trajectories between the corners of texts in video sequence over time. Each trajectory is considered as one node to form a graph for all trajectories and Delaunay triangulation is used to obtain edges to connect nodes of the graph (the first illustration in Fig. 4.25). In order to identify the edges that represent text regions, they propose four pruning criteria based on *spatial proximity*, *motion coherence*, *local appearance*, and *Canny rate*. Firstly, they believe that if two trajectories belong to the same text line region, they will remain in close proximity. So the length of the edge connecting them will be small in every frame of the time window. They use the maximum displacement between a pair of corner trajectories within a time window to represent the spatial proximity, which is defined as

$$Sp_{p,q} = max\left(len_{p,q}(t)\right) \; t \in [t_s, t_s + \tau - 1] \qquad (4.15)$$

where $Sp_{p,q}$ is the value of spatial proximity between node p and q, $len_{p,q}(t)$ is the length of edge between the two nodes at frame t, and t_s is the starting frame within the time window. If spatial proximity of the two connected trajectories is too large, then the edge connecting them will be pruned. This eliminates some of the false edges.

Secondly, they calculate the motion coherency of two connected trajectories. If two nodes of trajectories belong to the same text line region, the motion of them should be alike. Namely, the speed and direction of their motions will be approximate. In other words, the distance between these two nodes will always be the same within the time window. So they use the standard deviation of the distance between two trajectories over the time window to measure the dissimilarity with respect to motion coherency:

$$Cm_{p,q} = \sqrt{\frac{1}{\tau} \sum_{t_s}^{t_s+\tau-1} \left(len_{p,q}(t) - \overline{len_{p,q}}\right)^2} \tag{4.16}$$

where $Cm_{p,q}$ is the value of motion coherency between two nodes p and q, $\overline{len_{p,q}}$ is the mean value of length of edge between the two nodes within the time window. If motion coherency between two connected trajectory nodes is too large, then this edge connecting them will be pruned. With this criterion, they are able to distinguish those two text lines, which overlap with each other, but whose motion status is not the same as shown in Fig. 4.24, in which gradually two text lines are separated as time goes.

Thirdly, they calculate temporal variation of local appearance. As known, if text line region in a video remains in the same shape and size, it is just like a rigid thing, and its appearance remains the same during a period of time. So they utilize the

Fig. 4.24 Two text lines having overlap region but with their motion status not the same are distinguished [49]

temporal variation of local appearance to describe this property. In their method, the temporal variation of local appearance is measured to quantify the change in appearance of a sequence of small triangular patches bounded by three adjacent trajectories. They use the temporal variation of a hue-saturation color histogram of the Bhattacharyya distance between the color histogram $h(t)$, and the average color histogram $\bar{h}$ of the patch within the time window is used to define the dissimilarity $Tv_{p,q}$ for a sequence of patches as

$$Tv_{p,q} = \sqrt{\frac{1}{\tau}\sum_{t_s}^{t_s+\tau-1} d_{hist}^2\left(h\left(t\right),\bar{h}\right)} \qquad (4.17)$$

where $Tv_{p,q}$ is the value of temporal variation of local appearance and $d_{hist}(.,.)$ is the Bhattacharyya distance between two histograms.

Fourthly, they calculate the Canny rate for each edge between two connected nodes, which is used to further prune some more edges in the graph and only retain those represent text regions. They consider that there exists dense and orderly the presence of corner points in characters, especially at the turning of their strokes. These corner points always occur around a Canny line. They retain those edges in the graph whose two end points are the corner points at the turning of a character's strokes and near a Canny line, thus storing the structure of a character in the pruned graph. They then perform dilation operation on the Canny map to make the Canny line a little thicker to assure that the corner points near the original Canny line are in the dilated Canny line. After the dilation, they calculate the Canny rate over the time window for each edge in the graph. The Canny rate is defined as

$$Cr_{p,q} = \frac{\sum_{t=t_s}^{t_s+\tau-1}\left|E_{p,q}(t) \cap C_{p,q}(t)\right|}{\sum_{t=t_s}^{t_s+\tau-1}\left|E_{p,q}(t)\right|} \qquad (4.18)$$

where $Cr_{p,q}$ is the Canny rate of edge between node p and q. $E_{p,q}(t)$ and $C_{p,q}(t)$, respectively, represent the set of pixels belonging to edge between the two nodes and the set of pixels belonging to the Canny map within the time window. As a result, they get several small subgraphs as shown in the second illustration in Fig. 4.25, where two characters have two subgraphs correctly. Finally, they use depth-first search to collect corner points, which essentially represent text candidates. False positives are eliminated using heuristics and missing trajectories will be obtained by tracking the corners in temporal frames (the last illustration in Fig. 4.25).

In [29], the correlation between video frames is exploited to improve the results of the text detection phase. Their major goal is to refine the text detection in terms of removing false alarms in individual frames, interpolating the location of accidentally missed text characters and words in individual video frames, and further temporally localizing the beginning and end of each word as well as spatial location within each video frame. The overall architectural of their method is shown in Fig. 4.26.

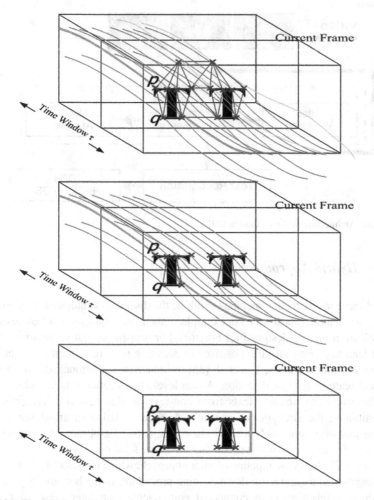

Fig. 4.25 The initial graph with trajectories, edges pruned graph, and the text line detected [49]

There are several more methods on video text detection by exploring temporal information, such as tracking video text [30], motion video text localization [31], utilization of temporal continuity of video text [32], and exploration of temporal features [33]. However, there is still much less work for video text detection by using temporal analysis as introduced generally. Temporal information is actually crucial in successfully detecting and tracking text from a large number of video frames. Sometimes it will be very useful in handling the discussed difficulties such as low video quality, occlusions, different font sizes, and even font style variations.

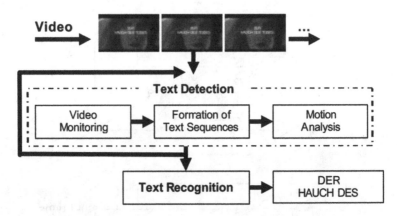

Fig. 4.26 Architecture of the method in [29]

4.2.5 Hybrid Approach

Hybrid scene text detection methods combine the discussed strategies for video text detection in a more robust way. For example, considering conventional features such as SWT are primarily designed for horizontal or near-horizontal scene texts which would lead to significant false positives in detecting texts of arbitrary orientations in complex natural images, Yao et al. [35] introduce two additional sets of rotation invariant features for text detection. A two-level classification scheme which then can effectively discriminate texts from non-texts is also designed. Accordingly, by combining the strengths of specially designed rotation invariant scene text features and discriminatively trained classifiers, texts of arbitrary orientations can be effectively detected without producing too many false positives.

Figure 4.27 shows the pipeline of their approach, which consists of a bottom-up grouping procedure and a top-down pruning procedure. In the bottom-up grouping procedure, pixels first form connected components, and later these connected components are aggregated into chains. Then, in the top-down pruning procedure, non-text components and chains are successively identified and eliminated. Essentially, the algorithm detects arbitrary orientation scene texts by the following four stages:

- *Component Extraction*: Edge detection is performed on the original scene image, and the edge map is input to SWT module to produce an SWT image. Neighboring pixels are grouped together to form connected components using a simple association rule.
- *Component Analysis*: This stage identifies and filters out those non-text components by a trained classifier of random forest [34]. The remaining components are taken as character candidates.

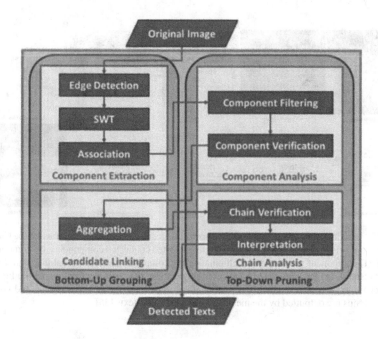

Fig. 4.27 Pipeline of the method, which consists of a bottom-up grouping procedure and a top-down pruning procedure [35]

- *Candidate Linking*: The character candidates are first grouped into a pair if they have similar geometrical properties and colors. Then, the candidate pairs are aggregated into chains in a recursive fashion.
- *Chain Analysis*: In this stage, the chains with low classification probabilities are discarded. Since the remaining chains may be in any direction, a candidate might belong to multiple chains, and thereby the interpretation step is aimed to dispel this ambiguity. The chains that pass this stage are the final detected scene texts.

For illustration, Fig. 4.28 shows the discussed text detection process from an example scene image. It is noticed that in the steps, the two-side aspects about the existing scene text detection algorithms are well solved: (1) methods built on heavy learning by training classifiers on a large amount of data reach certain but limited level of success, and (2) systems based on smart features, such as SWT, are robust to variations in texts, but they involve many hand tuning and are still far from producing all satisfactory results, especially for non-horizontal scene texts.

Mishra et al. [1] also present a hybrid framework that exploits both bottom-up and top-down cues in scene text detection. The bottom-up cues are derived from individual character detections from the image. They build a conditional random field model on these detections to jointly model the strength of the detections and the interactions between them. Then they impose top-down cues obtained from a lexicon-based prior of language statistics on the model. Accordingly, the optimal

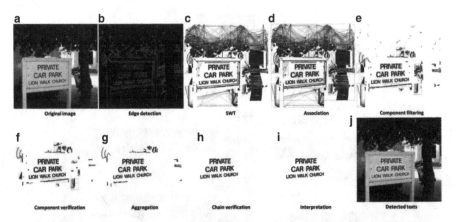

Fig. 4.28 Text detection process: (**a**) original scene image, (**b**) the edge map after using the Canny edge detector, (**c**) the resulting SWT image, (**d**) the detected connected components, (**e**) component filtering, (**f**) component verification by eliminating the components whose probabilities are lower than a threshold, (**g**) the candidate chains after aggregation, (**h**) chain verification, (**i**) the highest total probability will be remained if several chains compete for the same candidate, and (**j**) the survived chains are outputted by the method as detected scene texts [35]

word represented by the text image is obtained by minimizing the following energy function corresponding to the random field model:

$$E\left(\mathrm{x}\right) = \sum_{i=1}^{n} E_i\left(x_i\right) + \sum_{\varepsilon} E_{ij}\left(x_i, x_j\right) \tag{4.19}$$

where $x = \{x_i | i = 1, 2, \ldots, n\}$ represents the unary term, $E_{ij}(\cdot, \cdot)$ is the pairwise term, and ε represents the set of pairs of interacting detection windows, which is determined by the structure of the underlying graphical model. Each character detection window is represented by a random variable X_i, which takes a label x_i, and n is the total number of detection windows. Since the set of random variables includes windows representing not only true-positive detections but also many false-positive detections, they introduce a null label ϕ to account for the false windows:

$$\mathrm{x}_{\mathrm{i}} \in \kappa_\varphi = \kappa \cup \{\phi\} \tag{4.20}$$

The set κ_ϕ^n thus represents the set of all possible assignments of labels to the random variables. The energy function $\mathrm{E} : \kappa_\phi^n \to \mathrm{R}$ maps any labeling to a real number $E(\cdot)$ called its energy, which is commonly represented as the sum of unary and pairwise terms as in Eq. 4.20.

Figure 4.29 shows the summary of their approach. In Fig. 4.29a, a set of potential character windows are searched to build a random field model by connecting them with edges. The weight of an edge is computed based on the characteristics of the two windows it connects, as shown in either green or red in Fig. 4.29b. Based on

Fig. 4.29 Framework overview: (**a**) identification of potential character windows and (**b**) building a random field model by connecting the windows, where an edge in green indicates that the two windows it connects have a high probability of occurring together and an edge in red connects two windows that are unlikely to be characters following one another [1]

these edges and the SVM scores for each window, they infer the character classes of each window as well as the word.

4.3 Scene Character/Text Recognition

Scene text is a pervasive element in many environments, and accurate recognition of scene texts has a significant impact for real-life OCR applications. However, how to solve the problem of word recognition of scene texts is still a challenge and hard task. Even if the problem of text segmentation is to be ignored in this stage, the following characteristics of scene texts still need to be accounted for: (1) different font styles and thicknesses, (2) background as well as foreground color and texture, (3) languages, (4) partial occlusions, (5) camera position which can introduce geometrical distortions, (6) illumination changes, and (7) video resolution. Due to these factors, the traditional OCR techniques cannot be adopted to recognize scene texts directly.

Wang et al. [36] focus on a special case of the scene text problem where they are given a list of words (i.e., a lexicon) to be detected and read (see Fig. 4.30). They construct and evaluate two systems toward this target. The first is a two-stage pipeline consisting of text detection followed by a leading OCR engine, while the second is essentially a system rooted in generic object recognition. They show their

Fig. 4.30 The problem of word detection and recognition, where the input consists of a scene image and a list of words (e.g., "TRILE" and "DOOR"). The output is a set of bounding boxes labeled with words [36]

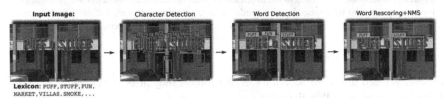

Fig. 4.31 An overview of the word detection and recognition pipeline. Starting with an input image and a lexicon, multi-scale character detection is performed. The words "PUFF" and "STUFF" appear in the image, while the other words in the lexicon can be thought of as "distractors." Next, word detection using a pictorial structure framework is performed by treating the characters as "parts" of a word. Finally, the detected words are rescored using features based on their global layout, and non-maximal suppression (NMS) is performed over words [37]

object recognition-based pipelines perform significantly better than the one using conventional OCR, and surprisingly, an object recognition-based pipeline achieves competitive performance *without* the need for an explicit text detection step.

The overview of their word detection and recognition pipeline is shown in Fig. 4.31. In the first step, they detect potential locations of altogether 62 characters in an image by performing multi-scale character detection via sliding window classification. Random ferns [37] are adopted as they are naturally multiclass and efficient both to train and test. To train their character detector, they generate 1,000 images for each character using 40 fonts. For each image, they add some amount of Gaussian noise and apply a random affine deformation. Next, to detect words in the image, they use the pictorial structure (PS) formulation that takes the locations and scores of detected characters as input and finds an optimal configuration of a particular word. The dynamic programming procedure for configuring a single word can be extended to find configurations of multiple words.

The final step in their pipeline is to perform non-maximal suppression over all detected words. The problems in this step mainly include (1) the obtained scores are not comparable for words of different lengths, and (2) the pictorial structure object function captures only pairwise relationships and ignores global features of the configuration. Therefore, they compute a number of features given a word and its configuration:

- The configuration score
- Mean, median, minimum, and standard deviation of character scores
- Standard deviation of horizontal and vertical gaps between consecutive characters
- Number of characters in a word

These features are fed into an SVM classifier and the output of which becomes a new score for the word. Parameters of the SVM are set using cross validation on the training data. Once the words receive their new scores, non-maximal suppression is performed. Some selected scene text recognition results on the ICDAR dataset are shown in Fig. 4.32.

González et al. [38] focus on the recognition of individual characters in scene images. After text detection and location, their framework takes each binarized character as input and then computes its feature vector, and the object is classified into a class using a KNN approach. Their feature is named as direction histogram (DH). They propose to detect the edge pixels of the binarized objects and then to compute the direction of the gradient for each edge pixel. As it is a binarized image, there is only gradient on the edge pixels, and therefore it is faster to compute. Next, they quantize the direction of the gradients in the edge pixels into eight bins and compute the histogram for each bin. Accordingly, the image is divided into 16 blocks in order to have spatial information, and the histograms for each block are concentrated into a 128-dimensional vector. Figure 4.33 shows the overview of feature extraction from an input binarized scene character. It can be found that the extracted features will not be affected by color neither intensity. Finally, their classification of scene

Fig. 4.32 Selected results of scene text recognition on the ICDAR dataset. The full system implemented in MATLAB takes roughly 15 s on average to run on an 800 × 1,200 resolution image with lexicon size of around 50 words [37]

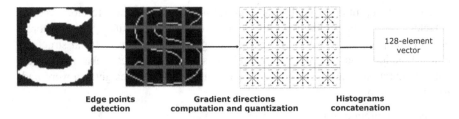

Edge points   Gradient directions   Histograms
detection   computation and quantization   concatenation

Fig. 4.33 Feature detection from a binarized scene character [38]

characters is based on a KNN approach. The training dataset is composed of 5,482 character samples extracted from the train set of the ICDAR 2003 Robust Reading Competition dataset, which has a wide diversity of fonts.

Similarly to [38], Campos and Bahu [39] tackle the problem of recognizing characters of natural scene images, which would traditionally not be well handled by OCR techniques. The problem is addressed in an object categorization framework based on a bag-of-visual-words representation. That is, after constructing the scene character corpus, they learn a set of visual words per class and aggregate them across classes to form the scene character vocabulary. Then, they map each feature extracted from an image onto its closest visual word and represent the image by a histogram over the vocabulary of visual words for scene character recognition. In their experiments, they learn five visual words per class for English scene characters, leading to a vocabulary of size 310. For Kannada, they learn three words per class, resulting in a vocabulary of 1,971 words. In [40], Feild and Learned-Miller further focus on improving the recognition rate.

Scene character or text recognition is the final step in developing useful real-life video scene text detection applications. Unlike OCR, the recognition faces a lot of difficulties, and the state-of-the-art methods still have to be improved both in accuracy and efficiency.

4.4   Scene Text Datasets

As discussed, commercial OCR systems have a good performance when recognizing machine-printed document text, but do not work well for reading text in natural scenes, where text is embedded in complex backgrounds. The ICDAR Robust Reading challenge is the first public dataset collected to highlight the problem of detecting and recognizing scene text.

The robust text reading problem in ICDAR 2003 is broken down into three subproblems consisting of *text locating*, *character recognition*, and *word recognition* [41, 42]. Images are captured by a variety of digital cameras with a range of resolutions and other settings. To allow management of the ground truthing or tagging of the images, a web-based tagging system is implemented. In ICDAR 2003, the scene word example *"Department"* in Fig. 4.34a is described by the fragment of

XML in Fig. 4.34b, where the *tagged rectangles* element contains a *tagged rectangle* element for each word in the image, and *x*, *y*, *width*, and *height* attributes specify the location (top left corner) and size of the word, while the *offset* and *rotation* specify the slant (e.g., for italicized text) and rotation of the word. Ideally, a text locating algorithm would identify five rectangles in image pixel coordinates, surrounding the words of "*Department*," "*of*," "*Computer*," "*Science*," and "1" in Fig. 4.34a.

The data in ICDAR 2003 are organized into *sample*, *trial*, and *competition* datasets for each competition of text locating, character recognition, and word recognition. Sample datasets are provided to give a quick impression of the data and also allow functional testing of different algorithms. Trial datasets have two intended uses. They can be used to get experimental results and are further partitioned into two sets: *TrialTrain* and *TrialTest*. The instructions are to use TrialTrain to train or tune algorithms and then quote results on TrailTest. The competition datasets are used to evaluate different algorithms.

Table 4.1 gives an idea of the level of interest in each problem in ICDAR 2003. The downloads column shows the number of downloads of the sample dataset for each problem. Note that the downloaded files for the text locating and robust reading contests are the same, and only in the case of the text locating problem do the expressions of interest (EOIs) translate to actual entries. The shortcomings of ICDAR 2003 mainly include: (1) missing ground truth information for some of the text elements, (2) mixed interpretation of punctuation and special characters as part of words, and (3) errors exist of bounding boxes around words.

A follow-up text reading competition was held at ICDAR 2005 [43] using the same dataset as that of ICDAR 2003. Again, only text locating problem received a sufficient number of entries. To track progress in text reading, a Robust Reading Competition was held at ICDAR 2011 dealing with two challenges. The first challenge deals with born-digital images (web, e-mail) whereas the second challenge deals with scene text recognition [44]. In ICDAR 2011, the dataset is extended with more images containing a variety of outdoor and indoor scenes. The dataset consists of 485 images containing text in a variety of colors and fonts on many different backgrounds and in various orientations. All the images are converted to gray level, and colored bounding boxes are used to mark the word location and saved as 24-bit PNG image. A simple ground truth GUI to annotate words in an image is prepared, which allows users to draw rough bounding boxes around words and label them with ASCII string. Accordingly, ground truth will be automatically generated using the colored image files and labels generated using the GUI by evaluating bounding boxes overlap for a given image file. The ground truth consists of bounding box coordinates which are stored in a separate text file for each of the image files. The word recognition dataset of ICDAR 2011 consists of 1,564 word images. These word images are actually cropped from images in the text localization dataset using word bounding box ground truth. Each word is stored in a separate file, and the ground truth transcription for these words is provided in a line-separated file.

The ICDAR 2013 edition of the Robust Reading Competition marks a new milestone in the series [50]. The two challenges on real scenes and born-digital images

```
b
<tagset>

    <image>

        <imageName>scene/ComputerScienceSmall.jpg</imageName>

        <resolution x="338" y="255" />

        <taggedRectangles>

            <taggedRectangle x="99" y="94" width="128" height="20"
                             offset="0" rotation="0">

                <tag>Department</tag>

                <segmentation>

                    <xOff>16</xOff>

                    <xOff>29</xOff>

                    <xOff>43</xOff>

                    <xOff>54</xOff>

                    <xOff>64</xOff>

                    <xOff>74</xOff>

                    <xOff>93</xOff>

                    <xOff>106</xOff>

                    <xOff>117</xOff>

                </segmentation>

            </taggedRectangle>

            ...

    </image>

    ...

</tagset>
```

Fig. 4.34 Word example in a scene image and its corresponding XML fragment in ICDAR 2003.
(**a**) The example word "*Department*" in the scene image and (**b**) its XML fragment to evaluate
scene text detection and recognition algorithms [41, 42]

Table 4.1 Measures of interest in each problem for text reading competitions in ICDAR 2003. In the competitions, the text locating competition has five entries, and other contests all have zero entries [42]

Problem	Downloads	EOIs	Entries
Text locating	394	7	5
Word recognition	228	4	0
Character recognition	218	5	0
Robust reading	394	0	0

are integrated, unifying performance evaluation metrics, ground truth specification and the list of offered tasks. A new challenge is established on text extraction from video sequences. Correspondingly, a new dataset of video sequences obtained under various activities and with diverse capturing equipment is added, together with a video-based ground truth for text detection in video. The competition of ICDAR 2013 consists of three challenges: reading text in born-digital images (challenge 1), reading text in scene images (challenge 2), and reading text in videos (challenge 3). Challenge 1 and challenge 2 offer tasks on:

- Text Localization: to detect the existence of text and return a boundary box location of it in the image
- Text Segmentation: to obtain a pixel-level separation of text versus background
- Word Recognition: to provide a transcription for a list of prelocalized word images

Challenge 3 offers a single task on text localization where the objective is to detect and track text objects in a video sequence. The difference between challenge 2 and challenge 3 is that although a video is a collection of images, videos are of different nature compared to static images. That is, video images are typically worse than static images due to motion blur and out of focus issues. Karatzas et al. [50] provide 28 videos in total, using different cameras for different sequences so that they can cover a variety of possible hardware used including mobile phones, handheld cameras, and head-mounted cameras. An ideal video text detection method should be able to detect all text words present at every frame and return their bounding boxes precisely. It should also keep consistent track of each word over time by assigning a unique ID which stays constant throughout the sequence. Thereby, their evaluation procedure is based on a mapping list of word-hypothesis correspondences, named CLEAR-MOT metrics calculated using the frame level mappings as

$$MOTP = \frac{\sum_{i,t} o_t^i}{\sum_t c_t} \qquad (4.21)$$

where o_t^i refers to the overlapping ratio of the ith correspondence in the mapping M_t and c_t is the number of correspondence in M_t and

$$MOTA = 1 - \frac{\sum_t (fn_t + fp_t + id\_sw_t)}{\sum_t g_t} \qquad (4.22)$$

where fn_t, fp_t, id_sw_t, and g_t refer to the number of false negatives, false positives, ID switches, and ground truth words at frame t, respectively. Additionally, the Sequence Track Detection Accuracy (STDA) is calculated by means of the sequence level mapping M as

$$STDA = \sum_{i=1}^{N_M} \frac{\sum_t m\left(W_i^t, H_i^t\right)}{N_{W_i \cup H_i \neq \phi}} \qquad (4.23)$$

where N_M is the number of correspondences in $M, N_{W_i \cup H_i \neq \phi}$ is the number of frames where either W_i or H_i exist, and $m(W_i^t, H_i^t)$ takes a value of 1 iff overlap $(W_i^t, H_i^t) > 0.5$ or 0 otherwise.

To evaluate the performance of character recognition from scenes, Campos and Bahu introduce another database of images containing English and Kannada text [39, 45]. Figure 4.35 shows some character examples extracted from the 1922 source scene images photographed, mostly of signboards, hoardings, advertisements, and products in supermarkets. In their dataset, individual characters are manually segmented by two types of segmentations: rectangular bounding boxes and finer polygonal segments. For English, they treat upper- and lowercase characters separately and include digits to get a total of 62 classes. Kannada does not differentiate between upper- and lowercase characters. It has 49 basic characters in its alphasyllabary, but consonants and vowels can combine to give more than 600 visually distinct classes. Altogether, their English dataset has 12,503 characters, of which 4,798 are labeled as bad images due to excessive occlusion, low resolution, or noise. Similarly, for Kannada, a total of 4,194 characters are extracted out of which only 3,345 are used.

To evaluate scene digit recognition algorithms, Netzer et al. [46] build the Street View House Numbers (SVHN) dataset to detect and read house-number signs in street view scenes. The SVHN dataset is obtained from a large number of street view scene images [47] using a combination of automated algorithms and the Amazon Mechanical Turk framework [48], which is used to localize and transcribe the single digits. A very large set of images from urban areas in various countries are downloaded. In total, the dataset comprises over 600,000 labeled characters and has been made available in two formats of (1) full numbers: the original, variable-resolution, color, house-number images as they appear in the image file and (2) cropped digits. The dataset has three subsets:

- SVHN train – 73,257 digits for training
- SVHN test – 26,032 digits for testing
- SVHN extra (train) – 531,131 additional, somewhat less difficult samples to use as extra training data

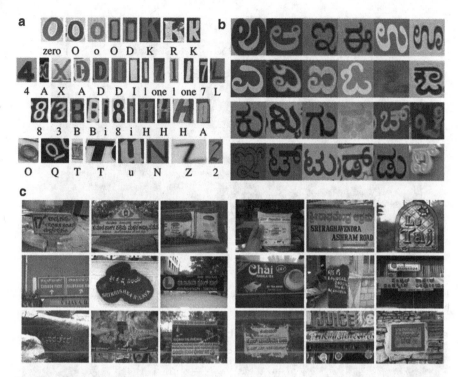

Fig. 4.35 Examples of Campos and Bahu's dataset for character recognition from scene images containing English and Kannada characters. (**a**) Examples of high visual similarity between samples of different classes of English characters, (**b**) examples of Kannada characters from different classes, and (**c**) sample source scene images [39]

Figure 4.36 shows samples from SVHN dataset. Comparing with other benchmarks, most digits in SVHN show vast intra-class variations and include complex photometric distortions that can evaluate scene digit recognition algorithms in a more comprehensive and challenging way.

There are some other scene text datasets, for example, the San Francisco city scene text dataset for use by blind and visually impaired subjects walking through city scenes [22]. The training dataset has 162 images of which 41 of them are taken by scientists from the Smith-Kettlewell Eye Research Institute (SKERI) and the rest taken by blind volunteers under the supervision of scientists from SKERI (see the examples in Fig. 4.37). The test dataset of 117 images is taken entirely by blind volunteers with a Nikon camera mounted on the shoulder or the stomach. They walked around the streets of San Francisco taking photographs. The camera was set to the default automatic setting for focus and contrast gain control.

Fig. 4.36 Samples from the SVHN dataset. *Blue* bounding boxes refer to AMT worker marked bounding boxes of the characters [46]

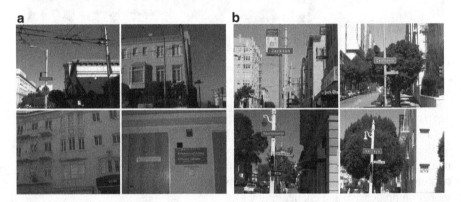

Fig. 4.37 Example scenes in the training dataset taken by (**a**) blind volunteers and (**b**) scientists from SKERI [22]

4.5 Summary

With the rapid growth of video-based applications on the Internet and portable devices, video scene text detection has gained increasing attention in recent years. Scene text carries semantic information, which provides valuable cues about the content of each static video frame image or a series of video frame sequences. Theoretically, it is due to the fact that viewers always tend to fixate on text when given a complex scene image containing both text and other visual objects.

Thus, detecting and recognizing scene text is indispensable for a lot of video text applications such as automatic navigation, video retrieval, and sign reading.

This chapter starts from the analysis of visual characteristics of scene text. Generally, humans can easily distinguish scene texts from their complex backgrounds in the same scene without difficulties. It indicates that humans can simultaneously process multiple channels of scene context and rapidly focus the attention on the visual characteristics of scene text. Inspired by this, we explore the salient visual characteristics of scene texts, especially focusing on imitating human perceptions through visual text saliency models. We introduce several typical saliency representations consists of probability-based maps (*Torralba's saliency map*, *Zhang's fast saliency map*), graph-based maps (*Harel's graph-based saliency map*, *Itti's saliency map*), and curvature-based maps (*Karaoglu's curvature saliency map* and *Shivakumara's gradient vector flow*), and finding visual text saliency computation greatly helps search for text regions from complex scenes in a reduced space to improve the efficiency. It can be considered as a preprocessing step adopted in the early stage of a scene text detection algorithm to search for interested text region candidates or used as a kind of visual feature to facilitate distinguishing scene text candidates from their complex backgrounds.

Next, we introduce the recent methods on scene text detection by roughly categorizing them into five classes, namely, *bottom-up*, *top-down*, *statistic and learning*, *temporal or motion analysis*, and *hybrid* approaches. A hybrid approach by combining the metrics of different methods may be a good choice in scene text detection, like simultaneously adopting a bottom-up grouping procedure to detect pixel-level connected components as character candidates and a top-down pruning procedure to successively identify non-text components using scene contexts. Nevertheless, even a lot of state-of-the-art methods have been proposed, most of them can only handle scene text detection under particular conditions due to the complexity of natural scenes. There still is a long way to develop a general scene text detection system to meet the real-life requirements.

Scene text or character recognition is also discussed in this chapter since accurate recognition of scene texts has a significant impact for real-life OCR applications. However, how to solve the problem of word recognition of scene texts is a challenge and hard task. It faces a series of difficulties, such as (1) different font styles and thicknesses, (2) background as well as foreground color and texture, (3) languages, (4) partial occlusions, (5) camera position which can introduce geometrical distortions, (6) illumination changes, and (7) video resolution. Due to these factors, the traditional OCR techniques cannot be adopted to recognize scene texts directly. We introduce several typical scene text or character recognition methods, and we believe the state-of-the-art methods still have to be improved both in accuracy and efficiency.

This chapter ends with the introduction of several typical scene text datasets. Most of the current methods focus on detecting text from static video images rather from a video sequence by using temporal analysis. Fortunately, ICDAR 2013 has noticed this problem, and a new video text detection competition (competition 3) has been set as a benchmark for evaluations.

References

1. Mishra A, Alahari K, Jawahar CV (2012) Top-down and bottom-up cues for scene text recognition. In: IEEE conference on computer vision and pattern recognition (CVPR), 2012
2. Yin X-C, Yin X, Huang K (2013) Robust text detection in natural scene images. arXiv preprint arXiv:1301.2628
3. Epshtein B, Ofek E, Wexler Y (2010) Detecting text in natural scenes with stroke width transform. In: IEEE conference on computer vision and pattern recognition (CVPR), 2010
4. Torralba A et al (2006) Contextual guidance of eye movements and attention in real-world scenes: the role of global features in object search. Psychol Rev 113(4):766–786
5. Shahab A et al (2012) How salient is scene text? In: 10th IAPR international workshop on document analysis systems (DAS), 2012
6. Harel J, Koch C, Perona P (2006) Graph-based visual saliency. In: Advances in neural information processing systems
7. Zhang L et al (2008) SUN: a bayesian framework for saliency using natural statistics. J Vis 8(7):32
8. Itti L, Koch C, Niebur E (1998) A model of saliency-based visual attention for rapid scene analysis. Pattern Anal Mach Intell IEEE Trans 20(11):1254–1259
9. Uchida S et al (2011) A keypoint-based approach toward scenery character detection. In: International conference on document analysis and recognition (ICDAR), 2011
10. Karaoglu S, Gemert J, Gevers T (2012) Object reading: text recognition for object recognition. In: Fusiello A, Murino V, Cucchiara R (eds) Computer vision – ECCV 2012. Workshops and demonstrations. Springer, Berlin, pp 456–465
11. Jain AK, Yu BIN (1998) Automatic text location in images and video frames. Pattern Recogn 31(12):2055–2076
12. Kim H-K (1996) Efficient automatic text location method and content-based indexing and structuring of video database. J Vis Commun Image Represent 7(4):336–344
13. Shivakumara P, Trung Quy P, Tan CL (2011) A Laplacian approach to multi-oriented text detection in video. Pattern Anal Mach Intell IEEE Trans 33(2):412–419
14. Shivakumara P et al (2013) Gradient vector flow and grouping based method for arbitrarily-oriented scene text detection in video images. Circ Syst Video Technol, IEEE Trans. **PP**(99):1
15. Shivakumara P et al (2010) Accurate video text detection through classification of low and high contrast images. Pattern Recogn 43(6):2165–2185
16. Pan J et al (2012) Effectively leveraging visual context to detect texts in natural scenes, In: Asian conference on computer vision (ACCV'12), 2012. Daejeon
17. Neumann L, Matas J (2011) A method for text localization and recognition in real-world images. In: Kimmel R, Klette R, Sugimoto A (eds) Computer vision – ACCV 2010. Springer, Berlin, pp 770–783
18. Yildirim G, Achanta R, Süsstrunk S (2013) Text recognition in natural images using multiclass Hough forests. In: 8th international conference on computer vision theory and applications (VISAPP). Barcelona, pp 737–741
19. Gall J et al (2011) Hough forests for object detection, tracking, and action recognition. Pattern Anal Mach Intell IEEE Trans 33(11):2188–2202
20. Kunishige Y, Yaokai F, Uchida S (2011) Scenery character detection with environmental context. In: International conference on document analysis and recognition (ICDAR), 2011
21. Leung T, Malik J (2001) Representing and recognizing the visual appearance of materials using three-dimensional textons. Int J Comput Vis 43(1):29–44
22. Xiangrong C, Yuille AL (2014) Detecting and reading text in natural scenes. In: CVPR 2004. Proceedings of the 2004 IEEE computer society conference on computer vision and pattern recognition, 2004

23. Drucker H, Schapire R, Simard P (1993) Boosting performance in neural networks. Int J Pattern Recognit Artif Intell 7(04):705–719
24. Jung-Jin L et al (2011) AdaBoost for text detection in natural scene. In: International conference on document analysis and recognition (ICDAR), 2011
25. Vezhnevets A, Vezhnevets V (2005) Modest AdaBoost-teaching AdaBoost to generalize better. Graphicon-2005, Novosibirsk Akademgorodok
26. Shivakumara P et al (2012) Multioriented video scene text detection through bayesian classification and boundary growing. Circ Syst Video Technol IEEE Trans 22(8):1227–1235
27. Shivakumara P et al (2011) A novel mutual nearest neighbor based symmetry for text frame classification in video. Pattern Recogn 44(8):1671–1683
28. Chenyang X, Prince JL (1998) Snakes, shapes, and gradient vector flow. Image Process IEEE Trans 7(3):359–369
29. Palma D, Ascenso J, Pereira F (2004) Automatic text extraction in digital video based on motion analysis. In: Campilho A, Kamel M (eds) Image analysis and recognition. Springer, Berlin, pp 588–596
30. Li H, Doermann D, Kia O (2000) Automatic text detection and tracking in digital video. Image Process IEEE Trans 9(1):147–156
31. Tsung-Han T, Yung-Chien C (2007) A comprehensive motion videotext detection localization and extraction method. In: IEEE 23rd international conference on data engineering workshop, 2007
32. Chen W, Hongliang W (2010) Utilization of temporal continuity in video text detection. In: Second international conference on multimedia and information technology (MMIT), 2010
33. Xiaoou T et al (2002) Video text extraction using temporal feature vectors. In: ICME '02. Proceedings of the IEEE international conference on multimedia and expo, 2002
34. Breiman L (2001) Random forests. Mach Learn 45(1):5–32
35. Cong Y et al (2012) Detecting texts of arbitrary orientations in natural images. In: IEEE conference on computer vision and pattern recognition (CVPR), 2012
36. Kai W, Babenko B, Belongie S (2011) End-to-end scene text recognition. In: IEEE international conference on computer vision (ICCV), 2011
37. Ozuysal M, Fua P, Lepetit V (2007) Fast keypoint recognition in ten lines of code. In: CVPR'07. IEEE conference on computer vision and pattern recognition, 2007
38. Gonzalez A et al (2012) A character recognition method in natural scene images. In: 21st international conference on pattern recognition (ICPR), 2012
39. Campos TED, Babu BR, Varma M (2009) Character recognition in natural images. In: Computer vision theory and applications, pp 273–280
40. Feild J, Erik G (2012) Learned-Miller, scene text recognition with bilateral regression. UMass Amherst technical report
41. Lucas SM et al (2003) ICDAR 2003 robust reading competitions. In: Proceedings of the seventh international conference on document analysis and recognition, 2003
42. Lucas S et al (2005) ICDAR 2003 robust reading competitions: entries, results, and future directions. IJDAR 7(2–3):105–122
43. Lucas SM (2005) ICDAR 2005 text locating competition results. In: Proceedings of the eighth international conference on document analysis and recognition, 2005
44. Shahab A, Shafait F, Dengel A (2011) ICDAR 2011 robust reading competition challenge 2: reading text in scene images. In: International conference on document analysis and recognition (ICDAR), 2011
45. A database of images. Available from: http://research.microsoft.com/~manik/
46. Netzer Y et al (2011) Reading digits in natural images with unsupervised feature learning
47. The Street View House Numbers (SVHN) Dataset. Available from: http://ufldl.stanford.edu/housenumbers/

48. Amazon Mechanical Turk framework. Available from: https://www.mturk.com/mturk/welcome
49. Wu L, Shivakumara P, Lu T, Tan CL Text detection using Delaunay Triangulation in video sequence. DAS 2014, to appear
50. Karatzas D, Shafait K, Uchida S, Iwamura M, Bigorda LG ICDAR 2013 robust reading competition. In: Proceedings of the 12th ICDAR, pp 1115–1124
51. Yin XC, Yin XW, Huang KZ, Hao HW (2013) Robust text detection in natural scene images. CVPR
52. Shi CZ, Wang CH, Xiao BH, Zhang Y, Gao S, Zhang Z (2013) Scene text recognition using part-based tree-structured character detection. CVPR

Chapter 5
Post-processing of Video Text Detection

The previous chapters describe how to detect text lines from video and natural scene images. This chapter introduces methods for text binarization and recognition as post-processing for text detection. Text binarization is an important step for improving recognition accuracy of characters because OCR engines basically accept only binary images. Therefore, this chapter discusses techniques to obtain binary images for the text lines detected by the text detection methods described in the earlier chapters. Since video and natural scene images suffer from low resolution and complex background, it is hard to develop effective binarization methods which preserve shapes of characters without losing text pixels. Therefore, there is a need to develop methods for character shape reconstruction. Hence, this chapter will also introduce a character reconstruction method using ring radius transform.

5.1 Text Line Binarization

Character recognition in document analysis has achieved great successes in the field of pattern recognition. However, OCR engines today still report poor accuracy for video scene characters because OCR technology was developed mainly for scanned document images containing simple background and high contrast. It was not meant for video images having complex background and low contrast. It is evident from the natural scene character recognition methods in [1–6] that the document OCR engine does not work for camera-based natural scene images due to failure of binarization in handling nonuniform background and insufficient illumination in some scene images. Therefore, poor character recognition rate (67 %) is reported for ICDAR 2003 competition data [7]. This shows that despite the fact that camera images are of high contrast, the OCR accuracy is at best 67 %. Considering that video images have both low contrast and complex background, the challenges are far greater because of the lack of good binarization methods which can tackle both low contrast and

© Springer-Verlag London 2014
T. Lu et al., *Video Text Detection*, Advances in Computer Vision
and Pattern Recognition, DOI 10.1007/978-1-4471-6515-6_5

complex background to separate foreground and background accurately [8]. It is noted that character recognition rate varies from 0 % to 45 % [8] if OCR is applied directly on video text. Experiments have been carried out using Niblack [9] and Sauvola [10] methods as baselines to show that direct thresholding techniques give poor accuracy for video and scene images. It is reported in [11] that the performance of these thresholding techniques is not consistent because the character recognition rate changes as the application and dataset change. In this chapter, a method for separation of foreground (text) and background (non-text) to facilitate OCR will be introduced.

There are several papers that addressed video text binarization and localization problem based on edge, stroke, color, and corner information to improve character recognition rate. Ntirogiannis et al. [12] propose a binarization method based on the text baseline and stroke width extraction to obtain the body of the text information. A convex hull analysis with adaptive thresholding is then done to obtain the final text information. However, this method focuses on artificial text where pixels have uniform color. Thus it will not work for artificial and scene text whose pixels do not have uniform color values. An automatic binarization method for color text areas in images and video based on convolutional neural network is proposed by Saidane and Garcia [13]. The performance of the method depends on the number of training samples. Recently, edge-based binarization for video text image is proposed by Zhou et al. [14] to improve the video character recognition rate. This method takes in the Canny map of the input image and uses a modified flood fill algorithm to fill the gap if there is a small gap on the contour. This method works well for small gaps but not for big gaps on the contours. Furthermore, the method's primary focus is graphics text and big font but not both graphics and scene texts.

The binarization methods above basically lack general capability in dealing with both graphics and scene texts together where one can expect much more variation in contrast and background compared to just graphics text alone. To meet this challenge, a recent method [15] known as the wavelet-gradient-fusion (WGF) method is described below.

5.1.1 Wavelet-Gradient-Fusion Method (WGF)

This method first uses the Laplacian approach and skeleton analysis [16] to segment the text lines from the video frames. The multi-oriented text lines segmented from the video frames are next converted to horizontal text lines based on the direction of the text lines. Hence, non-horizontal text lines are treated as horizontal text lines to make implementation easier. The resultant horizontal text lines form the input to the WGF method.

It is noted that wavelet decomposition is good for enhancing the low-contrast pixel in the video frame because of multi-resolution analysis which gives horizontal (H), vertical (V), and diagonal (D) information. The gradient operation of the same directions (i.e. H, V, and D) on the video image gives the fine details of the edge

Fig. 5.1 Flow diagram for the wavelet-gradient-fusion

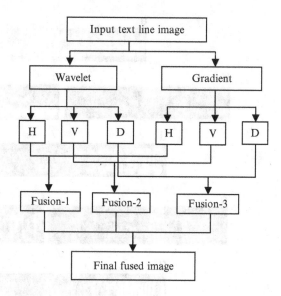

pixels in the video text line image. To overcome the problems of unpredictable video characteristics, the work presented in [17] suggested the use of fusion of the values given by the low bands of the input images to increase the resolution of the image. Inspired by this work, the WGF method proposes an operation that chooses the highest pixel value among low pixel values of different sub-bands corresponding to wavelet and gradient at different levels as a fusion criterion. It is shown in Fig. 5.1 where one can see how the sub-bands of wavelet fuse with the gradient images and the final fusion image is obtained after fusing the three fusion-1, fusion-2, and fusion-3 images. For example, for the input image shown in Fig. 5.2a, the method compares the pixel values in the horizontal wavelet (Fig. 5.2b) with the corresponding pixel values in the horizontal gradient (Fig. 5.2c), and it chooses the highest pixel value to obtain the fusion image as shown in Fig. 5.2d. In the same way, the method obtains the fusion image for the vertical wavelet and the vertical gradient as shown in Fig. 5.2e–g and the diagonal wavelet and the diagonal gradient images as shown in Fig. 5.2h–j. The same operation is performed on the above three obtained fused images to get the final fused image as shown in Fig. 5.2k where one can see that the text information is sharpened compared to the results shown in Fig. 5.2d, g, and j.

5.1.2 Text Candidates

It is observed from the result of the previous section that the WGF method widens the gap between text and non-text pixels. Therefore, to classify text and non-text pixels, the method uses k-means clustering with $k = 2$ by applying on each row and column separately as shown in Fig. 5.3a, b where the result of row-wise clustering

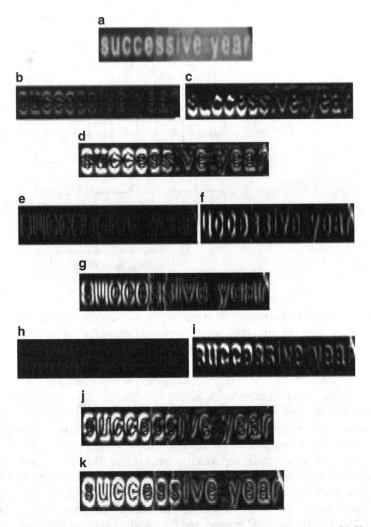

Fig. 5.2 Intermediate results for the WGF method. (**a**) Input text line image. (**b**) Horizontal wavelet. (**c**) Horizontal gradient. (**d**) Fusion-1 of (**b**) and (**c**). (**e**) Vertical wavelet. (**f**) Vertical gradient. (**g**) Fusion-2 of (**e**) and (**f**). (**h**) Diagonal wavelet (**i**) Diagonal gradient. (**j**) Fusion-3 of (**h**) and (**i**). (**k**) Fusion of Fusion-1, Fusion-2 and Fusion-3

loses some text information but not so for column-wise clustering. Here the cluster that has the higher mean between the two is considered the text cluster. This is the advantage of row-wise and column-wise clustering as it helps in restoring the possible text information. The union of row-wise and column-wise clustering results is considered as text candidates to separate and text and non-text information as shown in Fig. 5.3c though it is seen that the union operation still includes other background information in addition to text.

Fig. 5.3 Text candidates for text binarization. (**a**) k-means clustering row-wise. (**b**) k-means clustering column-wise. (**c**) Union of (**a**) and (**b**)

Fig. 5.4 Process of smoothing. (**a**) Gap identification based on mutual nearest neighbor criterion. (**b**) Disconnections are filled and identified noisy pixels. (**c**) Clear connected components

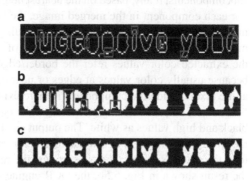

5.1.3 Smoothing

It is observed from the text candidates that the shape of the character is almost preserved, but it may contain other background information. Therefore, the method considers the text candidate image as the reference image to clean up the background. For this, the method uses the Canny map of the input image to smoothen the text information with the help of the reference image. The method identifies disconnections in the Canny map by testing a mutual nearest neighbor criterion on end points as shown in Fig. 5.4a where disconnections are marked with red color rectangles. The mutual nearest neighbor criterion is defined as follows: if P1 is near to P2, then P2 should be near to P1, where point P1 and point P2 are the two end points. This is because Canny operation gives good edge information for video text line images, but at the same time it gives lots of disconnections due to low contrast and complex background. The identified disconnections are matched with the same positions in the text candidate image locally to restore the missing text information since the text candidate image does not lose much text information compared to the Canny edge image as in Fig. 5.4b where almost all components are filled by a flood fill operation. However, one can see noisy pixels in the background. To eliminate them, the method performs a projection profile analysis which results in a clear text information with clean background as shown in Fig. 5.4c. Despite the above effort, if there are disconnections in the flood-filled image, then the method subtracts the flood-filled image with Canny operation to identify the disconnections, and the lost pixels are restored by referring to the text candidate image which results in a smoothed image.

5.1.4 Foreground and Background Separation

The method considers the text in the smoothed image as connected components, and it analyzes the components in order to fix a bounding box to merge the subcomponents, if any, based on the nearest neighbor criterion as shown in Fig. 5.5a. For each component in the merged image, the method extracts the maximum color information from the input image corresponding to pixels in the components of the merged image. It is found from the results of the maximum color extraction that the extracted color values refer the border/edge of the components. This is valid because usually color values at edges or near edges have higher values than those at the pixels inside the components if there exist holes inside the component. This observation helps in finding a hole for each component by making low values as black and high values as white. The output can be seen in Fig. 5.5b where the holes are created with the help of low and high color values. After separating text and non-text, the result is fed to OCR [18] to test the recognition results. For example, for the result shown in Fig. 5.5b, the OCR engine recognizes the whole text correctly as shown in Fig. 5.5c where recognition result is in quote.

5.1.5 Summary

A fusion method based on wavelet sub-bands and gradient of different directions is described. It is shown that this fusion helps in enhancing text information. The method uses k-means clustering algorithm row-wise and column-wise to obtain

(a). Color values of edge pixels and inside character

Fig. 5.5 Foreground and background separation by analyzing the color values at edge pixel and inside the components

(b) Foreground and background is separated

(c)"successive year"

text candidates. The mutual nearest neighbor concept is used to identify the true pair of end pixels to restore the missing text information. To separate foreground and background, the method explores the color values at edges and inside the components.

5.2 Character Reconstruction

It is observed from the previous section that it is hard to prevent disconnections and missing information in the binarization methods. Therefore, it is necessary to develop a character reconstruction method to restore the missing text pixels to enable OCR engine to recognize characters correctly. Thus, this section describes a method based on ring radius transform to reconstruct character shape.

Automatic recognition of text from natural scene images is currently an active field in the document analysis community due to the variety of texts, different font sizes, orientations, and occlusion [19–22]. To achieve better character recognition rate for the text in natural scene images, various methods have been proposed based on Gabor features and linear discriminate analysis [19], cross ratio spectrum and dynamic time wrapping [20], conditional random field [21], and Markov random field [22]. According to the literature on natural scene character recognition, the recognition rates of these methods have so far been unsatisfactory. This is due to the complex background in natural scene images. Furthermore, experiments show that applying conventional character recognition methods directly on video text frames leads to poor recognition rate [1, 8, 23]. This is because of several unfavorable characteristics of video such as high variability in fonts, font sizes, and orientations; broken characters due to occlusion, perspective distortion, and color bleeding; and disconnections due to low resolution and complex background [24]. In addition to this, concavity, holes, and complicated shapes make the problem more complex. For example, Fig. 5.6 shows the complexities of a video character compared to a document character. As a result, OCR does not work well for video images.

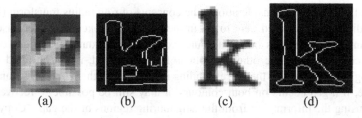

(a)   (b)   (c)   (d)

Fig. 5.6 Characters in videos (**a**) have poorer resolution, lower contrast, and more complex background than characters in document images (**c**). As a result, the former often has broken contours (**b**), while the latter has complete contours (**d**). Contours of (**a**) and (**c**) are shown in (**b**) and (**d**), respectively

As a result of the above problems, methods based on connected component (CC) analysis are not good enough to handle the problems of video characters. Therefore, this section looks into reconstruction of character contours from broken contours to increase the recognition rate because contours are important features which preserve the shapes of the characters. One way to reconstruct the broken contour is to exploit the symmetry of the character image shape, e.g., between the left- and right-hand sides of the contour or between the inner and outer contours of the same character image. Contour reconstruction based on symmetry of contours is motivated by the way the human visual system works. Research has shown that when an object is occluded, human beings are still able to recognize it by interpolating the observed incomplete contour with their knowledge about the shapes of the objects that they have seen before [25]. This symmetry can be observed in many kinds of objects, from real-world objects to industrial objects and even organs in the human body.

In the document analysis community, there are methods that fill small gaps caused by degradations and distortions in contour to improve character recognition. This is often done by utilizing the probability of a text pixel based on its neighbors and filling in the gap if required. Wang and Yan [26] propose a method for mending broken handwritten characters. Skeletons are used to analyze the structures of the broken segments. Each skeleton end point of a CC is then extended along its continual direction to connect to another end point of another CC. In a similar approach for broken handwritten digits, Yu and Yan [27] identify structural points, e.g., convex and valley points, of each CC. For each pair of neighboring CCs, the pair of structural points that have the minimum distance is considered for reconstruction. Different from the previous two methods, Allier and Emptoz [28] and Allier et al. [29] use active contour to reconstruct broken characters in degraded documents. Given a binary image, features extracted from Gabor filters are used for template matching. The lack of external forces (energy) at gap regions is compensated by adding gradient vector flow forces extracted from the corresponding region of the template. This compensation makes the snake (iterative method) converge to the character contour instead of going inside it. As the above methods are designed for document images, they rely heavily on CC analysis. However, this is not suitable for video images because it is extremely difficult to extract characters as complete CCs.

Based on the above considerations, the concepts of ring radius transform (RRT) and medial pixels are used here to fill in the gaps of a broken character based on the symmetry between its inner and outer contours. For example, if a gap occurs on one contour, while the other contour is fully preserved, it can be filled in by "copying" the pixels from the corresponding region of the other contour. As another example, if a gap occurs on both contours, it may still be possible to recover this gap by using the information from the neighboring regions of the gap. "Copying," as mentioned above, is achieved by introducing the concepts of RRT and medial pixels. For each pixel, RRT assigns a value which is the distance to the nearest edge pixel. The medial pixels are defined as the pixels at the middle of the inner and outer contours. In terms of radius values, they have the maximum values in their neighborhood because they are close to neither of the contours.

The method works in the following two ways. First, the method uses the symmetry information between the inner and outer contours to recover the gaps. This is a departure from the traditional approach of considering a broken character as a set of CCs and trying to connect these components. The second way lies in the concepts of RRT and medial pixels. The stroke width transform and medial axis concepts are explored for natural scene text detection in [30] using stroke width based on gradient information and distance transform. Similar idea is here applied on reconstruction of broken character image contours in video, and it works directly on the characters contours instead of the character pixels (in the form of CCs).

5.2.1 Ring Radius Transform

For reconstruction of character contour, the method in [31] is used for character segmentation from the video text line extracted by the text detection method [16]. This method treats character segmentation as a least cost pathfinding problem, and it allows curved segmentation paths. Therefore, the method segments character properly even if there is a touching and overlapping characters due to low contrast and complex background. Gradient vector flow is used to identify the candidate cut pixels. Then, a two-pass pathfinding algorithm is used for identifying true cuts and removing false cuts. In addition, the method has the ability to segment characters from multi-oriented text line. Therefore, the method treats non-horizontal characters as the same as horizontal characters. Thus, the method uses the output of segmentation method as input for character reconstruction.

The input for RRT is the edge map of the segmented character image. For a given edge map, RRT produces a radius map of the same size, in which each pixel is assigned a value according to the distance to the nearest edge pixel. The radius value is defined mathematically as follows:

$$\text{rad}(p) = \min_{q\,:\,f(q)\,=\,1} \text{dist}\,(p, q) \tag{5.1}$$

Here rad(p) returns the radius value of a pixel x in f, a binary image where edge pixels and background pixels are assigned values 1 and 0, respectively. dist (p, q) is a distance function between two pixels p, q. Figure 5.7 shows a sample radius map for the gap in the character on the right side. One can notice from Fig. 5.7 that the values marked by yellow color are text pixels having radius zero of the ring. It is also observed that the values between two zero radii marked by yellow color increase from zero (left text pixel) to the highest radius value (3) (this one being considered as the highest radius value which is the medial axis value) and again decrease in the same way to reach the zero radius value (right text pixel). Among the values returned in the radius map, the method requires the medial pixels, i.e., those that are at the middle of the inner and outer contours and thus have the

Fig. 5.7 Sample values in the radius map (using the chessboard distance function). The highlighted values (*yellow color*) are the text (*white*) pixels within the window

3	3	3	3	3	3	3	3	3	3	3
2	2	2	2	2	3	2	2	2	2	2
2	1	1	1	2	3	2	1	1	1	2
2	1	0	1	2	3	2	1	0	1	2
2	1	0	1	2	3	2	1	0	1	2
2	1	0	1	2	3	2	1	0	1	2
2	1	0	1	2	3	2	1	0	1	2
2	1	0	1	2	3	2	1	0	1	2
2	1	0	1	2	3	2	1	0	1	2

maximum radius values in their neighborhood. Horizontal medial pixels (HMPs) are the peak pixels compared to the neighboring pixels on the same row, while vertical medial pixels (VMPs) are defined with respect to the neighboring pixels on the same column (Fig. 5.7). Medial pixels are useful for analyzing character image regions with almost constant thickness. The medial pixels would lie along the center axes of the contours and have similar radius values, which are roughly half of the region widths. Potential gaps can then be identified by checking for contour pixels on both sides of the medial pixels based on the radius values.

It is clear from the above formulation that no character-specific features have been used. In other words, these concepts generalize well to any objects whose contours possess the symmetry property.

The method consists of six steps. In the first step, the method extracts the character contours from the input grayscale images using the method proposed in [32]. Based on these contours, the medial pixels are identified in the second step. The third step then uses the symmetry information from the medial pixels to reconstruct horizontal and vertical gaps. The fourth step uses both vertical and horizontal medial axes iteratively to fill large gaps. The fifth step fills the gaps in the outer contour. The sixth step fills in all the remaining small gaps. These steps can be seen in Fig. 5.8 where the flow diagram of the character reconstruction is given.

5.2.2   Horizontal and Vertical Medial Axes

In this step, the method applies RRT to the initial character contour image given by the method proposed in [31] using the chessboard distance function:

$$\text{dist}\,(p, p') = \max \left(\left| p.x - p'.x \right|, \left| p.y - p'.y \right| \right) \tag{5.2}$$

In other words, squares centered at p are used instead of rings, for ease of implementation. The output of Eq. 5.2 is shown in Fig. 5.9 where the horizontal and vertical medial axis values are indicated on the left and right sides, respectively. Medial pixels are then identified as described in previous step (ring radius transform for medial axis). The final medial axis with respect to the horizontal and vertical medial axis pixels can be seen in Fig. 5.10 on the left and right sides, respectively.

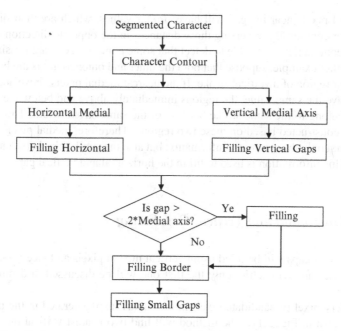

Fig. 5.8 Flow diagram of character reconstruction method for the segmented character

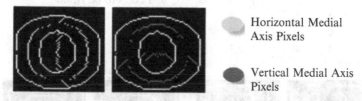

Fig. 5.9 Horizontal and vertical medial axis pixels marked by *green* and *red* color

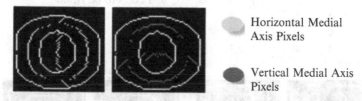

Fig. 5.10 Horizontal medial axis (*left*) and vertical medial

Medial pixels provide useful information about the symmetry between the inner and outer contours of a character. For example, suppose that a gap occurs at the outer contour while the inner contour is fully preserved during the extraction step.

The medial pixels near the gap will have similar values, which are their distances to the inner contour. By traversing those distances in the opposite direction (toward the outer contour), it is possible to detect that some contour pixels are missing.

As another example, suppose that both the inner and outer contours are broken at a particular region of a vertical stroke. If the nearest medial pixels above and below the gap have the same value, the regions immediately above and below the gap are likely to belong to the same stroke because of the same stroke width. The gap can then be reconstructed based on these two regions. Therefore, medial pixels help us to utilize not only the symmetry information but also the similarities between nearby regions. This information is used to fill in the horizontal and vertical gaps.

5.2.3   Horizontal and Vertical Gap Filling

The horizontal gaps will be filled using vertical medial pixels and vice versa. Since the two cases are symmetric, only the first one will be discussed in detail in this section.

For every pixel p (candidate pixel) in the radius map generated in the previous step as shown in Fig. 5.11a, the method will find two nearest vertical medial axis pixels (VMPs), one on the left of the pixel and the other on the right of the pixel as shown in orange color in Fig. 5.11a. If the original pixel and the two VMPs have exactly the same value r, it indicates that it is likely to be in the middle of a horizontal stroke of a character due to the constant thickness. The method will check two pixels, $(p.x - r, p.y)$ and $(p.x + r, p.y)$, and mark them as text pixels if

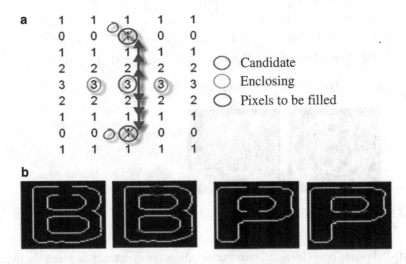

Fig. 5.11 Sample results of horizontal gap filling. (**a**) Illustration of horizontal gap filling based on VMP. (**b**) Horizontal gaps filled

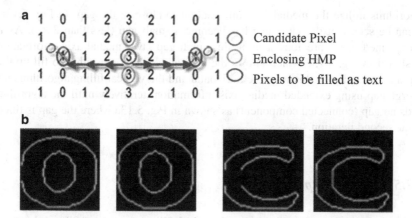

Fig. 5.12 Sample results of vertical gap filling. (a) Illustration of vertical gap filling based on HMP. (b) Vertical gaps filled

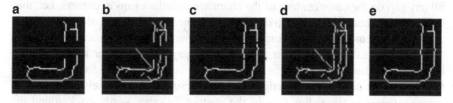

Fig. 5.13 Iterative filling helps to mend large gaps. (a) Input (b) Medial axis (c) 1st iteration results (d) Medial axis (e) 2nd iteration results

they are currently classified as non-text as shown in pixel to be filled as text by red color in Fig. 5.11a. The horizontal gap is thus filled as shown in the two examples in Fig. 5.11b. In the same way, the method uses horizontal medial axis pixels (HMPs) to fill the vertical gap as shown illustration in Fig. 5.12a, and the sample vertically filled results are shown in Fig. 5.12b.

5.2.4 Large Gap Filling

The above step fills horizontally and vertically if the contour of a character has gaps of $2 \times r$ where r is the medial axis pixel value. This is the advantage of the RRT method in filling gap compared to the other gap filling methods such as smoothing and morphological processing in document analysis. If a gap exceeds the size mentioned above, then it is considered as a large gap. It is observed that if there is a large gap as shown in Fig. 5.13a, the medial axis can be formed even in the gap. In Fig. 5.13b, it is observed that the medial axis (marked in yellow) is extended by a few pixels away down from the upper end pixels and a few pixels above the lower end pixels. In this situation, the horizontal and the vertical gap filling algorithms utilize the medial axis information to close in the gap. In Fig. 5.13c, it can be seen that the large gap has become a small gap (less than $2 \times r$). As it is explained in the previous section, this small gap gives medial axis information as shown in Fig. 5.13d which allows the horizontal filling algorithm to fill up the gap automatically. In this way, the horizontal and the vertical filling algorithms fill a large gap using extended medial axis information iteratively until the algorithm finds no gap (connected component) as shown in Fig. 5.13e where the gap is filled in the second iteration.

5.2.5   Border Gap Filling

It is true that the above horizontal and vertical filling algorithms fill only gaps in horizontal and vertical direction but not in diagonal direction which exists at the corners of the contours. Therefore, in this section, the method uses a criterion to fill any gap on the outer contour of the character including gaps at corners, i.e., the border of the character. This step describes the process of filling border gaps of the contours based on the radius information in both horizontal and vertical directions.

Every non-text pixel which is near the boundary of a character is represented by a high negative value in the radius map of the contour because for these pixels the boundary is nearer than the edge pixel. As a result, non-text pixels are assigned negative values in the radius map of the contour. In other words, background of noncharacter area is represented by high negative values as shown in Fig. 5.14a

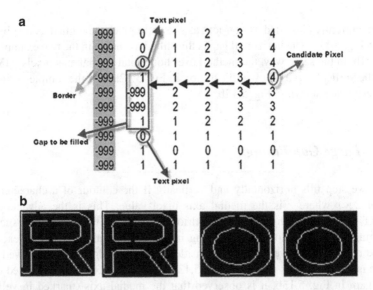

Fig. 5.14 Sample results of border gap filling. (a) Illustration of border gap filling. (b) Border gaps filled

(values marked in green color). From the medial axis values, the algorithm finds the outer contour and checks for any high negative values in the outer contour. It then fills the gap based on the criterion used in the horizontal and vertical filling algorithms. The sample results are shown in Fig. 5.14b where one can notice that the algorithm fills gaps at corners and other small gaps that are missed by the horizontal and vertical filling algorithms. Figure 5.14b shows that the gaps on the inner contour have not been filled by the algorithm as this algorithm fills gaps on the outer contour but not gaps on the inner contour. This is because once the algorithm fills the gaps on the outer contour, filling in the gaps on the inner contour becomes easy for this method. Note that for the character "R" shown in Fig. 5.14b, the algorithm also fills non-gap on the right side of the character. This causes problems for the next step of the algorithm. Hence, the method performs preprocessing to remove such extra noisy information.

5.2.6 Small Gap Filling

Most of the big gaps have been filled in the previous steps. The purpose of this step is to handle the remaining gaps, most of which are quite small and are missed by the above steps of the algorithms.

It is found that the result of the previous steps may contain extra information, e.g., small branches, loops, and blobs, which should be removed before filling in the gaps. Small branches are removed as follows: for each CC (usually a contour or part of a contour), only the longest possible 8-connected path is retained; all the other pixels are discarded as shown in Fig. 5.15a. Loops and blobs are removed if their lengths and areas are below certain thresholds, which are determined adaptively based on the estimated stroke widths (twice the radius values) as shown in Fig. 5.15b, c.

It is observed that if a character is not broken, there will only be closed contours (e.g., 1 contour for "Y," 2 contours for "A," and 3 contours for "B") and no end points at all. Therefore, after the image has been cleaned up, the small gaps are identified by looking for end points. A gap often creates two end points, and so the mutual nearest neighbor concept is used here again not only to find the end points but also to pair them up together. p1 and p2 are mutual nearest neighbors if p1 is the nearest edge pixel of p2 and vice versa. Each pair of the end points is connected

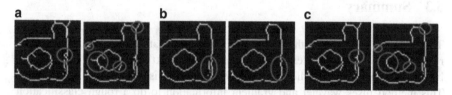

Fig. 5.15 Preprocessing steps during small gap filling. (a) Removal of small loops (b) Removal of small branches (c) Removal of small blobs

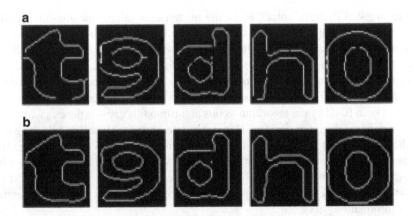

Fig. 5.16 Sample results of small gap filling. (**a**) Input images. (**b**) Gaps filled

by a straight line to fill in the gap between the two points as shown in Fig. 5.16. The preprocessing steps such as removing small branches ensure that the end points are true end points and thus the method avoids filling in false gaps. Figure 5.16 shows the small gap filling algorithm fills even large gaps also as shown by one example for the character "d." It is observed from Fig. 5.16 that the small gap filling algorithm does not preserve the shape of the contour while filling gaps. This is the main drawback of this algorithm. However, it does not affect the final recognition rate much because this algorithm is used in this work only for filling small gaps that remain after the horizontal and vertical filling algorithms but not for large gaps.

5.2.7   Summary

A method for reconstructing contours of broken characters in video images using RRT is described. RRT helps to identify medial pixels, which are used to fill in the horizontal, vertical gaps, large gaps, and border gaps. Finally, the remaining small gaps are reconstructed based on the mutual nearest neighbor concept.

5.3   Summary

This chapter presents methods for text line binarization and character shape reconstruction as post-processing to enhance video text recognition. For text line binarization, a wavelet-gradient-fusion (WGF) method is described as an example. This method fuses wavelet and gradient information to do a rough classification of text and non-text components followed by several refinements for contour smoothing. Character shape reconstruction aims to repair missing pixels and disconnections. A radius transform concept is presented as an example for character reconstruction. The method finds medial axis for each component by drawing rings for different radius values. Based on medial axis information, the method fills horizontal, vertical, large gap, and small gaps followed by the use of the nearest neighbor criterion for pairing of end pixels to complete the remaining gaps.

References

1. Doermann D, Liang J, Li H (2003) Progress in camera-based document image analysis. In: Proceedings of the ICDAR, pp 606–616
2. Zang J, Kasturi R (2008) Extraction of text objects in video documents: recent progress. In: Proceedings of the DAS, pp 5–17
3. Wang K, Belongie S (2010) Word spotting in the wild. In: Proceedings of the ECCV, pp 591–604
4. Tang X, Gao X, Liu J, Zhang H (2002) A spatial-temporal approach for video caption detection and recognition. IEEE Trans Neural Netw 13:961–971
5. Lyu MR, Song J, Cai M (2005) A comprehensive method for multilingual video text detection, localization, and extraction. IEEE Trans CSVT 15:243–255
6. Mishara A, Alahari K, Jawahar CV (2011) An MRF model for binarization of natural scene text. In: Proceedings of the ICDAR, pp 11–16
7. Neumann L, Matas J (2011) A method for text localization and recognition in real-world images. In: Proceedings of the ACCV, pp 770–783
8. Chen D, Odobez JM (2005) Video text recognition using sequential Monte Carlo and error voting methods. Pattern Recogn Lett 26:1386–1403
9. Niblack W (1986) An introduction to digital image processing. Prentice Hall, Englewood Cliffs
10. Sauvola J, Seeppanen T, Haapakoski S, Pietikainen M (1997) Adaptive document binarization. In: Proceedings of the ICDAR, pp 147–152
11. He J, Do QDM, Downton AC, Kim JH (2005) A comparison of binarization methods for historical archive documents. In: Proceedings of the ICDAR, pp 538–542
12. Ntirogiannis K, Gotos B, Pratikakis I (2011) Binarization of textual content in video frames. In: Proceedings of the ICDAR, pp 673–677
13. Saidane Z, Garcia C (2007) Robust binarization for video text recognition. In: Proceedings of the ICDAR, pp 874–879
14. Zhou Z, Li L, Tan CL (2010) Edge based binarization of video text images. In: Proceedings of the ICPR, pp 133–136
15. Roy S, Shivakumara P, Roy P, Tan CL (2012) Wavelet-gradient-fusion for video text binarization. In: Proceedings of the ICPR, pp 3300–3303
16. Shivakumara P, Phan TQ, Tan CL (2011) A Laplacian approach to multi-oriented text detection in video. IEEE Trans PAMI 33:412–419
17. Pajares G, Cruz JM (2004) A wavelet-based image fusion tutorial. Pattern Recogn 37:1855–1872
18. Tesseract http://code.google.com/p/tesseract-ocr/
19. Chen X, Yang J, Zhang J, Waibel A (2004) Automatic detection and recognition of signs from natural scenes. IEEE Trans Image Process 13
20. Zhou P, Li L, Tan CL (2009) Character recognition under severe perspective distortion. In: Proceedings of the ICDAR, pp 676–680
21. Pan YF, Hou X, Liu CL (2009) Text localization in natural scene images based on conditional random field. In: Proceedings of the ICDAR, pp 6–10
22. Pan YF, Hou X, Liu CL (2008) A robust system to detect and localize texts in natural scene images. In: Proceedings of the DAS, pp 35–42

23. Chen D, Odobez JM, Bourlard H (2004) Text detection and recognition in images and video frames. Pattern Recogn 37:595–608
24. Lee SH, Kim JH (2008) Complementary combination of holistic and component analysis for recognition of low-resolution video character images. Pattern Recogn Lett 29:383–391
25. Ghosh A, Petkov N (2005) Robustness of shape descriptors to incomplete contour representations. IEEE Trans PAMI 27:1793–1804
26. Wang J, Yan H (1999) Mending broken handwriting with a macrostructure analysis method to improve recognition. Pattern Recogn Lett 20:855–864
27. Yu D, Yan H (2001) Reconstruction of broken handwritten digits based on structural morphological features. Pattern Recogn 34:235–254
28. Allier B, Emptoz H (2002) Degraded character image restoration using active contours: a first approach. In: Proceedings of the ACM symposium on document engineering, pp 142–148
29. Allier B, Bali N, Emptoz H (2006) Automatic accurate broken character restoration for patrimonial documents. IJDAR 8:246–261
30. Epshtein B, Ofek E, Wexler Y (2010) Detecting text in natural scenes with stroke width transform. In: Proceedings of the CVPR, pp 2963–2970
31. Phan TQ, Shivakumara P, Tan CL (2011) A gradient vector flow-based method for video character segmentation. In: Proceedings of the ICDAR, pp 1024–1028
32. Shivakumara P, Ding Bei Hong, Zhao D, Lu S, Tan CL (2012) A new iterative-midpoint-method for video character gap filling. In: Proceedings of the ICPR, pp 673–676

Chapter 6
Character Segmentation and Recognition

The previous chapter assumes that segmented characters are available for character shape restoration and recognition. It is also noted that character segmentation from video text lines detected by the video text detection method is not as easy as segmenting characters from scanned document images due to low resolution and complex background of video. In this chapter, we discuss methods for word segmentation, character segmentation, and then character recognition. Segmenting characters and words reduces complexity of the background to facilitate binarization algorithms in achieving good results without losing much text pixels before feeding to the available OCR. We will give an overview of OCR for character recognition. We will then introduce a method for word segmentation followed by character segmentation. Next, we will describe another method that does character segmentation without the need for word segmentation. Finally, instead of using a traditional OCR, we will introduce a method that performs character recognition through a process of hierarchical classification.

6.1 Introduction to OCR and Its Usage in Video Text Recognition

There are two ways of recognizing characters in a text line detected by a text detection method. One way is to use an available OCR [1] to recognize the characters, and another way is to use a classifier to recognize the characters (video OCR). The former approach requires a good binarization method to obtain characters with well-defined shapes of the characters. The latter approach requires a large number of samples to train the classifier to recognize the characters. An advantage of the latter approach is that there is no need to segment words and characters such that a text line can be given to the classifier to recognize without binarization. However, this limits its ability to work on different datasets due to

© Springer-Verlag London 2014
T. Lu et al., *Video Text Detection*, Advances in Computer Vision
and Pattern Recognition, DOI 10.1007/978-1-4471-6515-6_6

the need for training with a large number of samples. Hence, this chapter adopts the first approach by doing binarization, segmentation of words and characters followed by the use of the available OCR to recognize the characters. Instead of using an available OCR, a character recognition method is also developed and described at the end of this chapter, using a set of features for English characters.

Character recognition plays a vital role in indexing and retrieval of videos to label events as close to its content. Without character recognition, content-based image retrieval methods work well for video labeling but fail to obtain actual meaning of the video's content of video to label the events. Therefore, character recognition-based labeling has become popular for video labeling as it gives meaning relevant to the video's content. With the proliferation of videos on the Internet, there is an increasing demand for search and retrieval. Both caption text and scene text (which appears on billboards, road signs, and so on) can be used to improve the retrieval of relevant videos, or even relevant frames.

According to [2], a video text detection and recognition system consists of five steps: (1) detection, (2) localization, (3) tracking, (4) extraction and enhancement, and (5) recognition. The first three steps focus on detecting and localizing text lines in video frames. Locations of the text lines are usually represented by their rectangular bounding boxes [3]. However, these boxes still contain both text and background pixels so the fourth step aims to make text easier to recognize, e.g., by binarization. These steps are discussed in the previous chapters. The fifth and final steps typically use an OCR engine to produce the final output as a string of characters.

OCR engines work well for document images, most of which contain monochrome text on a plain background. However, it does not produce satisfactory results for video images due to the poor resolution, low contrast, and unconstrained background of the text lines. Moreover, scene text is affected by lighting conditions and perspective distortions as introduced in Chap. 4. This chapter describes a method for video character segmentation and word segmentation, i.e., splitting a detected text line into individual characters and words. The motivation is twofold. First, it is an important step if a custom-built OCR with its own feature extraction scheme, e.g., [4], is used instead of a commercial OCR. Second, even if a traditional OCR engine is used, this step can still help to improve the recognition rate by performing enhancement methods, e.g., binarization, on individual character images instead of on the whole text line.

A common video character segmentation method is projection profile analysis [5]. Edge information (or other kinds of energy) in each column is analyzed to distinguish between columns that contain text pixels and gap pixels, based on the observation that the former have higher energy compared to the latter. Heuristic rules are proposed to further split and merge the segmented regions based on assumptions about the characters' widths and heights [6, 7]. Although these methods are simple and fast, it is difficult to determine a good threshold for images of different contrast (Fig. 6.1). In addition, because they work based on columns, they can only produce vertical cuts.

Fig. 6.1 The results of projection profile analysis are sensitive to threshold values. With a high threshold, true gaps are missed (*left*), while with a low threshold, many false gaps are detected (*right*)

To overcome this problem, a number of papers, inspired by works on touching handwritten characters, modeled the segmentation problem as a minimum-cost pathfinding problem. Kopf et al. [8] used Dijkstra's algorithm to perform pathfinding from the top row to the bottom row of the input image. A path's cost was defined as the cumulative absolute difference in grayscale intensities between consecutive pixels, based on the assumption that the background region had little variation in intensity. This method may not work well for images with complex backgrounds. In a similar approach, Tse et al. [9] applied pathfinding recursively until the segmented regions met the stopping criteria, e.g., their widths were below a threshold. However, this method requires binarization to get connected components, which is extremely difficult to do reliably, as aforementioned.

Finally, it should be noted that in the literature, there is another school of thought that leaves character segmentation to OCR engines and instead focusing on extracting character pixels more accurately, e.g., [10–12].

6.2 Word and Character Segmentation

Though many content-based retrieval algorithms have been developed for use in video indexing and retrieval in the field of image processing and multimedia, understanding video content and automatic annotations still remain an unsolved problem due to the semantic gap between the high-level and the low-level features. Therefore, automatic extraction of a video text, which aims at integrating advanced optical character recognition (OCR), is vitally useful for video annotation and retrieval systems [13]. Hence, video text extraction and recognition is crucial to the research in video indexing and summarization [13–17].

There are several algorithms that are reported in the literature for accurate text detection, and they have achieved good accuracy even for scene text detection [18–21] and multi-oriented text detection [3]. To recognize the detected video characters, it is necessary to reduce the complex background by segmenting words and characters properly even when the whole text string is already well located. Therefore, the third step mentioned earlier is important for real-time applications such as video events analysis and sports events analysis, etc. Text region extraction methods are generally classified into three groups. Methods in the first group use either global or local or multilevel thresholds to retrieve text regions. The second group uses stroke-based methods to retrieve text regions. The third group uses color-based methods. However, performance of these methods is poor because of the complex background and unfavorable characteristics of video images. Recently, a language-independent text extraction method [6] is proposed which works based on adaptive, dam point labeling, and inward filling. However, this method is sensitive to complex background images.

Chen et al. [14] proposed a two-step method for text recognition. The first step uses edge information to localize the text, and the second step uses features, and machine learning to recognize the segmented text. This method is not robust enough for complex backgrounds. Chen and Odobez [12] proposed a method based on Monte Carlo sampling for segmented text recognition. This method is expensive as it uses probabilistic Bayesian classifier for selecting thresholds. Another method [13] for low-resolution video character recognition is proposed based on a holistic approach and connected component analysis. However, it requires a large number of training samples. There are robust binarization methods which take the whole detected text region as input without segmenting a text region into words and characters to improve the recognition rate of video character recognition [22, 23]. Recently, Zhou et al. [23] developed a binarization method for video text recognition. This method uses the Canny information to binarize, and it achieves a reasonably good accuracy compared to conventional thresholding methods. The above methods focus on graphics text recognition rather than scene text recognition and hence their error rates are high if scene text is present in the image.

The above methods generally accept a whole text region detected by the text detection methods as input for binarization and recognition. Besides, these methods focus on graphics text and horizontal text. Hence, these methods are inadequate in handling complex background, multi-text and scene text in the video.

Therefore, a Fourier- and moments-based method for word and character extraction from video text lines in any direction is chosen here as an example for text segmentation because of its greater flexibility. The Fourier transform has the ability to enhance text pixels in video image as it gives high-frequency components for text pixels and low-frequency components for non-text pixels [24]. To further increase the gap between text and non-text pixels, the method uses moments on the inverse transfer of the Fourier image. Note that moment computation involves intensity and spatial information of the image, to widen the difference between text and non-text pixels [20]. For Fourier-moments features, the method introduces max-min clustering to obtain text cluster. The text cluster is combined with the Canny operation on the input text line image through a union operation to restore missing text candidates. The run-length concept is used for word extraction. Character extraction from the text candidate word image is done based on the fact that the text height difference at the character boundary column is smaller than the text height differences at other columns.

6.2.1　Fourier Transform-Based Method for Word and Character Segmentation

This method is chosen here for its ability to locate both graphics and scene text and multi-oriented text in complex video background despite low resolution of video images. The method takes advantage of the angle of text line determined by the text detection method during bounding box fixing. It then uses Bresenham's line drawing algorithm [25] to identify the text pixel direction. As a result, the method converts text lines of any direction into horizontal text lines. Hence, the problem of multi-orientation of text line has been simplified to the problem of horizontal text line.

The method is explained in four subsections. Bresenham's line algorithm for handling multi-oriented text is described in first subsection. The Fourier-moments combination features are explained in the second subsection to obtain text cluster. In the third subsection, the resultant text cluster is combined with a Canny operation on the input image to restore the missing text candidates for word extraction. The fourth subsection explains how characters are extracted from the segmented word image based on a thickness vector, a top distance vector, and a bottom distance vector.

6.2.2　Bresenham's Line Algorithm

Bresenham's line drawing algorithm [25] is used to determine the points in an n-dimensional raster that should be plotted to form a close approximation to a straight line between two given points. This algorithm works because it takes the coordinates of the bounding box determined by the text detection method to compute the direction of line which is then used to convert a text line of any given direction into a horizontal text line as shown in Fig. 6.2. However, the quality of image degrades somewhat. It can be seen in Fig. 6.2.

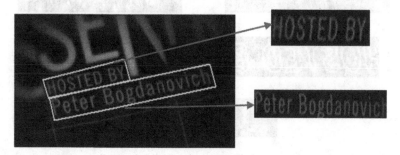

Fig. 6.2 Non-horizontal text line into horizontal text line

6.2.3   *Fourier-Moments Features*

Since video images have low resolution and complex background, the Fourier-moments combination is used to enhance low-contrast text pixels in order to differentiate text from the background. For a given horizontal text line image, the Fourier transform is applied to get high-frequency components for text pixels as the Fourier transform gives high energy for high-contrast pixels. Figure 6.3 shows a gray text image in (a), the Fourier spectra for text pixels in horizontal and vertical directions in (b), and the effect of inverse Fourier transform for the gray image in enhancing the brightness in (c), as compared to the input image. Note that for visualization, the binary form for the spectra of Fourier transform is shown in Fig. 6.3b.

Further, in order to increase the gap between text and non-text pixels, the method uses moments on the absolute inverse transfer of Fourier image shown in Fig. 6.3c. As we know that the moment computation involves intensity and spatial information of the image, which differs between text and non-text pixels.

The method uses a 3×3 sliding window on the resultant image of the absolute inverse Fourier transform (Fig. 6.3c) to calculate the moments with respect to mean and median as defined in equations (6.1) to (6.6). The respective features will be stored in different feature matrix. As a result, the method gets three Fourier-moments feature matrices for the text line image. Figure 6.3d shows the display of three feature matrices where it is noticed that text pixels appear brighter than non-text pixels. The effect of Fourier-moments is illustrated in Fig. 6.4 showing high-contrast values at text pixels and low-contrast values at non-text pixels. The gap representing the low-contrast values for the scan line 15 across the text in Fig. 6.4

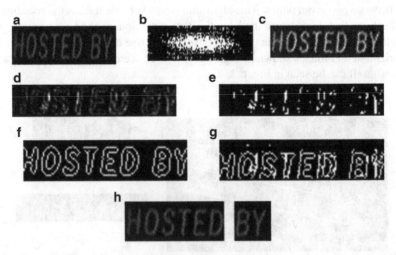

Fig. 6.3 Word extraction. (**a**) input, (**b**) Fourier, (**c**) inverse Fourier, (**d**) Fourier-moments, (**e**) max-min clustering, (**f**) Canny, (**g**) text candidates, (**h**) final output

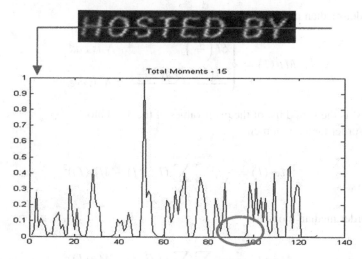

Fig. 6.4 Fourier-moments feature at gaps between the words

is marked by a green color oval. Hence, it is confirmed that Fourier-moments combination helps in classification of text and non-text pixels. To classify text pixels from non-text pixels, the method introduces the max-min clustering criterion instead of determining a threshold value for binarization. The result of max-min clustering is shown in Fig. 6.3e. The max-min clustering method selects max and min values in the feature matrix, and then it compares each value in the feature matrix with max and min chosen values to find its nearest neighbor, i.e., the value which is close to max is classified as text and the values which are close to min classified as non-text. This results in a text cluster as shown in Fig. 6.3e. Note that the method applies max-min clustering on three feature matrices separately to produce binary images. The results shown in Fig. 6.3e are the union of three binary images corresponding to three matrices.

First-order mean moment

$$M(I) = \text{Mean of the } 3 \times 3 \text{ block.} \tag{6.1}$$

Second-order mean moment

$$\mu_2(I) = \frac{1}{N^2} \sum_{i=0}^{N-1} \sum_{j=0}^{N-1} (I(i, j) - M(I))^2 \tag{6.2}$$

Third-order mean moment

$$\mu_3(I) = \frac{1}{N^2} \sum_{i=0}^{N-1} \sum_{j=0}^{N-1} (I(i, j) - M(I))^3 \tag{6.3}$$

First-order median moment

$$M\mu(I) = \begin{cases} SI\left(\frac{N^2}{2}\right) & , \ N \ is \ odd \\ \frac{SI\left(\frac{N^2-1}{2}\right)+SI\left(\frac{N^2+1}{2}\right)}{2} & , \ N \ is \ even \end{cases} \tag{6.4}$$

Where SI is the sorted list of the pixel values of the 3×3 block

Second-order median moment

$$Me_2(I) = \frac{1}{N^2}\sum_{i=0}^{N-1}\sum_{j=0}^{N-1}(I\,(i,j) - M\mu(I))^2 \tag{6.5}$$

Third-order median moment

$$Me_3(I) = \frac{1}{N^2}\sum_{i=0}^{N-1}\sum_{j=0}^{N-1}(I\,(i,j) - M\mu(I))^3 \tag{6.6}$$

where m and n are the number of rows and columns in the image, respectively, in the above equations.

6.2.4   Word Extraction

The max-min clustering gives a text cluster, but it is still not sufficient to identify the gap between words due to the sparsity of the matrices. To restore the lost text information, a union operation of the Canny edge map of the input image with the text cluster obtained by max-min clustering (Fig. 6.3e) is carried out. This union operation differs from the union operation mentioned in the Fourier-moments feature section where the method performs union operation on three different binary images obtained from the three feature matrices. This is done because the Canny operator definitely gives edges for text and that can be used for word segmentation (Fig. 6.3f) but not for character segmentation due to erratic edges at the character background. Hence, the union operation helps in filling the text region and leaving a gap between words as shown in Fig. 6.3g.

The gap between words is identified by introducing the concept of run length which is a well-known method for segmentation of text in document analysis. This idea is based on the observation that there is a large number of identical consecutive black pixels (background) between words, namely, gaps between consecutive words. Hence, this idea gives good results for word segmentation as shown in the sample results in Fig. 6.3h where it is observed that there is a clear space between the words.

Fig. 6.5 Character extraction. (a) input, (b) text candidates, (c) output

6.2.5 Character Extraction

The run-length concept used for word segmentation does not work for character extraction as it is noticed in Fig. 6.5b, which is the result of max-min clustering on Fig. 6.5a that there is no sufficiently large number of consecutive black pixels between characters. Here, another method based on text height difference (THd) vector, top distance and bottom distance vector of the above union operation is adopted. THd is defined as the distance between the topmost pixel and the bottommost pixel of each column in the restored word image. If THd is less than two pixels, the method considers the gap as a true character gap. If not, then the method checks the top and bottom distance vectors. The top distance vector (Td) is defined as the distance between the upper boundary and the topmost pixel of each column, and the bottom distance vector (Bd) is defined as the distance between the lower boundary and the bottommost pixel of each column. Then, the method finds the difference between consecutive distance values in Td and Bd to identify the depth (high difference when character boundary exists between the characters), which is denoted as Dtd and Dbd, respectively. When there is a gap between characters, both Dtd and Dbd give high values, and hence it is considered as a candidate gap. It can be seen in Fig. 6.6b that the candidate gaps are marked by red color dots for both Dtd and Dbd vectors, respectively. The use of Dtd and Dbd allows gaps between characters to be identified even if characters are touching. This is because touching between two characters usually exists near the midpoint of the character height rather than at the top or bottom. For Dtd and Dbd values, the method uses the same max-min clustering method used in the previous section for obtaining text cluster (Fig. 6.5b) for choosing candidate gap clusters (cluster with max value). For each candidate gap in the cluster belonging to the top distance vector, the method checks whether the corresponding candidate in the candidate gap cluster obtained from the bottom distance vector is also a candidate gap or not. If so, then the method considers it a true candidate gap for extracting the character as shown in sample results in Fig. 6.5c where the characters are segmented correctly.

6.2.6 Summary

In this section, a segmentation method based on Fourier-moments features for word and character extraction from text line image and word image is described.

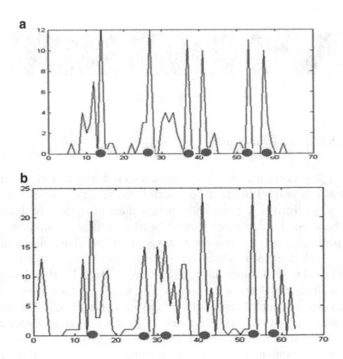

Fig. 6.6 Candidates for character gap identification. (**a**) top distance difference vector, (**b**) bottom distance difference vector

The combination of Fourier and moments facilitates classification of text pixels. The run-length concept is then applied on word gaps from the restored image. Next, a set of distance vectors are deployed for character extraction from words.

6.3 Character Segmentation Without Word Segmentation

The method in the previous section segments characters from words, and it uses binarization concept to segment the characters. However, it is noted that sometimes, binarization may lose text pixels and if any error exists during segmentation of words from text lines, the same error will affect the character segmentation. Therefore, this section describes a method that does not require words segmentation and binarization. The method works based on gradient vector flow by formulating character segmentation as a minimum-cost pathfinding problem. The method allows curved segmentation paths, and thus it is able to segment overlapping characters and touching characters due to low contrast and complex background. Thus, gradient vector flow is used in a way to identify candidate cut pixels. A two-pass pathfinding algorithm is then applied where the forward direction helps to locate potential cuts and the backward direction serves to remove false cuts, i.e., those that cut through the characters, while retaining the true cuts.

6.3.1 GVF for Character Segmentation

The GVF-based method accepts the output of the text detection method in [3], which is capable of extracting both horizontal and non-horizontal text lines. Similar to the Fourier transform method, any non-horizontal text line extracted will be converted to horizontal text line using Bresenham's algorithm [25] and normalized to a fixed height of 128 pixels. The GVF method consists of three steps: cut candidate identification, minimum-cost pathfinding, and false-positive elimination. The first step employs GVF to identify pixels that are potentially part of non-vertical cuts. In the second step, the method finds multiple least-cost paths from the top row to the bottom row of the image. The third step helps to remove false cuts that pass through the middle of the characters.

6.3.2 Cut Candidate Identification

GVF [26] is a popular method that is often used together with active contours or sometimes known as snakes [27] for nonrigid boundary modeling and motion tracking. Using normal gradient, there is only information at edges, and not in homogeneous regions. On the other hand, GVF propagates the gradient information, i.e., the magnitude and the direction, into homogeneous regions. As a result, there are enough forces to attract the snake model into concave regions. The propagation is done by minimizing the following energy function:

$$\varepsilon = \iint \mu \left(u_x^2 + u_y^2 + v_x^2 + v_y^2 \right) + |\nabla f|^2 \left| g - \nabla f^2 \right| \, dxdy \qquad (6.7)$$

where $g(x, y) = (u(x, y), v(x, y))$ is the GVF field and $f(x, y)$ is the edge map of the input image [14].

A gap between two characters can be thought of as a collection of points that lie in the middle of two edges, one from the character on the left-hand side and the other from the character on the right-hand side. Within a gap, there is more than one segmentation path that can separate the two characters. One way to define a good path is that it should stay as far as possible from the two character edges to allow room for errors if the edge information is not accurate or the character contours are partly broken due to low contrast.

Based on this idea, the method uses the GVF field to identify candidate cut pixels. It is observed that for edges, there are often two "arrows" (gradient directions) pointing toward each other, while for gaps, the arrows usually point away from each other (Fig. 6.7). This implies that on the left-hand side of a gap, the pixels are closer to the character on the left and thus attracted to that side, and similarly for the right-hand side. Because the gap pixel, being at the symmetry point, is equally far

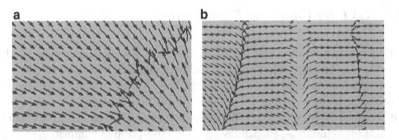

Fig. 6.7 GVF fields around an edge and a gap. (**a**) edge, (**b**) gap between two edges

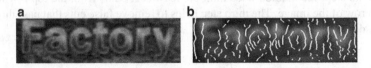

Fig. 6.8 Candidate cut pixels of a sample image. In (**b**), the image is blurred to make the (*white*) cut pixels more visible. (**a**) input, (**b**) candidate cut pixels

from both characters, it satisfies the criterion mentioned above. Consider a vertical symmetry point (x, y), the pixel at (x, y) is a candidate cut pixel if and only if

$$\begin{cases} u(x, y) < 0 \\ u(x + 1, y) > 0 \\ angle(g(x, y), g(x + 1, y)) > \theta_{min} \end{cases} \quad (6.8)$$

where *angle*(.) returns the angle between two vectors. In other words, the GVF vector at pixel (x, y) should point to the left-hand side, the GVF vector at pixel $(x + 1, y)$ should point to the right-hand side, and the angle between these two vectors should be sufficiently large, e.g., 15°.

Figure 6.8 shows the candidate cut pixels of a text line with complex background. GVF is able to detect pixels in the gaps between consecutive characters. Although these pixels do not form complete cuts yet, they play an important role in the pathfinding process, which is described in the next section, where the segmentation paths are encouraged to go through these pixels instead of other pixels in the same gap.

A side effect of (6.9) is that it also captures "medial" pixels, i.e., those that are in the middle of the character strokes (Fig. 6.8). However, it is still possible to distinguish between candidate cut pixels and medial pixels. Since medial pixels are part of a character, if a segmentation path tends to go through these pixels, it has to make several background-to-character and character-to-background transitions. This is not the case for candidate cut pixels because the segmentation path would only stay in the background.

The next section explains how the cost function is designed to encourage paths to go through candidate cut pixels and discourage paths from going through medial pixels.

6.3.3   *Minimum-Cost Pathfinding*

Following a method for segmenting merged characters in document images [28], the method formulates character segmentation as a minimum-cost pathfinding problem where from the top row, it costs less to go through a gap to reach the bottom row than cutting through a character.

The input image can be considered as a graph where the vertices are the pixels, and pixel (x, y) is connected to neighboring pixels in the left-down, down, and right-down directions, i.e., pixels $(x - 1, y + 1)$, $(x, y + 1)$, and $(x + 1, y + 1)$. The minimum-cost paths are found by dynamic programming as follows.

Let $I(x, y)$ be the grayscale input image, p_0 be a starting pixel on the top row, $c(p_1, p_2)$ be the cost of moving from pixel p_1 to pixel p_2, and $d(p)$ be the cumulative cost of the minimum-cost path from pixel p_0 to pixel p.

Initialization:

$$d(p) = \begin{cases} 0, & \textit{if } p = p_0 \\ +\infty, & \textit{otherwise} \end{cases} \tag{6.9}$$

Update rule:

$$d(p) = \min \begin{cases} d\left(p_{left-up}\right) + c\left(p_{left-up}, p\right) \\ d\left(p_{up}\right) + c\left(p_{up}, p\right) \\ d\left(p_{right-up}\right) + c\left(p_{right-up}, p\right) \end{cases} \tag{6.10}$$

where $p_{left-up} = (p.x - 1, p.y - 1)$, $p_{up} = (p.x, p.y - 1)$ and $p_{right-up} = (p.x + 1, p.y - 1)$. The cost function is defined as

$$c(p_1, p_2) = \begin{cases} 0 & \textit{if candidate } (p_2) \\ (I(p_1) - I(p_2))^2 & \textit{if } p_1.x = p_2.x \\ k \times (I(p_1) - I(p_2))^2 & \textit{otherwise} \end{cases} \tag{6.11}$$

where *candidate*(p) returns true if p is a candidate cut pixel and k is the diagonal move penalty (to be explained later).

As previously mentioned, the cost function is designed to encourage paths that go through candidate cut pixels. It is thus set to be zero at these pixels. For other pixels, the cost function is set to be the squared difference between two gray intensities because the method assumes that for text to be readable, there should be some contrast between the characters and the background. (The method uses the squared difference to penalize large differences more, instead of penalizing the differences linearly.) A large difference may indicate transitions between the background and the characters, i.e., cutting through the characters. Therefore, paths that go through medial pixels are discouraged by this cost function.

Curved segmentation paths are naturally allowed. However, in many cases, vertical paths are sufficient so k is set to $\sqrt{2}$ to avoid paths with excessive curvature.

An advantage of the proposed cost function is that it works directly on grayscale images and does not require binarization like many document analysis methods. In addition, by using the squared difference, it is able to handle text of different polarities, i.e., both bright and dark text.

Note that the above algorithm finds the best path for only one starting point on the top row. To segment all the characters, the method runs it multiple times with different starting points. Ideally, the method only needs to put a starting point every w pixels where w is the estimated character width (based on the height of the input image). However, because the characters have variable widths, e.g., "i" versus "m," and furthermore, the gaps between the words may not be a multiple of w, more frequent starting points are required. In implementation, a starting point is placed every $w/4$ pixels.

6.3.4 False-Positive Elimination

In the previous section, the cost function is carefully designed to discourage segmentation paths that cut through the characters. However, these false cuts may still occur for various reasons, e.g., low contrast which leads to a small difference in grayscale intensities of two consecutive pixels on the path. In this step, the method aims to remove these false cuts.

It is interesting to observe that if there are more starting points than required in a gap, the minimum-cost paths usually converge to the same end point (Fig. 6.9a). This suggests that end points are more reliable than the starting points, especially because the latter are placed according to a heuristic rule based on the estimated character width.

In order to verify whether a segmentation path is a true cut or a false cut (going through a character), the method performs backward pathfinding from the end points to the top row (similar to forward pathfinding, except that the directions of the edges are reversed). For true cuts, it is likely that the forward path and the backward path are close to each other because they both aim to pass through the candidate cut pixels in the background. However, for false cuts, instead of going the same route as the forward path, the backward path may switch to either side of the character because the cost would be lower since there are no background-to-character and character-to-background transitions (Fig. 6.9b).

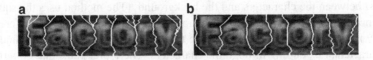

Fig. 6.9 Two-pass pathfinding algorithm. In (**a**), different starting points converge to the same end points. In (**b**), the false cuts going "F" have been removed, while the true cuts are retained. (**a**) forward pathfinding, (**b**) backward path verification

The proposed method can be considered as a two-pass pathfinding algorithm where the forward direction locates potential cuts and the backward direction verifies them.

6.3.5 Summary

A method for video character segmentation without word segmentation is described in this section. The method is able to produce curved segmentation paths and works directly on grayscale images, i.e., no binarization is required. GVF is used in a novel way to identify candidate cut pixels. A two-pass pathfinding process is then employed where the forward direction helps to locate potential cuts and the backward direction serves to verify the true cuts and remove the false cuts, i.e., those that go through the middle of the characters.

6.4 Video Text Recognition

As noted earlier, direct OCR on video text leads to poor recognition results typically between 0 and 45 % [12]. There are therefore attempts to enhance text lines before passing them to OCR engines. Tang et al. [15] proposed a method for video caption detection and recognition based on fuzzy-clustering neural networks, which make use of both spatial and temporal information. Wolf and Jolion [17] used gradient, morphological information and multiple frame integration for extraction and recognition for graphics text. Recently, a new approach for text detection and extraction from complex video scenes was proposed in [10] based on transient colors between graphics text and adjacent background pixel. Chen et al. [14] proposed a two-step method for text recognition. The first step uses edge information to localize the text. The second step uses features and machine learning to recognize the segmented text. Chen and Odobez proposed [12] using Monte Carlo sampling for text recognition. This method appears to be expensive as it uses probabilistic Bayesian classifier for selecting thresholds. It also requires a sequence of frames to achieve accuracy. Another method [13] for low-resolution video character recognition based on holistic approach and a connected component analysis is proposed. However, it requires a large number of training samples. In addition, there are methods which propose robust binarization algorithms to improve the recognition rate of video character recognition [22, 23, 29, 30]. However, these methods focus on graphics text recognition, and hence their error rates would be higher if there is scene text in the input images. Recently, Zhou et al. [23] developed a Canny-based binarization method for video text recognition, which achieved a reasonably good accuracy compared to the baseline thresholding methods. However, the assumption that the Canny operation gives fair edges in Zhou et al.'s method restricts the accuracy of video character recognition.

Most of the previous methods focus on only graphics text and high-contrast text instead of considering both graphics and scene text in video images. The performance of these methods depends on the enhancement step, and it is difficult to decide the number of frames used for enhancement. Most of the methods use traditional OCR engines to recognize the characters. Several methods use the text area detected by a detection algorithm for recognition. In this section, instead of using available OCR engines, we will introduce a method that does video character recognition without the use of any available OCR engine. The method uses a set of features for character recognition through hierarchical classification.

First the method takes in text lines detected by the text detection method [3] as input. It then uses vertical and horizontal cuts to identify gaps between characters. The hierarchical classification is done based on a voting method, which gives nine subclasses for 62 classes. The method uses a set of properties for each segment given by an eight-directional code of the edge character to study the shape of the segments and to obtain distinct features for each of the 62 classes of characters. In other words, eight-directional codes give eight segments for each character image. Finally, the method is evaluated by a varying number of sample images for different classes for training and testing.

6.4.1 Character Recognition

Character recognition is done in two steps. The first step performs hierarchical classification of the 62 character classes based on structural features. The second step proceeds to find features based on the characters' shapes for recognition.

6.4.2 Hierarchical Classification Based on Voting Method

A dataset is created by collecting a variety of sample character images segmented by the methods described in the previous character segmentation section. The sample size varies from 2 to 50 samples for each of the 62 characters which include 26 uppercase letters, 26 lowercase letters, and 10 digits. As a result, the method gets 62 labeled classes for classification. The method first resizes the input image to 64×64 pixels (Fig. 6.10b) and then computes its Canny edge image (Fig. 6.10c). It is observed that the Canny edge image preserves the shape of the characters after resizing. Resizing is done in order to standardize the characters of different font sizes. Large size of dataset, low contrast, and background variation make video character recognition complex and challenging. In addition, there may be disconnections and background noise due to low contrast. The structural features used are based on two criteria: (1) whether the centroid of the edge image falls on

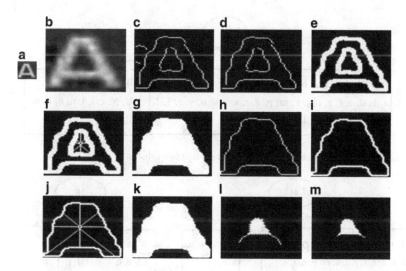

Fig. 6.10 Features for hierarchical classification: (**a**) input, (**b**) resized, (**c**) Canny, (**d**) filtered, (**e**) dilated, (**f**) 8 directions, (**g**) filled, (**h**) perimeter, (**i**) dilated, (**j**) 8 directions, (**k**) filled, (**l**) shrunk, and (**m**) end points removed

Table 6.1 Classification rates of uppercase letter classes (in %)

A	B	C	D	E	F	G	H	I
98	49.4	2.2	15.2	94.7	97.2	90.4	93.3	3.1
J	**K**	**L**	**M**	**N**	**O**	**P**	**Q**	**R**
100	53.8	97.2	49.5	97.7	6.6	86.6	66.6	97.7
S	**T**	**U**	**V**	**W**	**X**	**Y**	**Z**	
90.4	32.6	15.5	77.7	100	40	72.5	100	

the edge itself or not and (2) the outlet in eight directions from the centroid. These features are robust to disconnections, noise, font, font size, rotation, and scale.

To facilitate recognition, a voting scheme is used to divide the 62 classes into progressively smaller classes in a hierarchical way. If more than 50 % of the sample images in the class satisfy the criterion, say criterion 1, the method classifies the whole class into one group without testing the remaining images; otherwise, it classifies it into another group (binary tree classification). Using upper case characters as an example, the classification rate satisfying criterion 1 for each class of uppercase letters are reported in Table 6.1. For the uppercase letters A, E, F, G, H, J, K, L, N, P, Q, R, S, V, W, Y, and Z, the classification rate is more than 50 %; therefore, these characters are classified into one group. For B, C, D, I, M, O, T, U, and X, the classification rate is less than 50 %; therefore, these characters are classified into another group. The same classification applies to lowercase and other characters as shown in Fig. 6.11. This binary split continues for other features to form a binary tree of seven levels.

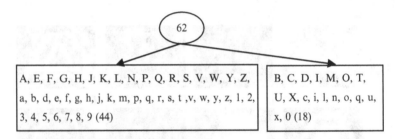

Fig. 6.11 Feature 1 classifies the 62-character set into two subsets

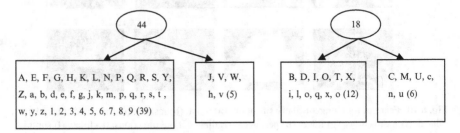

Fig. 6.12 Feature 2 classifies the sets of 44 and 18 characters into two subsets each

Feature 1 (F_1): This feature is the basis for criterion 1 which is tested on characters (Fig. 6.10d) after removing small noisy components (Fig. 6.10c). The method uses the voting criterion for feature 1 to classify 62 character classes into subclasses as shown in Fig. 6.11.

Feature 6.11(F_2): An interesting visual observation is to find outlets in eight directions. An outlet is defined as follows: from the centroid of the character edge image, if the method finds edge pixels in all eight directions as shown in Fig. 6.10f, then the method considers the character as having no outlets; otherwise, it has criteria 2. For characters like J, V, h, v, C, M, U, c, u, and n, one can expect an outlet as there is an open space, while other characters do not have such spaces. This feature is used for binary classification at the second level as shown in Fig. 6.12.

Feature 6.13 (F_3): This feature works based on the perimeter of the character edge image. Before finding the perimeter, the method dilates the Canny edge image in Fig. 6.10d as shown in Fig. 6.10e and fills the gap as shown in Fig. 6.10g. For the filled character shown in Fig. 6.10g, the method finds the perimeter as shown in Fig. 6.10h. The classification is then done as in feature 2 by testing criterion 1 (checking centroid falls on it or not). The result of classification is shown in Fig. 6.13. Note that a double enclosure denotes end of classification. A double circle indicates that a single character has been identified, while a double rectangle indicates that the set will not undergo further classification.

Feature 4 (F_4): Before testing criterion 2 (outlet in eight directions from the centroid), the method dilates the image in Fig. 6.10h to get the image in Fig. 6.10i. It tests the criterion 2 as shown in Fig. 6.10j for binary classification at the third level. The classification results are shown in Fig. 6.14b.

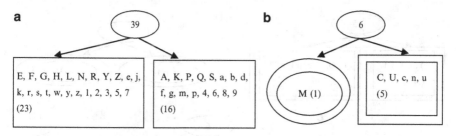

Fig. 6.13 (**a, b**) Feature 3 classifies only two groups containing 39 and 6 characters of the previous level, and for other two sets of 12 and 5 characters remain unchanged

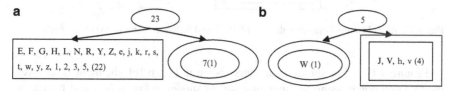

Fig. 6.14 (**a, b**) Feature 4 classifies the sets of 23 characters and 5 characters into two subsets each. It does not classify other sets such as the sets of 16 and 12 characters

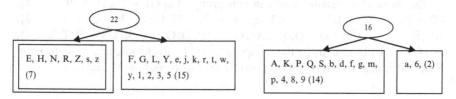

Fig. 6.15 Feature 5 classifies the sets of 22 and 16 characters into two subsets each, but other sets of 12 characters remains unchanged

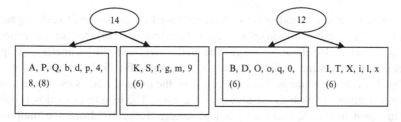

Fig. 6.16 Feature 6 classifies the sets of 14 and 12 characters into two subsets each. The sets of 15 and 2 characters remain unchanged

Feature 5 (F_5): For the dilated edge image shown in Fig. 6.10i, the method again uses flood fill function to fill the character as shown in Fig. 6.10k. The method then uses the function shrink to shrink the image as shown in Fig. 6.10l. After that, criterion 1 is used for classification. The classification results are shown in Fig. 6.15.

Feature 6 (F_6): For the result of the shrink function as shown in Fig. 6.10l, the method tests criterion 2 for classification. The results are shown in Fig. 6.16.

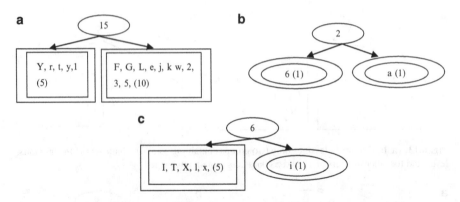

Fig. 6.17 (a–c) Feature 7 classifies the sets of 15, 2, and 6 characters into two subsets each

Feature 7 (F_7): For shrunk characters shown in Fig. 6.10l, the method removes the two end points using the spur function as shown in Fig. 6.10m and then tests criterion 1 for the result shown in Fig. 6.10m for classification. The classification results are shown in Fig. 6.17a–c.

The above classification results in nine groups. Let G1 = {E, H, N, R, Z, s, z}, G2 = {Y, r, t, y, 1}, G3 = {F, G, L, e, j, k, w, 2, 3, 5}, G4 = {A, P, Q, b, d, p, 4, 8}, G5 {K, S, f, g, m, 9}, G6 = {J, V, h, v}, G7 = {B, D, O, o, q, 0}, G8 = {I, T, X, l, x}, and G9 = {C, U, c, n, u} be the groups obtained by the hierarchical classification. Note that at this stage it is already possible to classify W, 6, a, M, and i.

6.4.3   Structural Features for Recognition

This section presents another set of features based on the shape of each segment determined by eight-direction splitting. For these features, the input is the perimeter of the character edge character image. The method segments the perimeter into eight subsegments according to eight directions as shown in Fig. 6.10j from the centroid of the character edge image. For each segment, the method studies its shape to find distinct features for each of the above nine groups. The feature extraction process is illustrated in Fig. 6.9 where C and M denote the centroid and the midpoint, respectively, of a segment. E1 and E2 denote the two end points of the segment.

The features are extracted based on the distance between the centroid and the end points, and the midpoint and the end points. Let D1 be the distance between C and E1, D2 be the distance between C and E2, D3 be the distance between C and M, D4 be the distance between M and E1, and D5 be the distance between M and E2 as illustrated in Fig. 6.18.

The method uses the following criteria to extract the properties to study the segment shape. If its centroid falls on the segment itself, then the method considers it as property St_1 else property Cur_1 ("St" and "Cur" stand for straight and cursive,

Fig. 6.18 Structural feature
extraction for each segment

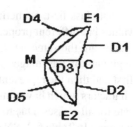

Table 6.2 Class representatives for G1 = {E, H, N, R, Z, s, z}

S.N	NoI	Cl	P	S-50 %	S-10 %	R-50 %	R-10 %
1	36	E	St-4	18	4	0.00	0.00
2	45	H	St-5	23	5	0.04	0.00
3	44	N	St-8	22	5	6.60	6.40
4	44	R	St-2	22	5	1.63	1.80
5	4	Z	St-6	2	1	13.0	12.0
6	27	s	Cur-6	14	3	0.00	0.00
7	4	z	Cur-7	2	1	0.50	0.00

respectively). If D3 < 1, then St_2 else Cur_2; if D1 ≤ D2, then St_3 else Cur_3; if D1 ≤ D3, then St_4 else Cur_4; if D2 ≤ D3, then St_5 else Cur_5; if D3 ≤ D4, then St_6 else Cur_6; if D3 ≤ D5, then St_7 else Cur_7; if D4 ≤ D5, then St_8 else Cur_8.

Based on observation and experiments, the method arrives at a total of 16 distinct properties for classification in this work. The assignment of a property to a particular class is by observation. For example, consider property St_4 (D1 ≤ D3) in Table 6.2 for the representative of class E. This property enforces the condition that segments in images belonging to E class should have. Note that one would expect more segments that satisfy the property D1 ≥ D3 for class E but not that satisfies the property St_4 which is designed to discriminate among the other classes. Hence in Table 6.2, class E representative has a small value (almost 0). Similar properties for each of the other classes are used to calculate a representative value for that class.

A representative for a class is determined by averaging the number of segments that satisfy a given property. In other words, given a training set for a particular class, the average number of segments over all images that satisfy the property corresponding to that class is the representative number of the class. Thus, a particular class is represented by a single number. Given an unknown character to be recognized, it is given the label of the class whose representative number is the closest to the number of segments in the unknown image. Representing a class of images by a single value has been studied earlier in scene category classification [31]. It is computed representatives for 10 %, and 50 % training samples per class for all nine groups. One such example for group 1 is shown in Table 6.2. Since the method knows class labels and their representative numbers, the method compares the number of segments of an unknown image of the class with a representative of that class first. Sometimes the group contains two or more same representative values but different properties. For instance, for class {E, H, s, z}, the representative values are the same but the properties are different. In this context, the number of segments of the images in class z is compared with the representative of class z first and then the representatives of others classes. This criterion helps in classifying characters which have similar shapes and hence the method gives a good recognition rate for all classes. Due to space constraint, representative tables for other groups are omitted. In Table 6.2, SN denotes the number of classes, NoI denotes the number of images in the class, P denotes property, S-10 % and S-50 % denote the number of samples considered for computing the average value (representative), and R-50 % and R-10 % denote the corresponding representatives.

6.4.4   Summary

This section describes a new method for recognition of video characters through hierarchical classification. For recognition of text lines detected by a text detection method, the method uses a segmentation algorithm which finds least-cost cuts by dynamic programming. Structural features that are invariant to geometrical transformation and robust to noise are used for classification and recognition. Voting criterion is adopted to classify the large number of classes into smaller groups based on structural features.

6.5   Summary

This chapter is concerned with word and character segmentation as well as character recognition from detected video text lines. Word and character segmentation are useful for improving character recognition rate since segmentation helps in reducing complex background for binarization method. This results in better separation of foreground and background. Then, an available OCR can be used for recognizing the characters.

In the first method for word segmentation, Fourier-moments features provide an indication of space between words such that computing the max and min values enables clustering of text and non-text. A run-length method is then used to count spacing between words to allow word segmentation. A set of column-wise distance vectors provides refined measures to dissect characters.

While this method proceeds from word segmentation to character segmentation, the second method actually proceeds straight into character segmentation without word segmentation. This is made possible by the use of gradient vector flow to identify gaps between characters. This is because GVF gives strong forces at edges or near edges but not at spaces between edges. This clue is exploited to identify seed points. With this, vertical and horizontal cuts with cost are obtained for identifying path between the characters. The cost is computed based on the neighbors' gray information. The advantage of this method is that the method works for complex background and distorted images well. However, its performance depends on seed point selection.

Finally, the third method described in this chapter performs character recognition without using the traditional OCR engine. The method uses a voting scheme to do a hierarchical classification to progressively classify character images into several subclasses using straightness and cursiveness of the characters. Structural features are extracted for each segment given by the eight-directional code to find representative for the classes. With the help of representatives, the method finds the minimum distance between the input character and representatives to classify the character into correct class. The advantage of this method is that the method does not require any classifier. However, hierarchical classification is expensive and if any error occurs in the beginning, the remaining steps of the method will classify characters wrongly.

References

1. OCR Engine used: http://code.google.com/p/tesseract-ocr/
2. Jung K, Kim KI, Jain AK (2004) Text information extraction in images and video: a survey. Pattern Recogn 37(5):977–997
3. Shivakumara P, Phan TQ, Tan CL (2011) A Laplacian approach to multi-oriented text detection in video. IEEE Trans PAMI 33(2):412–419
4. Mori M, Sawaki M, Hagita N (2003) Video text recognition using feature compensation as category-dependent feature extraction. In: Proceedings of the ICDAR, pp 645–649
5. Lienhart R, Wernicke A (2002) Localizing and segmenting text in images and videos. IEEE Trans Circ Syst Video Technol 12(4):256–268
6. Huang X, Ma H, Zhang H (2009) A new video text extraction approach. In: Proceedings of the ICME, pp 650–653
7. Miao G, Zhu G, Jiang S, Huang Q, Xu C, Gao W (2007) A real-time score detection and recognition approach for broadcast basketball video. In: Proceedings of the ICME, pp 1691–1694
8. Kopf S, Haenselmann T, Effelsberg W (2005) Robust character recognition in low-resolution images and videos. Technical report, University of Mannheim
9. Tse J, Jones C, Curtis D, Yfantis E (2007) An OCR-independent character segmentation using shortest-path in grayscale document images. In: Proceedings of the international conference on machine learning and applications, pp 142–147
10. Kim W, Kim C (2009) A new approach for overlay text detection and extraction from complex video scene. IEEE Trans Image Process 18(2):401–411
11. Saidane Z, Garcia C (2007) Robust binarization for video text recognition. In: Proceedings of the ICDAR, pp 874–879
12. Chen D, Odobez J (2005) Video text recognition using sequential Monte Carlo and error voting methods. Pattern Recogn Lett 26(9):1386–1403
13. Lee SH, Kim JH (2008) Complementary combination of holistic and component analysis for recognition of low resolution video character images. Pattern Recogn Lett 29:383–391
14. Chen D, Odobez JM, Bourland H (2004) Text detection and recognition in images and video frames. Pattern Recogn 37(3):595–608

15. Tang X, Gao X, Liu J, Zhang H (2002) A spatial-temporal approach for video caption detection and recognition. IEEE Trans Neural Netw 13:961–971
16. Doermann D, Liang J, Li H (2003) Progress in camera-based document image analysis. In: Proceedings of the ICDAR, pp 606–616
17. Wolf C, Jolion JM (2003) Extraction and Recognition of artificial text in multimedia documents. Pattern Anal Applic 6(4):309–326
18. Zang J, Kasturi R (2008) Extraction of text objects in video documents: recent progress. In: Proceedings of the DAS, pp 5–17
19. Jain AK, Yu B (1998) Automatic text location in images and video frames. Pattern Recogn 31:2055–2076
20. Li H, Doermann D, Kia O (2000) Automatic text detection and tracking in digital video. IEEE Trans Image Process 9:147–156
21. Kim KL, Jung K, Kim JH (2003) Texture-based approach for text detection in images using support vector machines and continuously adaptive mean shift algorithm. IEEE Trans PAMI 25:1631–1639
22. Saidane Z, Garcia C (2007) Robust binarization for video text recognition. In: Proceedings of the ICDAR, pp 874–879
23. Zhou Z, Li L, Tan CL (2010) Edge based binarization for video text images. In: Proceedings of the ICPR, pp 133–136
24. Jung K (2001) Neural network-based text location in color images. Pattern Recogn Lett 22:1503–1515
25. Hearn D, Pauline Baker M (1994) Computer graphics C version. 2nd edn. Prentice-Hall, Bresenham Line Drawing Algorithm
26. Xu C, Prince JL (1998) Snakes, shapes, and gradient vector flow. IEEE Trans Image Process 7(3):359–369
27. Kass M, Witkin A, Terzopoulos D (1987) Snakes: active contour models. Int J Comput Vision 1(4):321–331
28. Wang J, Jean J (1993) Segmentation of merged characters by neural networks and shortest path. In: Proceedings of the ACM/SIGAPP symposium on applied computing, pp 762–769
29. Su B, Lu S, Tan CL (2010) Binarization of historical document images using the local maximum and minimum. In: Proceedings of the international workshop on document analysis systems, pp 159–166
30. Bolan S, Shijian L, Tan CL (2010) Binarization of historical document images using the local maximum and minimum. In: Proceedings of the DAS, pp 159–165
31. Shivakumara P, Rajan D, Sadanathan SA (2008) Classification of images: are rule based systems effective when classes are fixed and known? In: Proceedings of the ICPR

Chapter 7
Video Text Detection Systems

Nowadays, a large number of video text detection systems have been developed for daily used video applications such as transportation surveillance, electronic payment, traffic safety detection, sport videos retrieval, and even commercial online advertisements, in which the existing closed-circuit television, road-rule enforcement cameras, or online videos can be the data sources.

For example, motorcycles are one of the most commonly used forms of transportation due to their low cost and the high concentration of people in cities. However, the increase in motorcycles results in new problems such as more thefts and traffic violations. According to the report from Taiwan [1], the owner of a motorcycle that is not examined for exhaust emission before a designated inspection date is subject to a US$65 fine. The police have to set up temporary monitoring stations along the roadside to conduct inspections; unfortunately when they approach these stations, most motorcyclists will accelerate to escape the inspection. Consequently, less than 50 % of all motorcycles have been inspected. Moreover, in 2007, there were 166,000 stolen motorcycles among the 12.8 million motorcycles registered in Taiwan. That is, on average a motorcycle is stolen every 3 min. Automatic video-based license plate recognition systems are accordingly necessary to help improve the convenience of checking motorcycle status at roadside and designated inspection points efficiently.

Another example is online video advertising. Driven by the advent of broadband Internet access, today's online video users face a daunting volume of video content from video sharing websites and personal blogs or from IPTV and mobile TV [2]. Demand for web video commercials accordingly has a rapid growth at marketing startups in the past several years. As reported in [3], in 2011, the total TV advertising market in the USA is worth more than $70 billion. In 2012, online video advertising has earned over $1.0 billion in the first two quarters, which has a 12.23 % increment comparing with the same two-quarter period in 2011. It is also believed the online advertising will, on average, more than double every year before 2017 in Japan and South Korea, behind only the USA and the UK. Online advertising revenues

© Springer-Verlag London 2014
T. Lu et al., *Video Text Detection*, Advances in Computer Vision
and Pattern Recognition, DOI 10.1007/978-1-4471-6515-6_7

are going up because more people are watching online video, and the people who provide that video are increasingly packaging it with "forced view" commercials at specific positions of video clips. According to [4], in Oct. 2012 alone, 183 million US Internet users watched more than 37 billion online content videos, while "video ad views reached nearly 11 billion." They also find that online videos 20 min or longer have an average of seven commercials and that viewers are watching 93 % of these ads in the entirety. Overall, averagely online ad viewing has grown by 49 % in 2012. Spending on online video advertising is dramatically increasing. Accordingly, how to develop advertising systems especially considering contextual video contents such as video text detection and visual/audio analysis techniques has become an urgent need.

The discussed systems have the same requirement of video content analysis, in which automatic video text detection is believed an essential task. The detected video texts can be recognized using OCR systems and further passed to a speech system, which potentially has other usages such as providing video services for blind people and automatic navigation for drivers. For example, in [5], Neumann and Matas present an end-to-end real-time text localization and recognition system, which achieves state-of-the-art results on the ICDAR2011 dataset. Their performance is achieved by posing the character detection problem with a linear computation complexity in the number of pixels. Accordingly, the recognition results will be passed to a speech system to read them aloud real time.

In this chapter, we introduce several typical video text detection systems, including license plate recognition systems (Sect. 7.1), navigation assistant systems (Sect. 7.2), sport video analysis systems (Sect. 7.3), and online video advertising systems (Sect. 7.4). Actually, the discussed techniques in this chapter can be similarly adopted or extended to many other real-life applications such as video content retrieval [6, 7], person identification from videos [8, 9], E-education or E-meeting [10–12], and even karaoke music [13].

7.1 License Plate Recognition Systems

As discussed at the beginning of this chapter, license plate recognition (LPR) systems play an important role in numerous real-life applications such as unattended parking lots, security control of restricted areas, and traffic safety enforcement [41]. Take car parking as an example, number plates are used to calculate the duration of the parking in an automatic manner. When a vehicle enters the gate, license plate is automatically recognized and stored in database. On leaving, the license plate is recognized again and compared with the stored numbers in the database. The time difference is thus calculated and then used for showing the parking fee. Figure 7.1 shows an example of LPR systems for checking the annual inspection status of motorcycles from the images taken along the roadside and at designated inspection stations [1]. Both a UMPC (ultra-mobile personal computer) with a webcam and desktop PC are used as hardware platforms.

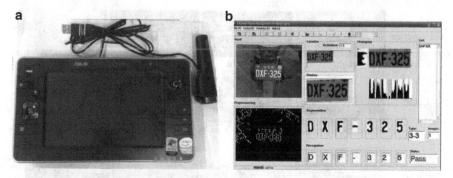

Fig. 7.1 The hardware in a mobile license plate recognition system for checking the annual inspection status of motorcycles: (**a**) the UMPC and webcam, (**b**) user interface [1]

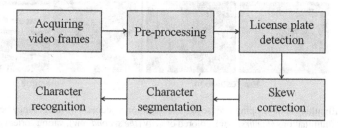

Fig. 7.2 Block diagram of license plate recognition systems

Generally, a typical LPR system consists of four steps after capturing video frames from a digital surveillance camera, the block diagram of which are shown in Fig. 7.2:

1. **Preprocessing**: LPR systems have to face video data of different qualities. Preprocessing techniques are thereby necessary to improve the quality of video frames, such as removing shadows, reducing noises, and transforming color spaces.
2. **License plate detection**: This stage aims at locating license plates by searching in a preprocessed image. Note that license plates may be available in various styles in different countries and therefore a LPR system in general is appropriate for a specific vehicle license plate format.
3. **Skew correction**: This stage is performed to correct the recognized license plates with tilts which are very common in LPR systems since a video camera cannot always take pictures without any tilt especially for running vehicles.
4. **Character segmentation and recognition**: It is the procedure of extracting the characters from the LP image and then recognizing them using OCR techniques.

Note that the development of video text detection systems for real-life usages is actually quite challenging. For LPR systems, they have to face the diversity of plate formats and the nonuniform outdoor illumination conditions during video

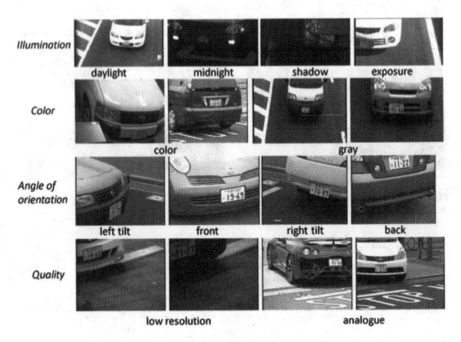

Fig. 7.3 Difficulties in developing license plate recognition systems. The images may be captured by different illuminations (*the first row*), colored or *gray (the second row)*, various orientations (*the third row*), or varied resolutions (*the last row*) [14]

acquisition, such as backgrounds, illumination, vehicle speeds, and distance ranges between the camera and the vehicle. For example, in Fig. 7.3, the images in the first row are captured by different illuminations, which include daylight, night, shadow, and exposure conditions [14]. The second-row images indicate that the license plate images may be colored or gray. The third-row images show that the images captured from various angles of orientation. The image resolution may be low in the last row images due to the filming equipment. Therefore, most LPR approaches have to work only under restricted conditions such as fixed illumination, limited vehicle speed, designated routes, and stationary backgrounds to assure the accuracy or improve the robustness of a real system.

7.1.1 Preprocessing of LPR Systems

Before the license plate detection stage, several preprocessing techniques have to be performed to improve the quality of video frames.

Binarization is one of the most widely used techniques in LPR systems, which segments an acquired frame image into several subregions to highlight characters and suppress background simultaneously. Binarization is performed mainly for two purposes: to highlight characters and to suppress background. Chang et al. [15]

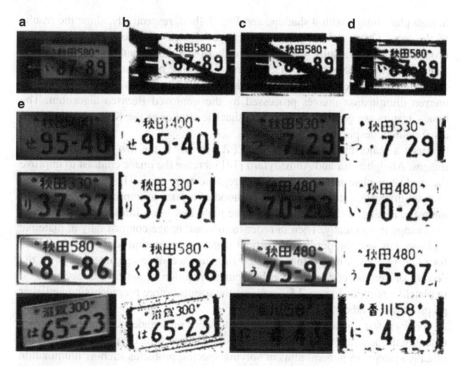

Fig. 7.4 Shadow images and binary results in the LPR system: (a) the original image with a shadow, (b) result by the local Otsu from (a), (c) result by the global Otsu from (a), (d) result by the differential binary from (a), and (e) examples processed by the improved Bernsen algorithm under uneven illumination [14]

employ a variable thresholding technique to avoid losing important license plate information during binarization, in which a local optimal threshold value is determined for each image pixel so as to avoid the problem originated from nonuniform illumination. Although locally adaptive thresholding methods cannot completely compensate for the loss of information, it at least preserves the details that may be lost when using a simple constant binarization method. Anagnostopoulos et al. [16] use locally adaptive thresholding to convert a grayscale image to a binary one. The value of threshold mainly depends on the local statistics like range, variance, and surface fitting parameters. In the case of badly illuminated areas, the calculated threshold value will be relatively low, and thus regions of interest can be successfully detected even under in the ambient illumination conditions. Sometimes a global threshold value is chosen instead of an adaptive one as in [17] to minimize the computational time of preprocessing.

Since the processed license plates are obtained under various illumination scenarios and complex backgrounds, shadows and uneven illumination are unavoidable on the license plates [14]. Hence, shadow or uneven illumination removal becomes another necessary step. In [14], an improved Bernsen algorithm for uneven illumination, particularly for shadow removal, is proposed. Figure 7.4a shows a license plate image with a shadow, and Fig. 7.4b–d, respectively, show the results of the local Otsu, global Otsu, and differential local threshold binary methods. From these binary results, it can be seen that these traditional binary approaches cannot effectively remove the shadow, and the license plate cannot be successfully detected and segmented. As a comparison, Fig. 7.4e shows some examples of uneven illumination images processed by the improved Bernsen algorithm. The binary results are good, and it is noted that the strokes of the Kana characters are also retained, despite fewer pixels.

Since a major cause of failure for LPR systems is the low quality of vehicle images, Abolghasemi and Ahmadyfard [18] increase the image contrast to improve the quality of plate images during the preprocessing stage. They use the variance of pixel intensities at the local neighborhood of a pixel to improve the variance of intensity, aiming at the pixels in a license plate that has a limited range and does not change dynamically. Then in order to increase image contrast only at platelike regions, they use the density of vertical edges as a criterion to detect candidates for plate regions. Finally, they replace the variance of image intensity with the density of vertical edges in the enhancement function to increase image contrast in platelike regions. Figure 7.5 compares the results before preprocessing and after preprocessing in their LPR system.

As discussed, most LPR systems have to work only under restricted conditions to assure the accuracy or improve the robustness. Therefore, the preprocessing stage of LPR systems in general aims at solving specific problems such as illumination

Fig. 7.5 Increasing the image contrast to improve the quality of plate image: (**a**) the original car image, (**b**) the plate before preprocessing, and (**c**) the plate after preprocessing [18]

variations, shadows, or complex background interferences. We here introduce several typical preprocessing techniques for LPR systems, and a more general introduction for preprocessing may refer Chap. 2 for details.

7.1.2 License Plate Detection

Styles of license plates are variable especially from different countries. Figure 7.6 gives some license plate examples for Japan, American, China, the UK, and Germany. The main differences among these license plates are the following [14]: (1) Most license plates may include two or three types of characters, such as English and numeric characters on the American license plate and Chinese, English, and numeric characters on the Chinese license plate. (2) Most license plates have only a line of characters such as on the plates from Germany, the UK, and other European nations. For those license plates where there may exist two lines of characters, most existing LPR systems only process the second line which is generally larger than the first line of characters.

The situations of license plate images in real applications are complex, thereby license plate characters that are helpful for automatic detection have to be well explored. Xu and Zhu [19] consider there are three facts that attract human attentions: the first one is that the characters and the bottom surface of vehicle license have a big gray level change; the second is that the size and the position of license plates are indefinite in different images, but the change of plate size has a certain scope within a particular scene; the rest is that the areas of license around the license plate mainly include horizontal edges. Based on these observations, they divide a license plate detection system into two stages, namely, rough segmentation to locate the regions by SUSAN corner detection and edge extraction to detect license plates.

Huang et al. [1] first accumulate horizontal x-axis projections. Since the license plate is in general located at the lower part of an image, the projection histograms are scanned from the bottom to the top such that the height of the license plate can

| Japan | American | China |

| United Kingdom | Germany |

Fig. 7.6 License plate images from different countries [14]

Fig. 7.7 Locate the license plate through vertical projection using a search window under the prior observation that the width-to-height ratio of a license plate is about 3 to 1: (**a**) without search window (**b**) with search window [1]

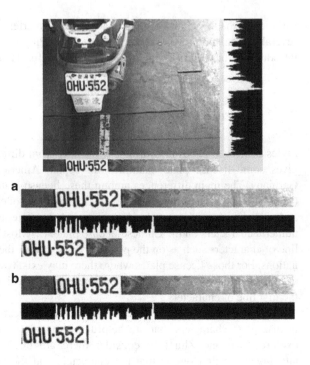

be quickly identified. Then, they locate the license plate through vertical projection using a search window under the prior observation that the width-to-height ratio of a license plate is about 3 to 1 (see Fig. 7.7). Finally, they use platelike filters in which license plate characteristics and plate characters are defined to avoid misrecognizing irrelevant areas as part of the license plate. In [20], connected component labeling (CCL) is used for license plate detection. CCL scans the image and labels the pixels according to pixel-level connectivity. Then, a feature extraction algorithm is used to count the similar labels, and the region with the maximum area is considered as a possible license plate region.

7.1.3   Skew Correction

Since the video camera and the license plate are not always located at the same height (also potentially because of road slope and vibration of the vehicles), the images of license plate exhibit a certain degree of skew. To correct such skews, Jin et al. [21] first scan the left half of the image and calculate the average height of white pixels, denoted as *leftaver*, and then scan the right half to calculate *rightaver*. Next, the slope is determined by

$$slope = (leftaver - rightaver) / (nWidth/2) \tag{7.1}$$

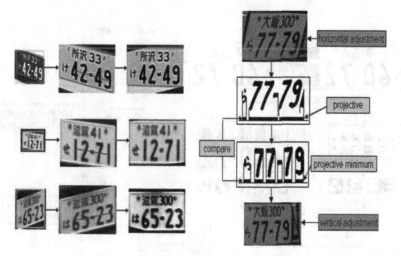

Fig. 7.8 Skew correction examples in LPR systems: (**a**) horizontal correction and (**b**) vertical correction [14]

where *nWidth* is the width of the license plate. Wen et al. [14] correct both the horizontal and the vertical corrections for recognized license plates. In the case of horizontal correction, the large numerals are detected and the tilt angle between two central points of the numerals is found. After calculating the average tilt angle, 2-D rotation is performed. For vertical correction, projective minimum is calculated. Figure 7.8 shows some example result of their tilt corrections in their LPR system.

7.1.4 Character Segmentation

The purpose of this stage is to segment the characters and numbers in the license plate region obtained from the license detection step. Figure 7.9a shows the flow chart of character segmentation for a license plate. Before segmenting characters from a located license plate, image enhancement can be again implemented by knowing the plate has either white characters and black background or reversely black characters and white background [14]. Then, after segmenting the license plate by using the projection technique into two blocks, specific characters will be extracted from each block. Finally, the characters will be resized to a uniform size for further analysis. As a result, illustration Fig. 7.9b presents the examples after license plate segmentation.

Character segmentation results will be sent to the character recognition module for outputting the final vehicle information in LPR systems. In this sense, the character segmentation stage has a great influence on the recognition module. Note

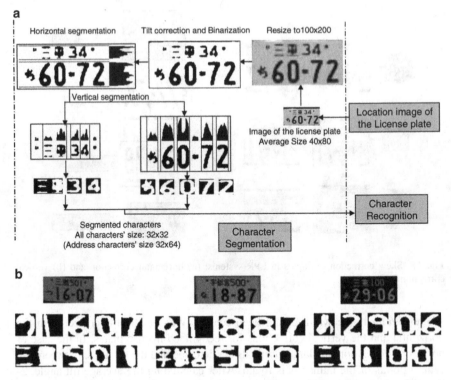

Fig. 7.9 Character segmentation in LPR systems: (**a**) flow chart of character segmentation in LPR systems, which consists of horizontal-vertical segmentations, image enhancement by knowing the plate type, resize of the plate, and character segmentations, and (**b**) successful examples after character segmentation [14]

that there are now no standards or benchmarks to determine whether a character segmentation method works well. Thereby in some LPR systems, this stage is considered as a part of character recognition but not an independent module.

7.1.5   Character Recognition

Typically, template matching and neural networks are the two main categories of methods frequently used for character recognition in LPR systems. The former technique requires a library of a wide variation of character fonts and thicknesses and is thus not very practical for developing real-life systems. The latter is trained for a large amount of sample characters. For example, probabilistic neural networks (PNNs) are introduced in the neural network literature in [16]. These types of neural networks can be designed and trained faster, as the hidden-layer neurons are defined by the number of the training patterns and are only trained once. PNN for LPR

Fig. 7.10 Features of
visually similar characters:
(**a**) "D" and "0"; (**b**) "B" and
"8"; (**c**) "I" and "1" [1]

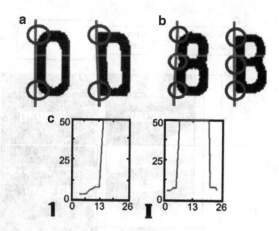

is first introduced in an early version of an LPR system where two PNNs, i.e.,
one for alphabet recognition and the other for number recognition, are trained and
tested.

Although most license plate characters can be successfully recognized using
template matching or neural networks methods, particular characters such as "B"
and "8," "1" and "I," and "0" and "D" may be still hard to distinguish. In [1],
the most significant difference between the characters "0" and "D" lies at their
upper and lower left corners as shown in Fig. 7.10. A straight line is thus posted
to the character as the baseline to respectively accumulate the numbers of white
pixels at the upper and at the lower left corners. If the volume of accumulated white
pixels is greater than a predefined threshold, then the character is recognized as "0";
otherwise it is recognized as "D." The same strategy is applied to distinguish the
characters "B" and "8" as shown in Fig. 7.10. For the normalized characters "1" and
"I," the x-axis project histogram of "1" is right skewed while the histogram of "1" is
more symmetric as shown in Fig. 7.10. Then, the ratio of left to right side histograms
is defined as $Ratio_{1,1}$. When the ratio $Ratio_{1,1}$ is greater than a predefined threshold,
the character is recognized as "1," otherwise "I." Through the two-step recognition
processes, the recognition rate can be improved in LPR systems.

How to develop the character recognition modular on hardware is another
challenge especially in developing mobile LPR systems. In [20], Cancer et al. use
self-organization map (SOM) to recognize characters, which is a process that will
produce similar outputs for similar inputs. An ordinary SOM has the following
two layers: an input layer and a computation layer. The computation layer has
the processing units, and the weight matrix of the SOM is calculated during the
learning phase. In their hardware designed for embedded license plate recognition,
they use the 2-D SOM algorithm. Since it is very difficult to implement the product
and square root operations in hardware, the Euclidean distance is implemented
using the Manhattan metric to reduce the hardware computation cost. Then, the
output character is the node that has the minimum distance, and parallel processing
operations in their hardware make the minimum distance calculation quite efficient.

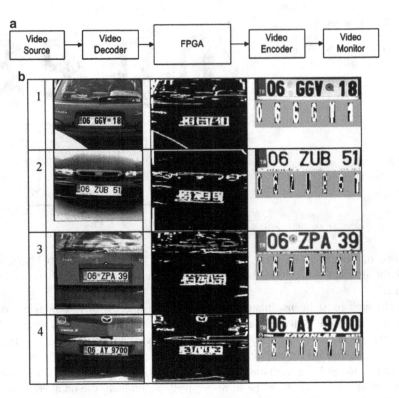

Fig. 7.11 Hardware design and actual tests: (**a**) hardware block diagram, (**b**) tests performed and results [20]

In their hardware design, they use a Virtex IV FPGA in the core of the hardware, video decoder and video encoder. A video board is designed and implemented for this purpose. Each step of the recognition is pipelined to speed up such as toll collection in a fast-flowing traffic. Their hardware block diagram is shown in Fig. 7.11, where a video decoder is needed for the video input interface between the video source and the FPGA. The input of the video decoder is a composite/s-video signal in PAL/NTSC format, and the PAL format is used throughout their design. The encoder/decoder processes the signal and receives/sends the video from/to the FPGA with 8 bits in ITU-R BT 656 video standard. The output of the video encoder is a composite/s-video signal in PAL format. Video monitors and video encoders are used to display the output to test and debug the operation of the system. Their actual tests and experimental results performed on the hardware of Xilinx Virtex IV FPGA are shown in Fig. 7.11b.

LPR systems have been widely used in daily life and proved useful in many applications. However, most current LPR systems can only work in restricted environments as discussed. New methods and approaches are still required to improve the robustness of the systems and reduce the errors.

7.2 Navigation Assistant Systems

A system capable of localizing and reading aloud text embedded in urban or highway environments can be very helpful for both drivers and pedestrians. We take text detection from road signs to assist safely driving as an example. As reported in [22], the statistic data relevant to road safety show that the 36.3 % road facilities are from hit object type crashes, 17.2 % are from head-on type crashes, and 14.8 % are from angle-type crashes. Many of these crashes could be avoided by timely finding and recognizing road sign texts, which is now becoming increasingly important for assessments of road safety risk. Essentially, text on road signs carries information that is useful for driving by describing the current traffic situations, giving right-of-way warnings about potential risks, or showing avoidance of dangerous situations. Road sign text detection can thereby keep a driver aware of traffic situations by highlighting signs. Moreover, such a mobile video text detection system can provide a driver with audio services by reading out text on road signs that are ahead or have been passed or further integrating with a navigation system as a GPS-assistant map tool.

Generally, there are three essential requirements for a text-based navigation assistant system: (1) the detection accuracy should be high enough with a low false hit rate; (2) text on road signs should be detected and recognized in real time to provide driving assistant information; (3) the environment of a driver should be recognized to accordingly provide probable services automatically. However, finding and recognizing road sign texts has always been a challenge to system developers, with existing solutions less than ideal in accuracy and capability. A mobile video text detection-based driving assistant system may face several challenges:

- The appearance analysis of sign texts may be disturbed by various factors such as font, size, color, orientation, and even occlusions of other vehicles. Moreover, text can be distorted by slant, tilt, and shape of road signs. Sometimes the size of road sign may seem too small even for human driver to distinguish from a relatively long distance.
- For driving systems, text will move fast in video and potentially be blurred from motion.
- Road environment is also relatively difficult to analyze, especially distinguishing road signs from complex backgrounds. Outdoor lighting conditions, raining or snowing variations, and even crowded vehicles in video always worsen the task.
- Relatively low resolution of video images and the noises in them make automatic sign text detection more challenging.

In order to address the difficulties, Wu et al. [23] propose incremental text detection system from video. They employ a two-step strategy of first locating road signs by using discriminative features like sign areas and color, then detecting text within the candidate road sign areas, and fusing the detection results with the help of a feature-based tracker. Specifically, a set of discriminative points are found for

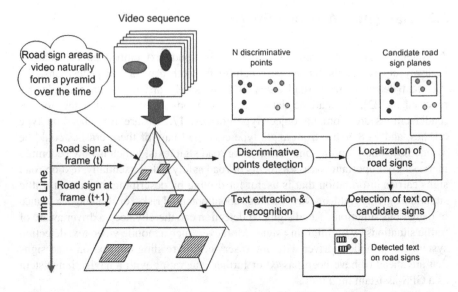

Fig. 7.12 An illustration of the road sign text detection system [23]

each video frame and clustered based on local region analysis. Then, a vertical plane criterion is applied to verify road sign areas in video by recovering the orientations of possible planes. Through the sign location step, the number of the false positives caused by "text-like" areas will be reduced. Next, they use a multi-scale text detection algorithm to locate text lines within candidate road sign areas. For every detected text line, a minimum bounding rectangle is fitted to cover it, and previously selected points inside the rectangle are tracked. Figure 7.12 shows the overview of the system. By taking full advantage of spatiotemporal information in video and fusing partial information for detecting text from frame to frame, the system iterates the process for every video frame and tracks text on signs over the time.

Marmo and Lombardi [24] develop a system for the detection of milepost signs that are a specific type of road sign showing distance on Italian highway. Their first step concerns the identification of rectangular sign by optical flow analysis. Then in the second step, they search for gray discontinuity on image and Hough transform. Classification is based on the analysis of surface color on the inner part, and the detection of rectangular border around the sign. Verma and Stockwell [25] present a neural network-based automated system that can analyze vehicle-mounted video data for improving road safety. The main target of their system is to segment roadside data obtained from vehicle-mounted video into regions of interest, classify roadside objects, and estimate the risk factor based on roadside conditions and objects for various crashes. Recently, in [42], digital maps that are provided by Google Map are automatically labeled and used in a wide variety of electronic devices such as navigation systems and mobile phones by street signs capturing and detection.

A text detection system can also be helpful for blind or visually impaired persons, especially with the advances in modern information technology and digital signal processing techniques. For example, a GPS-based navigation system can provide support to blind persons when they go outside without assistance through reading aloud texts on a road directly. Pazio et al. develop such a text detection system for the blind [26]. Street information boards, shop signboards, text signs besides the office entrances, and traffic signs with a text content (such as "stop" signs) are considered as the source of important and/or helpful text messages that can be detected and accordingly read aloud to a blind person by their video-based text reading system. Their experiments performed in urban environments by blind volunteers show that, in addition to providing path planning and online guidance, such portable navigation devices can play a very important role in exploring the surrounding environment. Moreover, after combining with the electronic map and its embedded city road database, the navigation unit allows blind users to learn about their whereabouts, e.g., to get information about the surrounding buildings, shopping services, bus stops, offices, and hospitals. It illustrates that such information support aspect of navigation systems is very much helpful for blind or visually impaired persons.

7.3 Sport Video Analysis Systems

Sports video has a large audience base, especially considering that there are numerous sport games archived and many types of sports attracting huge numbers of fans worldwide every day [27]. Text analysis is an essential process in sports video content understanding systems. As described in [28], sometimes the fans cannot watch a live broadcast or rebroadcast of a game, thereby they would like to watch excerpts of the game, such as the summary and highlights. They might also hope to directly search a broadcast video for the scenes that show specific events like score variations, the decisive moments of the winner, or even the behavior of a particular player. Unfortunately, sport videos are not organized in a structured format with such meaningful annotations, which make them relatively difficult for content analysis. The huge amount of video content produced for sport games aggravate the challenge. How to increase the accessibility especially for daily accumulated sport videos has become another urgent need both for content owners and sport fans.

Utilizing the external source information of game videos is a feasible way for sport content understanding. Such external source information in general includes the well-defined sport rules, professional reports, and textual commentaries that are reported on games. In this way, sport video content analysis will be considered on the following two levels: (1) the low-level visual or audio cues that will be involved in the detection of specific events in a sports game video and (2) the external source information that is parsed as high-level sports keywords or textual summarizations to provide comprehensive details of the game. Moreover, a mechanism between the two levels can be developed to complement one another. Currently, most of sport video analysis systems are developed by following either one or both these two considerations.

We take the baseball game video analysis as an example. As introduced in [28], the Major League Baseball, which is a professional baseball organization in the USA and Canada, is comprised of 30 teams. Each team plays 162 games in a regular season, and each game usually lasts more than 2 h. Since about 5,000 h of video data is generated every season, manual annotation would obviously be too cumbersome and impractical. A baseball game is played by two teams and comprises regular nine innings, each divided into a top half-inning and a bottom half-inning. In a half-inning, the offensive team "bats," and the other defensive team "fields." In a next half-inning, the two teams alternate between batting and fielding. A half-inning ends when three offensive players are recorded out. Accordingly, the useful video content in baseball games in general can be dissected into two types of segments, namely, *a pitch segment* and *an event segment*. A baseball video event (e.g., home run, strikeout, and groundouts) is generally composed of a series of video scenes (e.g., infield, outfield, player, and pitching), and each scene is further composed of several video shots. An example of the structure of baseball video content of a half-inning is shown in Fig. 7.13, where a pitch segment shows a pitcher throwing the baseball toward his/her home plate to start the game, while the subsequent event segment shows the batter's action.

From Fig. 7.13, we can conclude that baseball video content cannot be analyzed in a common manner in video analysis systems due to the nature of the game itself, namely, (1) the time stamp information of baseball games is preserved in neither video content nor external source information, and (2) no changes of the offensive attacks exist in a baseball's half-inning because the offensive team is always the same. These two characteristics make the attack-based alignment methods and the change detections of the offensive team in soccer and basketball videos invalid in baseball sport video analysis. Moreover, frame-based or shot-based methods are hard to detect baseball events effectively since a baseball video event (e.g., home run, strikeout, and groundouts) is generally composed of a series of video scenes.

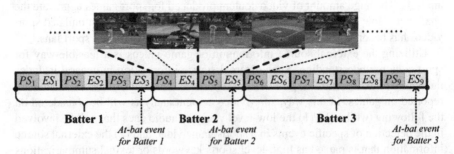

Fig. 7.13 Structure of the video content of a half-inning, which comprises nine pairs of pitch segments (*PS*) and event segments (*ES*). Batters 1, 2, and 3 occupy three, two, and four pitch/event segments, respectively [28]

To detect more general baseball events composed of a series of game scenes, Lien et al. [29] first segment the baseball video into many video shots. Then, various visual features including the image-based features, object-based features, and global motion are extracted to analyze the semantics for each video shot. Each video shot is then classified into the predefined semantic scenes according to its semantics. Finally, they apply the hidden Markov model to detect general baseball events by regarding the classified scenes as observation symbols. The average recall ratio and precision of their method outperform Han's method [30], but the number of detected semantic events is much fewer. It is potentially multimedia features including text, image, and audio that are not integrated to detect general baseball events. Takahashi et al. [31] develop an automatic pitch-type recognition system by analyzing ball trajectories by using automatic ball tracking and the catcher's stance. Similarly, text information is not considered, potentially making their method lack semantic details for baseball video content interpretation and only depending on visual motion analysis.

Scoreboard recognition seems to be a good choice for accurate baseball video content analysis. A scoreboard appears in baseball games to show the audience with the current status of score, counts of strikes or outs, and the inning number, which can be considered as an external source information type to understand baseball sport videos. Figure 7.14 shows examples of superimposed caption text in baseball, which is typically called scoreboard information. Zhang and Chang [32] develop a system for baseball video event detection and summarization using scoreboard caption text detection and recognition. The system detects different types of semantic level events in baseball video, which has two components of scoreboard text-based event recognition and event boundary detection. It is the one of the early systems achieving accurate detection of multiple types of high-level semantic events in baseball videos by developing video text detection techniques.

Chiu et al. [28] develop another baseball video annotation system by video segmentation and video text alignment. They align high-level webcast text with low-level video content to facilitate baseball content analysis. Webcast text has well-defined metadata structures and thereby can be considered as a type of external source information used in soccer, basketball, and football games. Figure 7.15 shows two versions of webcast text in baseball games, where the basic version shown in Fig. 7.15a is from the Chinese Professional Baseball League, containing the basic half-inning information including the names of batters, bats (left/right handed), and at-bat events. Figure 7.15b gives the details from the Major League Baseball, which

Fig. 7.14 Scoreboard in baseball videos [32]

a

局数	比賽內容

(Chinese webcast text screenshot, baseball basic version)

b

— Top 1

1. Kosuke Fukudome strikes out swinging.

	Pitcher M. Scherzer	Batter K. Fukudome		
	Speed		Pitch	Result
1	92		Fastball (Four-seam)	Foul
2	94		Fastball (Four-seam)	Ball
3	93		Fastball (Four-seam)	Called Strike
4	85		Changeup	Foul
5	95		Fastball (Four-seam)	Swinging Strike

2. Jason Kipnis singles on a ground ball to right fielder Magglio Ordonez.

	Pitcher M. Scherzer	Batter J. Kipnis		
	Speed		Pitch	Result
1	92		Fastball (Four-seam)	Foul
2	88		Slider	Ball
3	94		Fastball (Four-seam)	Ball

Fig. 7.15 Examples of webcast text. (**a**) *baseball* (a basic version), (**b**) *baseball* (a detailed version) [28]

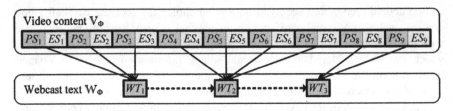

Fig. 7.16 Example of mapping between video content and webcast text [28]

records each batter's pitch count and each pitch's speed, type, and other events in additional to the basic version. Accordingly, the authors convert the task of baseball video annotation to the alignment problem between video content and webcast text.

Specifically, they formulate the alignment problem as a bipartite graph that models the mapping between baseball video content that is represented by pitch segment and event segment pairs and webcast text items. Then, given baseball video and the webcast text, the content of video is analyzed by the two steps of pitch segment detection and batter extraction. In the first step, they capture the properties of pitch segments adaptively with applying any rule or training data beforehand by using hierarchical clustering and Markov random walk. In the second step, they search for clues to distinguish between the batters in the detected pitch segments. Each batter's personal appearance and batting posture that are unique to distinguish him/her from other batters are extracted, instead of unreliable face recognition techniques since batter face images are in general too small in baseball videos. After baseball content analysis, they further extract cues from the video content and webcast text through multimodal alignment. Two alternative methods of batter clustering and a genetic algorithm are selected to search for the best solution to the alignment problem. Figure 7.16 shows an example of the mapping relation between baseball video and webcast text. It can be found that properly defined webcast text greatly helps understanding the content of a baseball video.

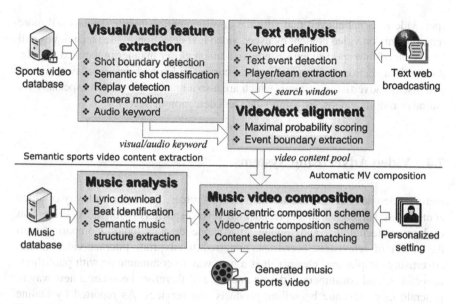

Fig. 7.17 Personalized music sports video generation framework [33]

Wang et al. [33] propose another automatic approach for personalized music sports video generation. Two research challenges are addressed, specially the semantic sports video content extraction and the automatic music video composition. They use audio, video, and text feature analysis and alignment techniques to detect the semantics of events in broadcast sports video for the first challenge. While for the second challenge, they introduce the video-centric and music-centric music video composition schemes and propose a dynamic-programming-based algorithm to perform fully or semiautomatic generation of personalized music sports video. Figure 7.17 shows their two-level music sports video generation framework. In the low-level "semantic sports video content extraction" block, the "visual/audio feature extraction" module extracts A/V features from the input sports video, the "text analysis" module detects the event and identifies the player/team information from the text source, and the "video/text alignment" module aligns the detected text event with A/V features to recognize video segment boundaries for each event. In their high-level "automatic music video composition" block, the "music analysis" module analyzes the input music clips to obtain "beat," "lyric," and "semantic music structure" boundaries, and the "content selection/matching" module uses a dynamic-programming-based algorithm to select suitable video and music content to generate video-centric and music-centric results.

In general, sports video has a wide market both due to many types of sports in the world and the huge numbers of sport fans. The numerous sport videos on the Internet make manually annotation impossible and thereby video text detection technique potentially plays an important role in sport video analysis systems, such as content summarization, sport story restoring, and even automatic advertising in sport videos. It is believed that with the development of mobile devices and more requirements on video content by users, video text detection-related techniques will be combined into sport video systems in a much closer manner in the next decade. As the final section to introduce typical current video text detection systems, we will discuss advertising systems, which are also a much wide market especially for online or mobile videos, by using video text detection in Sect. 7.4.

7.4   Video Advertising Systems

Online video has become one of the primary sources, and online delivery of video content has surged to an unprecedented level especially with the development of Internet techniques and mobile smartphone devices today. Comparing with the media of television, broadcast, and traditional print, Internet video makes advertising simpler and cheaper. It is a new way to communicate with publishers, advertisers, and consumers with one another and therefore becomes a new way to generate more revenue by selling products and services. As reported by Online Publisher Association [34], the majority (66 %) of Internet users have ever seen video ads, while 44 % have taken some action after viewing video ads, showing a big chance to develop online advertising systems to take advantages of the video form of information representation. As a result, advertisers are increasingly relying on various modes of online video-related technology to advertise and promote their products and services.

There are in general three ways for developing an online video advertising system [35]:

- Displaying video ads at the beginning or the end of a video is an intuitive technique which is adopted by most current video websites. However, for the perspective of user experience, this approach is inflexible without taking less intrusiveness of users into consideration.
- Advertising according to video content is a more natural approach by embedding contextual relevance ads at less intrusive positions within the video stream. Essentially, it is always preferable to distribute ads that are relevant to the video or web page rather than unrelated generic ads both for publishers, advertisers, and online video users/consumers.
- Providing the opportunity to instantaneously advertise, executing a sale, and collecting payment in an interactive way. User preferences of searching and navigating through commercial Internet websites will be customized to facilitate the interactive advertising between video and users.

By considering online video content as an effective information carrier, we find the more compelling the video contents, the more audience will view them to accordingly generate more market benefits from video-driven contextual advertising [35]. Some existing video providers such as YouTube, AOL Video, Yahoo! Video, and Metacafe provide content-related video advertising services. Most of them

Fig. 7.18 Example of an online source video with contextually relevant ads embedded. The *yellow bars* below the timeline indicate video ads being inserted at these points. The thumbnails with *red box* in a filmstrip view correspond to video ads. The candidate ads are listed in the *right* panel in which only the highlighted ads are inserted into the source video [2]

match the ads with videos by textual analysis techniques, which are essentially contextual relevance to video contents. For example, Mehta et al. name the computation problem of assigning user queries to advertisers to maximize the total revenue as the Google's AdWord or AdSense problem in [36]: when returning results of a specific query, the search engine company needs to immediately determine what ads to display on the side.

Mei et al. believe ads should be inserted at appropriate positions within video streams rather than only at the fixed positions. Moreover, ads should be contextually relevant to online video content in terms of multimodal relevance (i.e., textual, visual, and audio relevance) [2]. For example, when viewing an online music video, users may prefer a relevant ad with the similar editing style or audio tempo style to the video, which cannot be measured only by textual information. They believe this capability will enable delivering the ads with much higher relevance. Motivated by the observations, they develop a contextual in-video advertising system *VideoSense* (see Fig. 7.17) to automatically associate the relevant video ads and seamlessly insert the ads at the appropriate positions within an individual video. In Fig. 7.18, since the content provider of this source video has tagged it "Lexus," some candidate ads listed at the right panel are related to "car." One of the candidate ads has been inserted into this video, i.e., the highlighted thumbnail with yellow box in the filmstrip view. Since this ad is inserted at the boundary of two scenes, as well as both the source video and ad are related to "car," they propose that the ad is less intrusive and more contextually relevant.

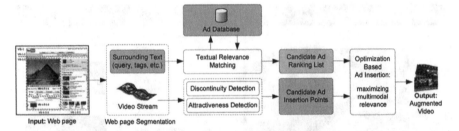

Fig. 7.19 System overview of VideoSense, which consists of four major components, namely, web page segmentation, candidate ad ranking, candidate ad insertion points detection, and optimization-based ad insertion. The output is a XML description file of the augmented video in which the ads are embedded [2]

Figure 7.19 shows the system overview of VideoSense. Given a web page containing a source video, the system segments the page into several blocks and extracts textual information related to this source video. Then, VideoSense selects candidate ad insertion points within the video based on content discontinuity and attractiveness, selects candidate ads according to textual relevance, and associates the ads with the insertion points in an optimization way. The surrounding texts consist of two parts: (1) direct texts such as the query used to search the video, keywords, descriptions, and expansions, as well as transcripts which are provided by content providers if available, and (2) hidden texts such as the text categories and corresponding probabilities which are automatically recognized by text categorization based on a predefined vocabulary, as well as concept texts which are recognized by concept detection. The candidate ads are ranked according to the textual relevance derived from textual information, while the candidate ad insertion points are detected based on the combination of video content discontinuity and attractiveness. Note that the ad insertion process aims to maximize the overall multimodal relevance including global textual relevance and local visual-audio relevance in VideoSense. Finally, the output is an XML description file about the augmented video in which the selected ads are embedded.

In [37], Srinivasan et al. develop a next-generation video ad system that analyzes the video to find appropriate changes where ads can be inserted. The context of each ad insertion point is determined through high-level analysis of the surrounding video segment thereby making ads contextual. Their vADeo system implements two novelties on the user side, namely, ad bookmarking and delayed interaction, to encourage ad clicks without disrupting the video viewing experience. However, in their system, the problem of finding ad insertion points is simply reduced to detect scene changes without considering the content importance. Moreover, the ads are associated with the insertion points based on face recognition technique, which is relatively difficult to be extended to a large-scale video set. More advertising systems depending on video texture analysis or integrating more modalities can refer [38–40].

Similar to other discussed systems, video advertising market increases sharply due to the daily accumulated videos on Internet, which in turn requires video text techniques being systematically and deeply explored to provide accurate video content analysis results. It is widely believed that more video text analysis methods will be proposed and used in the systems in practice in the future.

7.5 Summary

Video text detection has become one of the hot spots in computer vision and pattern recognition especially in the past several years. It is actually due to the great development of Internet technologies, mobile hardware devices, and huge numbers of video from daily life. In this chapter, we introduce several typical video text detection systems, including license plate recognition systems (Sect. 7.1), navigation assistant systems (Sect. 7.2), sport video analysis systems (Sect. 7.3), and online video advertising systems (Sect. 7.4). There are many other systems in which video detection techniques can be used, such as surveillance systems in hospital and elderly people assistance systems especially considering a lot of countries will step into the aging society in the next several decades.

Text in video provides the most intuitive information comparing with other visual characteristics, thereby for developing robust and accurate real-life systems, video text detection has to be further explored, especially focusing on how to improve the accuracy under different scene conditions in video and simultaneously reduce the computational cost to provide users with real-time information. The discussed techniques in this chapter can also be similarly adopted or extended to many other real-life applications such as video content retrieval, person identification from videos, and E-education or E-meeting.

References

1. Huang Y-P et al (2009) An intelligent strategy for checking the annual inspection status of motorcycles based on license plate recognition. Expert Syst Appl 36(5):9260–9267
2. Tao M, Xian-Sheng H, Shipeng L (2009) Video sense: a contextual in-video advertising system. IEEE Trans Circ Syst Vid Technol 19(12):1866–1879
3. IAB internet advertising revenue report. Available from: http://www.iab.net/insights_research/industry_data_and_landscape/adrevenuereport
4. FreeWheel manages the economics of content for the enterprise-class world of entertainment. Available from: http://www.freewheel.tv/
5. Neumann L, Matas J (2012) A real-time scene text to speech system, in computer vision – ECCV 2012. In: Fusiello A, Murino V, Cucchiara R (eds) Workshops and demonstrations. Springer, Berlin, pp 619–622
6. Weiming H et al (2011) A survey on visual content-based video indexing and retrieval. IEEE Trans Syst Man Cybern C Appl Rev 41(6):797–819

7. Chua T-S, Ruan L-Q (1995) A video retrieval and sequencing system. ACM Trans Inf Syst 13(4):373–407
8. Poignant J et al (2011) Text detection and recognition for person identification in videos. In: 9th international workshop on content-based multimedia indexing (CBMI), 2011
9. Ming-yu C, Hauptmann A (2004) Searching for a specific person in broadcast news video. In: Proceedings (ICASSP '04). IEEE international conference on acoustics, speech, and signal processing, 2004
10. Erol B, Ying L (2005) An overview of technologies for e-meeting and e-lecture. In: ICME 2005. IEEE international conference on multimedia and expo, 2005
11. Quanfu F et al (2011) Robust spatiotemporal matching of electronic slides to presentation videos. IEEE Trans Image Process 20(8):2315–2328
12. Dorai C, Oria V, Neelavalli V (2003) Structuralizing educational videos based on presentation content. In: ICIP 2003. Proceedings of the international conference on image processing, 2003
13. Zhu Y, Chen K, Sun Q Multimodal content-based structure analysis of karaoke music. In: Proceedings of the 13th annual ACM international conference on Multimedia 2005, ACM, Hilton, Singapore, pp 638–647
14. Ying W et al (2011) An algorithm for license plate recognition applied to intelligent transportation system. IEEE Trans Intell Transp Syst 12(3):830–845
15. Shyang-Lih C et al (2004) Automatic license plate recognition. IEEE Trans Intell Transp Syst 5(1):42–53
16. Anagnostopoulos CNE et al (2006) A license plate-recognition algorithm for intelligent transportation system applications. IEEE Trans Intell Transp Syst 7(3):377–392
17. Shapiro V, Gluhchev G, Dimov D (2006) Towards a multinational car license plate recognition system. Mach Vis Appl 17(3):173–183
18. Abolghasemi V, Ahmadyfard A (2009) An edge-based color-aided method for license plate detection. Image Vis Comput 27(8):1134–1142
19. Zhigang X, Honglei Z (2007) An efficient method of locating vehicle license plate. In: ICNC 2007. Third international conference on Natural computation, 2007
20. Caner H, Gecim HS, Alkar AZ (2008) Efficient embedded neural-network-based license plate recognition system. IEEE Trans Veh Technol 57(5):2675–2683
21. Jin L et al (2012) License plate recognition algorithm for passenger cars in Chinese residential areas. Sensors 12(6):8355–8370
22. Road safety statistics. Available from: http://www.tmr.qld.gov.au/Safety/Transport-and-road-statistics/Road-safety-statistics.aspx
23. Wu W, Chen X, Yang J Incremental detection of text on road signs from video with application to a driving assistant system. In: Proceedings of the 12th annual ACM international conference on Multimedia 2004, ACM, New York, pp 852–859
24. Marmo R, Lombardi L (2007) Milepost sign detection. In: CAMP 2006. International workshop on computer architecture for machine perception and sensing, 2006
25. Verma B, Stockwell D (2011) An automated system for the analysis of the status of road safety using neural networks. In: Lu B-L, Zhang L, Kwok J (eds) Neural information processing. Springer, Berlin, pp 530–537
26. Pazio M et al (2007) Text detection system for the blind. In: 15th European signal processing conference EUSIPCO
27. Wang JR, Parameswaran N Survey of sports video analysis: research issues and applications. In: Proceedings of the Pan-Sydney area workshop on visual information processing 2004, Australian Computer Society, Inc., pp 87–90
28. Chih-Yi C et al (2012) Tagging webcast text in baseball videos by video segmentation and text alignment. IEEE Trans Circ Syst Vid Technol 22(7):999–1013
29. Lien C-C, Chiang C-L, Lee C-H (2007) Scene-based event detection for baseball videos. J Vis Commun Image Represent 18(1):1–14
30. Han M et al An integrated baseball digest system using maximum entropy method. In: Proceedings of the tenth ACM international conference on Multimedia 2002, ACM, Juan-les-Pins, pp 347–350

31. Takahashi M, Fujii M, Yagi N (2008) Automatic pitch type recognition from baseball broadcast videos. In: ISM 2008. Tenth IEEE international symposium on multimedia, 2008
32. Zhang D, Chang SF Event detection in baseball video using superimposed caption recognition. In: Proceedings of the tenth ACM international conference on Multimedia 2002, ACM, Juan-les-Pins, pp 315–318
33. Jinjun W et al (2007) Generation of personalized music sports video using multimodal cues. IEEE Trans Multimedia 9(3):576–588
34. Online Publisher Association. Available from: http://www.online-publishers.org
35. McCoy S et al (2007) The effects of online advertising. Commun ACM 50(3):84–88
36. Mehta A et al (2007) AdWords and generalized online matching. J ACM 54(5):22
37. Srinivasan SH, Sawant N, Wadhwa S vADeo: video advertising system. In: Proceedings of the 15th international conference on Multimedia 2007, ACM, Augsburg, pp 455–456
38. Mei T et al (2012) Image sense: towards contextual image advertising. ACM Trans Multimedia Comput Commun Appl 8(1):1–18
39. Albayrak S et al (2011) Towards "Semantic IPTV". In: Prasad AR, Buford JF, Gurbani VK (eds) Advances in next generation services and service architectures, River Publishers, pp 197–230
40. Ulges A, Borth D, Koch M (2013) Content analysis meets viewers: linking concept detection with demographics on YouTube. Int J Multimedia Inf Retr 2(2):145–157
41. Gilly D, Raimond K (2013) A survey on license plate recognition systems. Int J Comput Appl 61(6):34–40
42. Joakim Kristian Olle Arfvidsson, Sriram Thirthala. Labeling features of maps using road signs. US patent (US8483447 B1)

Chapter 8
Script Identification

While most works on text detection reported in the literature focus on English text as test beds, there has been a number of methods that are meant for detecting specific scripts such as Chinese, Korean, Japanese, Arabic, and Indian scripts. In more recent times, there have been attempts to deal with videos containing multiple scripts. In such cases, techniques to extract texts of several predetermined scripts in video will be needed for such applications. On the other hand, a challenge would be to develop capability in detecting texts from multilingual video yet without prior knowledge of their origins of language and script. In this case, text detection irrespective of languages, scripts, and orientations may be considered a preprocessing step for script identification and recognition. Script identification of an extracted text line allows the user to choose the appropriate OCR engine to recognize the text line. Hence, there are two issues here. One is in language-/script-independent text detection and the other involves script identification of the text extracted. This chapter introduces these two problems and describes relevant methods to deal with the two problems. We will first discuss language-dependent text detection methods. To do so, we will first survey several methods each specifically for a particular script including Chinese, Arabic/Farsi, and Korean. We will then describe an India script-dependent text detection method in more detail to illustrate how specific features of a particular script play an important role in text detection. Next, we will discuss language-independent text detection methods with details given on a method that can deal with multi-oriented text as multi-oriented text may be common for some scripts such as Chinese which can appear in vertical text lines. Finally, we will discuss methods of script identification with an example method in greater details.

© Springer-Verlag London 2014
T. Lu et al., *Video Text Detection*, Advances in Computer Vision
and Pattern Recognition, DOI 10.1007/978-1-4471-6515-6_8

8.1   Language-Dependent Text Detection

Before we examine language-independent approaches to text detection, we will describe a few methods that are specific to a particular language, to draw insights to language-independent features. We then take a closer look of a method that is dependent on two Indian scripts.

Liu et al. [1] have proposed a method for multi-oriented Chinese text detection in video. This method first uses wavelet features to identify text candidates in video. It then uses color and spatial information to detect text lines from these text candidates. This is done by merging horizontal, vertical, slant, curved, or arc text lines based on arrangement structures of multi-oriented text lines in the text candidate regions. Character segmentation will then automatically choose the best-fit strategies based on Chinese character structure analysis which follows single, up-down, left-right, encircling of character components. Finally, it uses an SVM classifier to remove false-positive elimination, which in turn improves the overall text detection accuracy. Moradi et al. [2] have proposed Farsi/Arabic text detection in video using corners of the text information. The approach is based on the intrinsic characteristics of Farsi and Arabic text lines. It finds edges first using edge masks of different directions. It then performs morphological operations on edges' images to find connected components. For connected components, the method detects corners to identify text candidates. Finally, profile features are used to detect text lines. False positives are removed based on geometrical properties of Farsi/Arabic texts. Agnihotri and Dimitrova [3] have proposed a method for Korean text detection in video using edge detection, image enhancement, edge filtering, character detection, text box detection, and finally text line detection. The method uses geometrical properties of Korean text for detection. The above methods basically take advantage of structural or geometrical information of a specific script in question to detect the text line of that script. The following methods, on the other hand, are tailored to a range of multiple languages in their detection.

Lyu et al. [4] have proposed a method for multilingual video text detection using edge detection, local thresholding, and hysteresis edge recovery. Though it claims to have multilingual capability, the method actually deals with Chinese and English texts specifically. It makes use of language-dependent characteristics due to the alphabetic literals in English text and the ideographic features in Chinese text for detection of text regions in video. This entails considering differences in language-dependent characteristics in terms of stroke density (more uniform for English), font size (large font size for Chinese), aspect ratio (greater constraint for Chinese), and stroke statistics (involving four stroke directions and more stroke intersections for Chinese).

Fig. 8.1 Examples of text lines of Indian script. (**a**) Example of Bangla text line (Indian script), (**b**) example of Devanagari text line (Indian script)

8.1.1 Method for Bangla and Devanagari (Indian Scripts) Text Detection

We will now introduce a text detection method which is dependent on two Indian scripts to show how specific features of the scripts are used in text line detection. This is because features that are used for English may not work well for Indian scripts due to more cursive nature of the Indian characters. The method [5] presented below is for detection of Bangla and Devanagari text lines in natural scene images as well as video. The reason to choose Bangla and Devanagari for text detection out of several Indian scripts here is that Devanagari and Bangla are the two most popular Indian scripts used by more than 500 million and 200 million, respectively, in the Indian subcontinent. Besides, a unique and common characteristic of these two scripts is the existence of certain headlines as shown in Fig. 8.1 where (a) and (b) show sample text line images of Bangla and Devanagari, respectively. Therefore, the method's focus is to exploit headline features for text detection in images. Since headline is a unique feature of the Bangla and Devanagari scripts, the method may not be useful for other scripts and English as well. Thus, the method is language dependent and it is good only for Bangla and Devanagari text detection.

8.1.2 Headline-Based Method for Text Detection

The objective of this method [5] is to explore headline features which are unique for the Bangla and Devanagari for text detection. As a result, the method initially obtains binary image by applying Otsu thresholding on the foreground and background pixels separately as shown in Fig. 8.2b for the images shown in Fig. 8.2a. However, foreground and background pixels are separated by the adaptive

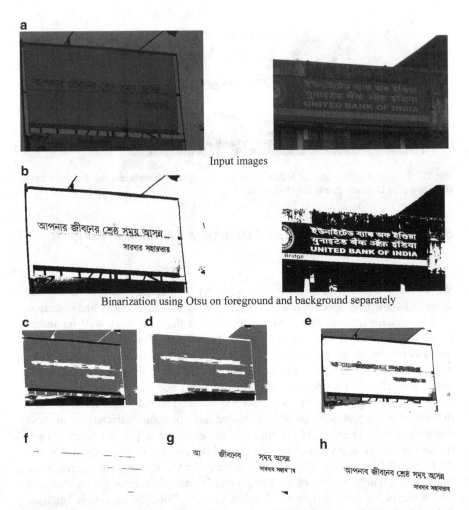

Fig. 8.2 Intermediate results of text detection method: (**a**) Input images, (**b**) Binarization using Otsu on foreground and background separately, (**c**) all lines segments obtained by morphological operation, (**d**) set of candidate headlines, (**e**) all the components minus the respective candidates headlines, (**f**) true headlines, (**g**) components selected corresponding to true headlines, and (**h**) final set of selected components (Courtesy of [5])

thresholding. Since adaptive thresholding is not good for perfect binarization when the images have complex background resulting in loss of significant text pixels, the method uses the output of adaptive thresholding to separate foreground and background pixels. Then the method deploys Otsu thresholding on both the foreground and background separately to recover the loss of text pixels. This gives better results than applying Otsu thresholding directly on the input image because text in video and image may not have bimodal distribution.

Next, the method performs morphological operation on the binary images given by the Otsu thresholding to group text components in the respective text lines as shown in Fig. 8.2c where the two lines are separated. The method finds the largest headline for each segmented text lines as shown in Fig. 8.2d. The headlines are subtracted from all the components in the text lines as shown in Fig. 8.2e, which results in true headlines as shown in Fig. 8.2f. The components corresponding to the true headlines are chosen as shown in Fig. 8.2g. This gives the final text detection as shown in Fig. 8.2h where the two text lines are detected.

8.1.3 Sample Experimental Results

Sample qualitative results of the method are shown in Fig. 8.3 where (a) shows input images containing Bangla and Devanagari text and (b) shows text detection results corresponding to the input images in (a). It is observed from Fig. 8.3 that the method gives good results for the different images. This is because the method extracts headlines as the specific feature to identify text components.

8.1.4 Summary

This section discusses language-dependent text detection methods. It then presents details of a language-dependent method for Bangla and Devanagari text line detection based on a particular set of features of the scripts, namely, headline

Fig. 8.3 Sample experimental results of the method. (a) Sample input image, (b) text detection results for the images shown in (a)

features. The Otsu thresholding is applied on the foreground and background separately to prevent loss of information from direct thresholding on the image. The headline features are studied to obtain text candidates. From the text candidates and the headlines, the method obtains true headlines. The true headlines are then used to find exact text information in the images.

8.2   Methods for Language-Independent Text Detection

Video text detection methods since the early days were mainly language/script independent as they explored general text features such as edges, gradients, texture, and connected components with no particular regard to any language or script. However, most methods were mainly tested on English text due to the much greater availability of English video text datasets. Most of the English text lines in video are in horizontal layout and hence most methods have been confined to horizontal text detection. It is only in recent years that we see interests in multi-oriented text line detection video which opens up flexibility for language-independent text detection, as some ideographic scripts such as Chinese and Japanese can appear in vertical orientation.

Therefore, Shivakumara et al. [6, 7] have proposed several methods for detection of any script text line. The method in [6] combines Laplacian and Fourier techniques to identify text candidates in video frames using the maximum difference concept for merging small components of text as one component. This is useful for scripts such as Chinese and Japanese Kanji characters which may comprise of smaller components known as radicals. Connected and component analysis with skeleton concept is explored to segment text lines from the text components which allow non-horizontal text lines to be traced and detected. This method is good for all types of text though to a lesser accuracy for Chinese characters. To overcome this problem, the same authors have proposed a method for multi-oriented text detection in video using a Bayesian classifier [7]. In this method, a combination of Sobel and Laplacian methods has been used for enhancing text information in video frames. Then the Bayesian classifier is deployed to classify text pixel correctly. Next boundary growing is used to allow video text lines to grow in any direction without being confined to horizontal direction only. However, this method assumes text lines, be they horizontal or non-horizontal, are in straight line alignment. To deal with non-straight text lines such as circle- or arc shaped text, the method in [8] relies on gradient vector flow to detect arbitrary text lines in video. This method uses two-stage grouping to solve the problem of arbitrary orientation thus offering even greater flexibility in script independence.

Another approach to language-independent multi-oriented text detection is to explore the space inside characters and in between characters and words. This is based on the assumption that space between characters and words of any text line irrespective of orientation and scripts is almost constant and uniform. The method reported in [9] uses run length to compute intra- and inter-character space to achieve this objective. We will now examine the method in [9] in greater details.

8.2.1 Run Lengths for Multi-oriented Text Detection

This method works on the basis that intra-character, inter-character, and interword spaces have regular spacing. The method uses Sobel operation of the input image for computing the run lengths because Sobel edge operator is known to be good for high-contrast text pixels, and text pixels usually have high contrast compared to its background. To solve the multi-oriented text detection problem, the method uses the idea of selecting potential run lengths with the help of the run lengths computed on the Sobel edge image of an ideal horizontal text image. Boundary growing is then performed to fix the bounding box for the multi-oriented text. Since input image contains complex background, boundary growing sometimes groups adjacent text lines if the space between text lines is small. The method overcomes the problem of touching text lines by finding zero crossing in the output of boundary growing.

8.2.2 Selecting Potential Run Lengths

To identify the potential run lengths for text candidates from the multi-oriented text input image, the method chooses an ideal horizontal text image as shown in Fig. 8.4a for which the method gets the Sobel edge image as shown in Fig. 8.4b. Then the method computes horizontal run lengths by counting the number of consecutive black pixels between white pixels in the Sobel edge image. Next the method uses max-min clustering to classify the frequencies of run lengths which represent text pixels as shown in Fig. 8.4c where one can see text patches for the text regions. Here max-min clustering algorithm chooses the max and min frequencies from the array of run lengths, and then the frequencies in the array are compared with the max and the min to choose the frequency that is close to the maximum frequency. The basis of max-min clustering is that text has a much higher frequency of run lengths than non-text since the run lengths are computed based on regular spacing between the intra- and inter-characters. This is true because high frequencies of run lengths usually occur when there is a text due to transition from background to text and text to background. This results in ideal run lengths for the multi-oriented text detection as shown in Fig. 8.4c where ideal run lengths are displayed as white patches. For multi-oriented text input image shown in Fig. 8.4d, the method applies the same horizontal run-length criteria on the Sobel edge image (Fig. 8.4e) of the input image Fig. 8.4d to find ideal run lengths with the help of max-min clustering algorithm as shown in Fig. 8.4f where the ideal run lengths are displayed as white patches for the multi-oriented text. It is noticed from Fig. 8.4c and f that just the ideal run lengths do not give better results for multi-oriented text image. Therefore, the method proceeds to obtain potential run lengths from the ideal run lengths by comparing the ideal run lengths of the multi-oriented text with the ideal run lengths of horizontal text obtained from the horizontal input image shown in Fig. 8.4c. The resultant potential run lengths are in Fig. 8.4g where clear text patches can be seen compared to the text patches in Fig. 8.4f. The horizontal ideal run lengths are computed only once for the image shown in Fig. 8.4a. The ideal horizontal image is chosen based on experimental study on both horizontal and non-horizontal images with the help of visual inspection.

8.2.3   Boundary Growing Method for Traversing

For the text patches obtained from the previous section shown in Fig. 8.4g, the method performs boundary growing (BG) to traverse multi-oriented text lines along

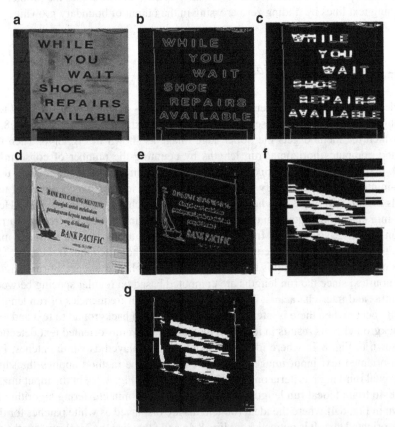

Fig. 8.4 Run-lengths for multi-oriented text. (**a**) Horizontal input, (**b**) Sobel edge, (**c**) ideal run-lengths, (**d**) multi-oriented text, (**e**) Sobel edge, (**f**) run-lengths, (**g**) potential run-lengths

the text direction to extract text lines in the image. BG is used because projection profile approach does not work for multi-oriented text. For each component in the text patches shown in Fig. 8.4g, BG fixes a bounding box first and then it allows boundary to grow pixel by pixel until it reaches a pixel of the neighboring component. This is based on the observation that the space between characters is less than the space between words and lines. Similarly, BG will continue across words based on interword spacing along the text line direction until it reaches the end of the text line. End of the line is determined based on experiments on space between characters and words. The process of BG is illustrated in Fig. 8.5a–f where BG-1–BG-5 show the process to extract the first text line in Fig. 8.4g. Figure 8.5g shows all text lines which are extracted by BG after eliminating false positives.

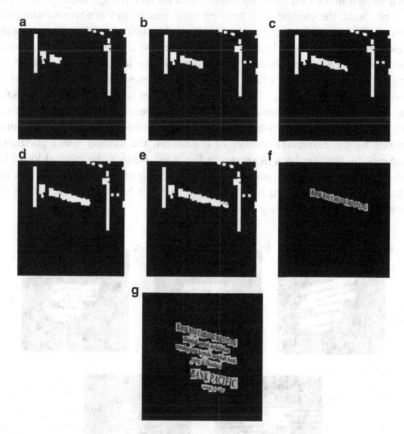

Fig. 8.5 Boundary growing (*BG*) for multi-oriented text lines. (**a**) BG-1, (**b**) BG-2, (**c**) BG-3, (**d**) BG-4, (**e**) BG-5, (**f**) BG text line, (**g**) BG-for all text lines in Fig. 8.4d

8.2.4 Zero Crossing for Separating Text Lines from Touching

Due to complex background of natural scene images in video, BG sometimes connects adjacent text lines that are too close shown in Fig. 8.5g where the top four lines are connected and form one component. As a result, fixing bounding box for each text line has become hard. To overcome this problem, the method fills white pixels for the results obtained by BG as shown in Fig. 8.6a, where binary multi-oriented text patches can be seen. For each component in the image shown in Fig. 8.6a, the method computes its angle using principal component analysis (PCA) by passing the coordinates of each component. The average of the angles of all the components is considered as the actual angle of the whole image. The image is then rotated to the horizontal direction based on this average angle as shown in Fig. 8.6b. Next, the method uses zero crossing which does not require complete spacing between text lines to fix the boundary for such text lines. Zero crossing means transition from 0 to 1 and 1 to 0. The method counts the number of such transitions in each column from top to bottom for the image shown in Fig. 8.6b. Next, it chooses the column which gives the maximum number of transitions to be the boundary for the text lines. This column is shown as the vertical line in Fig. 8.6c. Here, method ignores transition if the distance between two transitions is too small. With the help of the number of transitions between 0 and 1 in the column identified by the maximum number of transitions, the method draws horizontal boundaries for the text lines as shown in Fig. 8.6d. Further, the method looks for spacing between the text components within two horizontal boundaries to draw the vertical boundary for the text lines as shown in Fig. 8.6e, where all text lines are separated within their bounding boxes.

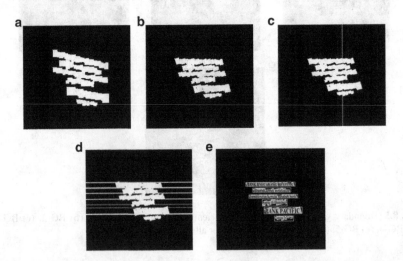

Fig. 8.6 Zero crossing method for rotated multi-oriented touching text line segmentation. (**a**) Multi-oriented text with touching, (**b**) text line segments, (**c**) column-maximum zero crossing, (**d**) text line separation, (**e**) text detection

8.2.5   Sample Experiments

The method is tested on high-resolution multi-oriented camera images (HMCI), low-resolution multi-oriented mobile camera images (LMMI), high-resolution horizontal text camera images (HHCI), low-resolution mobile camera images (LMCI), and the standard dataset ICDAR-2003 competition data [10] to evaluate the performance of the method. Sample results for the above categories are shown from Figs. 8.7, 8.8, 8.9, 8.10, and 8.11.

Fig. 8.7   Sample results for high-resolution multi-oriented camera images

Input   Text detection

Fig. 8.8 Sample results for low-resolution multi-oriented mobile camera images

8.2.6 Summary

A run-length-based method with boundary growing and zero crossing for multi-oriented text detection in both high- and low-resolution images is presented. Simple horizontal run lengths are computed in comparison with an ideal horizontal text image to identify the potential run lengths for multi-oriented text detection. The touching between text lines is solved with the help of angle information of the text given by the boundary growing process and zero crossing computation between text lines.

Fig. 8.9 Sample results for high-resolution horizontal camera images

8.3 Script Identification

In multilingual video text recognition or script-independent video text recognition, it is necessary to know the script to be recognized in order to deploy the appropriate OCR engine. Currently, there is no universal OCR for recognizing multiple script frames in video. Therefore, to enhance the capability of the current OCR readability for multilingual video, it is necessary to identify scripts before sending the detected text lines to the appropriate OCR engine. This section deals with video script identification for this purpose. Though there have been works on script identification for document images with reasonable accuracy, video presents great challenges for

Input   Text detection

Fig. 8.10 Sample results for low-resolution horizontal mobile camera images

script identification due to low resolution, complex background, orientation, and varying font types and sizes [11–13]. Nevertheless, we will first review the methods for document images to draw insights for video script identification.

An overview of script identification methodologies based on structure and visual appearance in document images is presented in [14]. As noted in the review, these methods do not work for video frames due to their low contrast and complex background. Tan [15] proposed a set of rotation invariant features based on Gabor filter for automatic script identification involving six scripts. Busch et al. [16] have explored a combination of wavelet and Gabor features to identify scripts. However, their method expects a large number of training samples to achieve good classification rate. Lu and Tan [17] have proposed a method for script identification in noisy and degraded document images based on document vectorization. Although the method is tolerant to various types of document degradations, it does not perform

Input   Text detection

Fig. 8.11 Sample results for ICDAR-2003 competition data

well for Tamil because of the complexity of the script. Texture features based on Gabor filter and discrete cosine transform are used for script identification at the word level in papers such as [18–20] which expect high-contrast documents for segmentation of words. Similarly, a study of character shape for identifying scripts is proposed in [21, 22]. These methods perform well as long as segmentation works well and the character shape is preserved. Online script identification is addressed in [23] where the spatial and temporal information is used to recognize the words and text lines. Recently, composite script identification and orientation detection for Indian text images is proposed by Ghosh and Chaudhuri [24]. This method considers eleven scripts with plain background and high contrast for identification purposes. The features used are derived from connected component analysis with the assumption that character shapes are preserved. Generally, script identification in document images requires shapes to be preserved in order to effectively identify a script apart from others. This is possible with the high contrast and clean background usually found in document images. However, this is not achievable with video due to its low resolution and complex background. Video thus presents great challenges to script identification.

Addressing these challenges, there have been attempts in the literature to do script identification in video. The method [25] takes text lines detected by text detection methods as input and uses statistical and texture features with a k-nearest neighbor classifier to identify Latin and ideographic text in images and videos. This method works well for English and Chinese but not for other scripts. In addition, its performance depends on the classifier. Phan et al. [26] proposed the use of text features, namely, smoothness and cursiveness, without classifier for video script identification. This method considers only English, Chinese, and Tamil scripts, and it is noted from the experimental results that the features are not adequate to handle more than three scripts present in video frames. Recently, the method in [27] for video script identification at word level is proposed using gradient and Zernike moments together with an SVM classifier. However, the scope is restricted to only two Indian languages, namely, Bengali and Hindi together with English. The methods reported in the literature thus so far have been restricted to a small number of predetermined scripts. In the following subsections, we will describe in some details a method [28] that is capable of identifying six scripts, namely, Arabic, Chinese, English, Japanese, Korean, and Tamil. Essentially, this method makes use of spatial and gradient features of text as a basis of identification.

8.3.1 Spatial-Gradient-Features for Video Script Identification

This method first divides the whole video frame of size 256×256 into 16 blocks of size 64×64 as described in [29]. It then analyzes each block based on wavelet-moments and mutual nearest neighbor concept to identify the text blocks among the 16 blocks. The reason for choosing the block size of 64×64 is to capture at least a few words in each block. Dividing into blocks also simplifies and speeds up computation. This is because generally, text does not occupy an entire video frame. But rather it scatters in the frame in small clusters. The advantage of this method is that it identifies the text block irrespective of scripts, fonts, font size, and orientation. It expects at least one block to satisfy the criteria to identify the frame of a particular script.

8.3.2 Text Components Based on Gradient Histogram Method

For each pixel in a block as shown in Fig. 8.12a, the method obtains gradient values by convolving Sobel horizontal mask and vertical mask shown in Eq. 8.1 over the block to increase the contrast as shown in Fig. 8.12b, c, respectively. Gradient

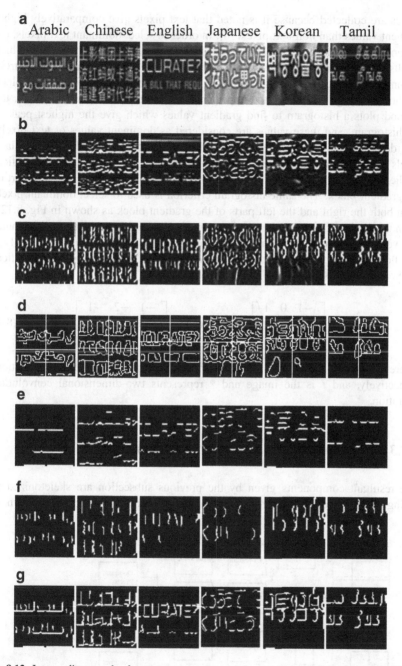

Fig. 8.12 Intermediate results for text components. (**a**) Input blocks. (**b**) Horizontal gradient values. (**c**) Vertical gradient values. (**d**) Canny edge maps values. (**e**) Dominant gradient pixels by horizontal division. (**f**) Dominant gradient pixels by vertical division. (**g**) Text components (horizontal + vertical dominant pixels)

values are collected because it is noted that text pixels give comparatively higher gradient values than non-text pixels [6]. In order to select dominant text pixels, the method divides the horizontal gradient block at the centroid horizontally, which results in two equal parts, namely, the upper part and the lower part. The centroid is computed based on the edge pixels in the Canny edge map of the input block as shown in Fig. 8.12d. For the upper and the lower part of gradient block, the method plots a histogram to find gradient values which give the highest peak in the histogram, and these values are considered as dominant values of text pixels. The dominant text pixels are represented as white pixels and the rest as black pixels as shown in Fig. 8.12e. In the same way, the method divides the vertical gradient block vertically at the centroid to obtain the left part and the right part of the gradient block. The same histogram criterion is used to select dominant pixels from both the right and the left parts of the gradient block as shown in Fig. 8.12f. Then the method combines the dominant pixels obtained from the above horizontal and vertical divisions to obtain the total text information as shown in Fig. 8.12g. The flow diagram for the selection of text components from horizontal and vertical gradient division is shown in Fig. 8.13.

$$G_x = \begin{bmatrix} -1 & 0 & 1 \\ -2 & 0 & 2 \\ -1 & 0 & 1 \end{bmatrix} * I, \quad G_y = \begin{bmatrix} -1 & -2 & -1 \\ 0 & 0 & 0 \\ 1 & 2 & 1 \end{bmatrix} * I \quad (8.1)$$

where G_x and G_y represent gradients in the horizontal and vertical direction, respectively, and I is the image and $*$ represents two-dimensional convolution operation.

8.3.3 Candidate Text Components Selection

The resultant components given by the previous subsection are skeletonized to a single pixel width in order to preserve the components' shapes as shown in

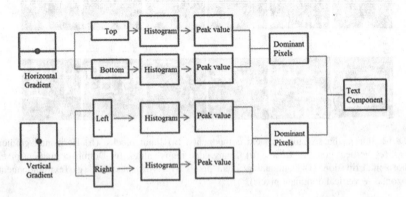

Fig. 8.13 Flow diagram for text components selection using gradient histogram

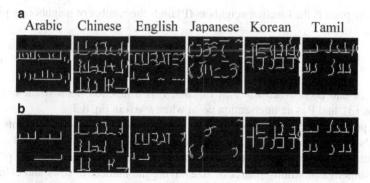

Fig. 8.14 Candidate text components. (a) Skeletons of text components, (b) candidate text components after filtering

Fig. 8.14a. This is to facilitate identification of end points, junction, and intersection points of the components accurately. The components are then grouped into two clusters based on their areas using k-means algorithm with $k = 2$. Components in the cluster with the lower mean are considered as noise as defined in Eq. 8.2 and hence eliminated. This results in candidate text components as shown in Fig. 8.14b for use in the next subsection:

$$\mu_{NC} = \min(\mu_{C1}, \mu_{C2}) \qquad (8.2)$$

where $\{\mu_{C1}, \mu_{C2}\}$ are the means of the two clusters and μ_{NC} is the mean of the noise cluster.

8.3.4 Features Based on Spatial Information

It is observed from the candidate text components in the block of six scripts that the spatial distribution of end points, intersection points, junction points, and pixels exhibit distinctive appearances among the different scripts. For instance, between English and Chinese candidate text components, end points in Chinese have closer proximity than English. This is because Chinese components contain many subcomponents leading to closer proximity between end points, while English components generally have single components with fewer end points. To extract such observations, the method computes four variance features with respect to end points, intersection points, junction points, and pixels. The method finds distances from each end point to the remaining end points, thereby generating a proximity matrix for all end points. The same is done for intersection points, junction points, and pixels. Then a single vector comprising the four variance features is formed. The end points, junction, and intersection points are defined as follows.

For any pixel P, the function neighbors (P) finds the number of neighboring pixels connected to P:

$$k = \text{Neighbors (P)} \qquad (8.3)$$

P is an end point when $k = 1$ in Eq. 8.3. P is a junction point when $k = 3$ in equation (3), and P is an intersection point when $k = 4$ in Eq. 8.3.

The proximity matrices for end points, junction points, intersection points, and all pixels are defined as follows. The end point proximity matrix is a distance matrix that contains distances between every end point to all the remaining end points. This results in a proximity matrix of size having the number of rows and columns equal to the number of points (let it be n, as in Eq. 8.4 below). Each element of the end point proximity matrix $ED_{i,j}$ represents the distance between end points i and j. Similarly, elements of proximity matrices for junction points, intersection points, and all pixels are represented by $JD_{i,j}$, $ID_{i,j}$, and $PD_{i,j}$, respectively. In the same way, the variances for proximity matrices are computed as follows. The variance of proximity of end point distances is represented by $Var(ED)$ where ED is the set of all end point distances and μ_{ED} is the mean of all the end point distances in the end point proximity matrix:

$$Var\,(ED) = \frac{1}{n^2}\sum_{i=1}^{n}\sum_{j=1}^{n}\left(ED_{i,j} - \mu_{ED}\right)^2 \qquad (8.4)$$

where n is the number of rows or columns in the proximity matrix. The variance of junction point distances, intersection point distances, and all pixel distances represented by $Var(JD)$, $Var(ID)$, and $Var(PD)$, respectively, is computed as in Eq. 8.4.

8.3.5   Template Formation for Script Identification

The method chooses 50 frames randomly from each class of scripts for template creation as suggested in [17] in which script identification for camera images is addressed. The four variance features are computed for the blocks corresponding to the 50 frames of each script class. Then the average of the variance features of the blocks of 50 frames, which contain text information chosen manually for each script, is computed as defined in Eq. 8.5 below:

$$Avg(Var) = \frac{1}{50}\sum_{i=1}^{50}Var_i \qquad (8.5)$$

This gives six templates (vectors) for the six scripts containing four average variance features in each template. For the given block, the method extracts four

variance features and compares them with the six templates to find the minimum
Euclidean distance to classify the frame into a particular class. This procedure
gives a confusion matrix for the six scripts. The sample templates for the scripts
Arabic, Chinese, English, Japanese, Korean, and Tamil can be seen, respectively, in
Fig. 8.15a–f where all the six templates have distinct features.

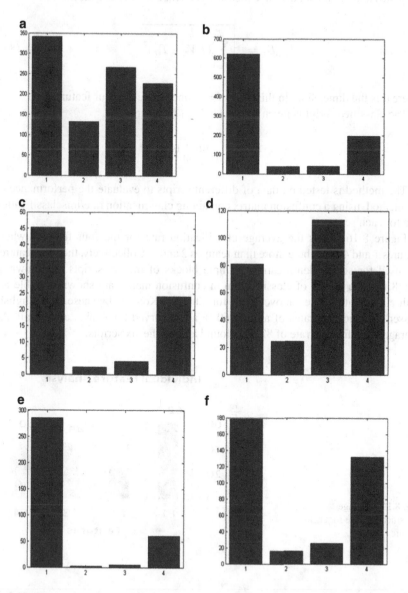

Fig. 8.15 Six templates for script identification. (**a**) Arabic, (**b**) Chinese, (**c**) English, (**d**) Japanese,
(**e**) Korean, (**f**) Tamil

We will now compute the Euclidean distance measure between each extracted feature vector and each of the six templates constructed above for the six scripts. For a query text of unknown script, let FV_r be its feature vector of feature r where feature refers to end points, junction points, intersection points, and all pixels. Let T_{ir} be the template vector of feature r for script i. We will compare FV_r with the six templates and obtain six distance measures D_i (for $i = 1$–6) as follows:

$$D_i = \sqrt[2]{\sum_{r=1}^{d}(FV_r - T_{ir})^2} \tag{8.6}$$

where d is the dimension, in this case, $d = 4$ since there are four features.

The classified script is given by $S \in \{1, 2 \ldots 6\}$ where

$$D_s = \min_{i \in \{1,2,\ldots,6\}} (D_i)$$

The method is tested on data of different scripts to evaluate the performance of the method, using a confusion matrix containing classification rate/misclassification rate for each script.

Figure 8.16 shows the average classification rate for the four features where features 1 and 4 contribute more than features 2 and 3. Collectively, the four features are used for script identification. Sample blocks of the six scripts are shown in Fig. 8.17. The results of classification in confusion matrix are shown in Table 8.1 with classification rates above 90 % for Chinese, Korean, Japanese, and English. Lesser classification rates of around 60 % are observed for Arabic and Tamil. An average classification rate of 82 % is found among the six scripts.

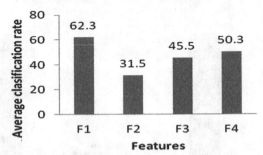

Fig. 8.16 Average classification rate for each feature

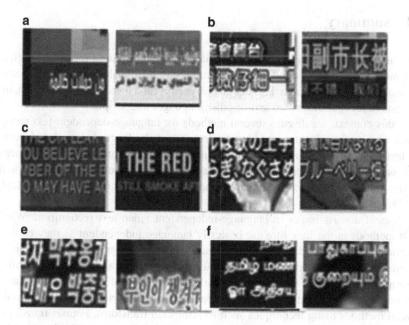

Fig. 8.17 Sample blocks for six scripts from database. (**a**) Arabic, (**b**) Chinese, (**c**) English, (**d**) Japanese, (**e**) Korean, (**f**) Tamil

Table 8.1 Confusion matrix of the method (in %)

Scripts	Arabic	Chinese	English	Japanese	Korean	Tamil
Arabic	66	3	1	4	0	4
Chinese	7	94	1	3	1	4
English	11	1	96	7	5	17
Japanese	1	0	0	83	2	4
Korean	7	0	1	2	90	7
Tamil	4	2	1	1	2	64

8.3.6 Summary

This section describes a set of spatial-gradient-features for identifying six scripts. The dominant text pixel selection is done based on the histograms of horizontal gradient and vertical gradient. The four variance features with respect to distances between end points, intersection points, junction points, and pixel in the block are used for script identification.

8.4 Summary

This chapter concerns video text recognition involving multiple scripts. Traditionally, most video text recognition works are based on English due to much greater availability of English video datasets. In the recent years, there have been increasing interests in recognizing video text of other languages and scripts.

In this context, we discuss several methods for language-dependent text recognition which take advantage of specific features of the language/script concerned for text recognition. Examples of scripts in the respective methods in our general discussion include Chinese, Arabic/Farsi, and Korean. We then take a closer look in greater details of a method for Indian script video text recognition involving Bangla and Devanagari scripts.

We next discuss issues in language-independent video text recognition. While most methods in the literature are basically language independent as they explore general text features such as edges, gradients, texture, and component connectivity, a recent interest has been on multi-oriented text recognition to allow greater flexibility in script detection other than the traditional horizontal text alignment. For instance, scripts like Chinese and Japanese can appear in vertical orientation. We describe several methods using techniques such as Laplacian transform, Fourier transform, and gradient vector flow to enable multi-oriented text detection. We also examine a method in detail that is based on run-length computation to explore intra- and inter-character spaces, which are generally constant among different scripts.

Finally, we discuss the need for script identification for multi-script video text recognition in order to determine the appropriate OCR engine for the script identified. While script identification has been well researched in the community of document image analysis, video script identification presents challenges due to low resolution and complex background in video images. With a brief survey of document script identification, we take note of scanty works in video script identification due to its challenges. We then describe a method in detail that makes use of spatial-gradient-features for identification of six scripts. The reported average classification rate of 82 % shows promise for further work in this direction.

References

1. Liu Y, Song Y, Zhang Y, Meng Q (2013) A novel multi-oriented Chinese text extraction approach from videos. In: Proceedings of the ICDAR, pp 1355–1359
2. Moradi M, Mozaffari S, Oruji AA (2010) Farsi/Arabic text extraction from video images by corner detection. In: Proceedings of the MVIP, pp 1–6
3. Agnihotri L, Dimitrova N (1999) Text detection for video analysis. In: Proceedings of the CBAIVL, pp 109–113
4. Lyu MR, Song J, Cai M (2005) A comprehensive method for multilingual video text detection, localization, and extraction. IEEE Trans CSVT 15:243–255
5. Bhattachatya U, Parui SK, Mondal S (2009) Devanagari and Bangla text extraction from natural scene images. In: Proceedings of the ICDAR, pp 171–175

6. Shivakumara P, Phan TQ, Tan CL (2011) A Laplacian approach to multi-oriented text detection in video. IEEE Trans PAMI 33:412–419
7. Shivakumara P, Sreedhar RP, Phan TQ, Lu S, Tan CL (2012) Multi-oriented video scene text detection through Bayesian classification and boundary growing. In: Proceedings of the IEEE Trans CSVT, pp 1227–1235
8. Shivakumara P, Phan TQ, Lu S, Tan CL (2013) Gradient vector flow and grouping based method for arbitrarily-oriented scene text detection in video images. IEEE Trans CSVT 23:1729–1739
9. Basavanna M, Shivakumara P, Srivatsa SK, Hemantha Kumar G (2012) Multi-oriented text detection in scene images. Int J Pattern Recognit Artif Intell (IJPRAI) 26(7):1–19
10. Lucas SM, Panaretos A, Sosa L, Tang A, Wong S, Young R (2003) ICDAR 2003 robust reading competitions. InProceedings of the ICDAR, pp 1–6
11. Doermann D, Liang J, Li H (2003) Progress in camera-based document image analysis. In: Proceedings of the ICDAR, pp 606–616
12. Zang J, Kasturi R (2008) Extraction of text objects in video documents: recent progress. In: Proceedings of the DAS, pp 5–17
13. Jung K, Kim KI, Jain AK (2004) Text information extraction in images and video: a survey. Pattern Recognit 977–997
14. Ghosh D, Dube T, Shivaprasad AP (2010) Script recognition-review. IEEE Trans PAMI 32:2142–2161
15. Tan TN (1998) Rotation invariant texture features and their use in automatic script identification. IEEE Trans PAMI 20:751–756
16. Busch A, Boles WW, Sridharan S (2005) Texture for script identification. IEEE Trans PAMI 27:1720–1732
17. Shijian L, Tan CL (2008) Script and language identification in noisy and degraded document images. IEEE Trans PAMI 30:14–24
18. Jaeger S, Ma H, Doermann D (2005) Identifying script on word-level with informational confidence. In: Proceedings of the ICDAR, pp 416–420
19. Pati PB, Ramakrishnan AG (2008) Word level multi-script identification. Pattern Recogn Lett 1218–1229
20. Chanda S, Pal S, Franke K, Pal U (2009) Two-stage approach for word-wise script identification. In: Proceedings of the ICDAR, pp 926–930
21. Chanda S, Terrades OR, Pal U (2007) SVM based scheme for Thai and English script identification. In: Proceedings of the ICDAR, pp 551–555
22. Li L, Tan CL (2008) Script identification of camera-based images. In: Proceedings of the ICPR
23. Namboodiri AM, Jain AK (2002) on-line script recognition. In: Proceedings of the ICPR, pp 736–739
24. Ghosh S, Chaudhuri BB (2011) Composite script identification and orientation detection for Indian text images. In: Proceedings of the ICDAR, pp 294–298
25. Gllavata J, Freisleben B (2005) Script recognition in images with complex backgrounds. In: Proceedings of the IEEE international symposium on signal processing and information technology, pp 589–594
26. Phan TQ, Shivakumara P, Ding Z, Lu S, Tan CL (2011) Video script identification based on text lines. In: Proceedings of the ICDAR, pp 1240–1244
27. Sharma N, Chanda S, Pal U, Blumenstein M (2013) Word-wise script identification from video frames. In: Proceedings of the ICDAR, pp 867–871
28. Zhao D, Shivakumara P, Lu S, Tan CL (2012) New spatial-gradient-features for video script identification, In: Proceedings of the DAS, pp 38–42
29. Shivakumara P, Dutta A, Trung Quy P, Tan CL, Pal U (2011) A novel mutual nearest neighbor based symmetry for text frame classification in video. Pattern Recognit 44:1671–1683

Chapter 9
Text Detection in Multimodal Video Analysis

Access to video repositories has attracted attentions in the past decade, and the existing approaches for video analysis are based on a wide range of techniques, ranging from the selection of visual features to the retrieval or indexing of video clips automatically. These methods analyze video data by different ways but follow a similar principle: independently using low-level visual cues such as color, shape, and texture as visual features or low-level audio characteristics from the raw video data. However, considering the multimodal nature of video data, theoretically the choices here should both include mono-modal analysis, i.e., using one modality data stream, and multimodal analysis, i.e., using two or more modality data streams, in which the latter tends to be omitted in the past research. Actually, it has been proved that using mono-modal low-level visual cues alone only achieves a fairly low accuracy on unconstrained datasets; therefore, multimodal strategy can be addressed as a new approach for video content analysis by simultaneously taking advantage of different modalities that potentially appear in the same video explicitly or implicitly. Text is one of the typical modalities embedded in a video. For example, a single name, a street, or a building text sometimes has the ability to provide cue about the presence of a person in video, rather than solving the traditional mono-modal computational problem like face recognition or speaker recognition which may be hard to accurately figure out. Similarly, the task of efficient visual or auditory retrieval can be potentially improved by narrowing the search space from a large number of raw video data after detecting the texts that indicate video semantics or categories.

Most video streams involve more than one modality for conveying hints related to the nature of the underlying contents. In general, video data is composed of three low-level modalities, namely, the *visual modality* (i.e., visual objects, motions, and scene changes), the *auditory modality* which can be structural foreground or unstructured background sounds in audio sources, and the *textual modality* such as natural video texts or man-made overlapped dialogues. Since perceptual attention is easily attracted by changes in the involved modalities in video streams like

© Springer-Verlag London 2014
T. Lu et al., *Video Text Detection*, Advances in Computer Vision
and Pattern Recognition, DOI 10.1007/978-1-4471-6515-6_9

visual scene transitions or audio variations, the concurrent analysis of multimodal information modalities has thus potentially emerged as a more efficient way in automatic video content access especially in the recent years.

Essentially, multimodal video data originated from the same source tend to be correlated [1, 2, 48]. It means that different modalities can take a complementary role on solving video content analysis tasks, and the presence of one modality can help understand certain semantics of others. For example, a video retrieval system that exploits modalities consisting of audio, image, and text may in general achieve better performance in both accuracy and efficiency than one which exploits either one or the other [3, 4], due to the fact that each modality may compensate for weakness of the other. As a result, multimodal correlation has been given a growing attention in video content analysis research in the past years [5, 6], and much efforts have been made to detect video semantics such as story, location, people, and event.

However, negotiating the "semantic gap" between low-level feature descriptors and high-level contents by effective combination of multimodality video data streams still remains a great challenge [7]. First, the traditionally preferred representations of low-level feature vectors extracted from multimodal objects in video stream are heterogeneous and thereby cannot be correlated directly. Let us take a look at the characteristics of the three modalities in video sequentially. The audio volume in video stream typically includes structural sounds like speech and music and more complex environmental audio scenes that are simultaneously composed of structural foreground and unstructured background sounds. The analysis of audio volume uses the temporal or spectral domain feature vectors for audio signals to predict the structures inside speech or music sounds or searches for the set of best feature subspaces to provide maximum dissimilarity information between different unstructured auditory scene classes from all mutually orthogonal subspaces. The visual volume in video stream will be initially decomposed into a set of feature volumes, namely, color, intensity, textual, and spatiotemporal optical flows, by using the introduced preprocessing techniques in Chap. 2. Moreover, volumes for each visual feature can be decomposed into multiple scales and the pyramidal theory allows the model to represent smaller or larger visual objects on different scales for visual representations. Unlike the audio and visual modalities, the textual modality in video stream consists of scene text embedded in visual scenes and graphics text of subtitles which include transcripts of the audio track as well as time stamps in movies, TV, or karaoke videos. The detection and recognition of video text in general adopts techniques from natural language processing, such as syntactic text analysis and probability-based text frequency prediction models of latent semantic analysis (LSA), probabilistic latent semantic analysis (PLSA), and latent Dirichlet allocation (LDA). It can be found that even the effective combination of multimodality video content is likely to enable video semantic concept detection methods to become more powerful; the low-level features from different video modalities are relatively difficult to integrate together due to their heterogeneous essences. Second, directly merging the heterogeneous multimodal features is also not preferred since high dimensionalities of multimodal feature vectors always cause the problem of "curse of dimensionality." Besides, the over-compression problem [8] will occur when the sample vector is very long and the number of training samples is small, which results in loss of information in the dimension reduction process.

Following the mentioned considerations, we introduce text detection in multimodal video analysis in this chapter as follows. We first introduce the relevance of different modalities existing in video, namely, the auditory, the visual, and the textual modalities in Sect. 9.1. General multimodal data fusion schemes for video analysis are discussed, and two examples for connecting video texts and other modalities are given in this section. Then we give a brief overview on the recent multimodal correlation models which integrate the video textual modality in Sect. 9.2. In Sect. 9.3, we discuss multimodal video applications of text detection and OCR for person identification from broadcast videos, multimodal content-based structure analysis of karaoke, text detection for multimodal movie abstraction and retrieval, and web video classification through text modality. Finally, we conclude this chapter in Sect. 9.4.

9.1 Relevance of Video Text and Other Modalities in Video Analysis

In video streams, the three modalities in general have a contextual co-occurrence characteristic in essence. Wu et al. [7] consider that video data exhibit this characteristic by intra-shot context correlation and inter-shot context propagation. On the one hand, although the multimodality data of continuous visual video frames, overlapped transcripts, and audio signal may not occur at the same time, they still convey the similar video content over a period of time in the same shot. Obviously, it will be helpful to analyze video semantics by correlating the temporal-associated multimodalities. On the other hand, the connections of inter-shots can potentially be reinforced by propagating the complementary multiple modalities among inter-shots. For example, although the video shots of swimming and football are visually distinguished by their dominant colors of blue and green, they can still be easily classified to the same concept of *sport* since the text modality appearing in the two shots may show their connections. That is, the text modality may represent more similarity than the visual one in this case. So the similarities between the visually distinguished video shots could be correspondingly propagated through the analysis from multiple modalities.

How to incorporate the visual and auditory modalities together with the embedded video texts detected in the video streams through a novel multimodal correlation scheme to improve the accuracy of video analysis such as indexing and retrieval has become an interesting task in the recent years. We take the following example that can be used in real-life applications to further explain it. Suppose a building often has its name on the wall and the picture of a street often contains signs showing the street names. From the human perception point of view, it might be convenient to directly utilize the detected textual names to conclude the concepts in video stream or at least help improve the accuracy of video content analysis. Conversely, the knowledge of detected video contents can be used to help in the accurate detection of video texts or provide robust OCR results.

Unlike the visual feature descriptors of color histograms, textures and Canny edges in Chap. 2, or the acoustic feature descriptors like spectral centroid, roll-off, flux, zero crossings and Mel frequency cepsrtral coefficient (MFCC), the source text in video stream is either directly tracked from video frames or indirectly recognized from speeches and then properly organized as a bag of words using text-based feature descriptors, such as the TF-IDF with a vocabulary of terms which appears in the whole video dataset. Due to the fact that the number of such textual words is generally very large and the characteristics of natural language processing, correspondingly, the dimension of text-based features will be much larger than the features of other modalities. Therefore, probability-based text frequency prediction models like the widely used latent semantic analysis techniques of LSA, PLSA, and LDA are often first applied to reduce the dimension of text features.

Generally, a multimodal analysis approach for semantic interpretation of video streams inevitably includes a fusion step to combine the results of several single-modality analysis procedures. Rather than focusing on rule-based combination for multimodal fusion, Snoek et al. [9] identify two general fusion strategies for semantic video analysis, namely, *early fusion* and *late fusion*, differing in the way they integrate the results from feature extraction on the various modalities. Specifically, the methods that rely on early fusion first extract unimodal features. Then after analysis of various unimodal streams, the extracted features are combined into a single representation as a combination of unimodal features. Correspondingly, they define early fusion as the fusion scheme that integrates unimodal features before learning concepts. Early fusion yields a truly multimedia feature representation since the features are integrated from the start. A disadvantage of the approach is the difficulty to combine features into a common representation due to the heterogeneity of different modalities. The general scheme for early multimodal fusion on visual, auditory, and textual features for video analysis is shown in Fig. 9.1.

Instead, the late fusion in [9] is defined as the scheme that first reduces unimodal features to separately learned concept scores, and then these scores are integrated to learned concepts. The approaches relying on late fusion also start with extraction of unimodal features, but in contrast to early fusion where features are then combined into a uniform multimodal representation, approaches for late fusion learn semantic concepts directly from unimodal features. For example in [10], separate generative probabilistic models are learned for the visual and textual modalities, respectively. Then the scores are combined afterward to yield a final detection score. In general, late fusion schemes combine the learned unimodal scores into a multimodal representation, where unimodal concept detection scores are fused into a multimodal semantic representation rather than a feature representation. For example, the latent semantic analysis techniques of LSA, PLSA, and LDA can be first separately adopted for visual, audio, and text modalities, and then multimodal

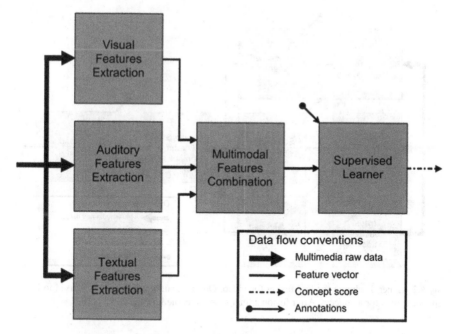

Fig. 9.1 General scheme for early fusion for video. Outputs of unimodal analysis on visual, auditory, and textual features in video are fused before learning concepts [9]

data will be correlated on a higher level in the latent aspect space [2] to avoid the discussed difficulty in analyzing heterogeneous low-level feature vectors or the "curse of dimensionality" problem. However, a big disadvantage of late fusion schemes is its expensiveness in terms of the learning effort, as every modality requires a separate supervised learning stage. Another potential disadvantage of the late fusion approach is the potential loss of correlation in mixed feature space [9]. A general scheme for late fusion is illustrated in Fig. 9.2.

The interesting connection examples between low-level visual cues and detected texts can be described as follows. First, for the purpose of video content understanding, a video dataset often contains some relevant text information, such as person names, road signs, taxi plate numbers, etc. The text embedded in video scenes of the same category may show some uniform patterns over text colors, sizes, locations, orientations, languages, textures, etc. It indicates that the texts in video are sometimes more robust to be detected and understood to provide cues or other useful information for helping general visual understanding. Second, the detected texts themselves can be better interpreted if we know the classification of their associated visual scene. Inspired by the observations, Zhu et al. [11] propose a multimodal fusion framework using visual cues and texts for visual categorization. For a given image, they first perform image classification using a bag-of-words model which is based on the low-level visual cues. The outcomes of this step are

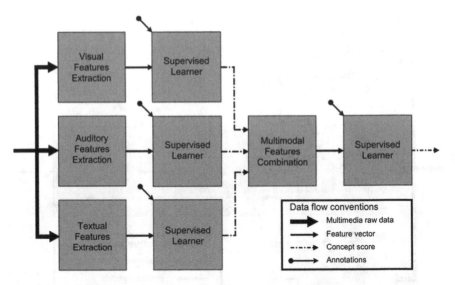

Fig. 9.2 General scheme for late fusion for video. Output of unimodal analysis is used to learn separate scores for a concept. After fusion a final score is learned for the concept [9]

the probabilities of this image belonging to each semantic category. Meanwhile, a text detector is used to locate the text lines in this image. Then an SVM-based classifier is used to fuse the information of two different models together. Since the bag-of-words model is a generative approach and proved to be successful for scene classification and, on the contrary, the SVM model is typically selected for a discriminative approach, their proposed framework can be viewed as an implicit way of combining a generative model and a discriminative model in fusing visual cues and texts. Karaoglu et al. [12] further evaluate multimodal object recognition based on visual features fused with text recognition on the IMET dataset [11] which consists of around 2,000 examples. The IMET dataset contains natural scene images with text somewhere in them. The detected text is converted to characters and words, which in turn are used in a bag-of-character-bigrams text classifier. Then this text classifier is further combined with a bag-of-visual-words image representation (see Fig. 9.3). Their experimental results show that text recognition from natural scenes helps object classification if there is text in the image and if the text is not too specific to a single object. As a possible application, they show in Fig. 9.4 the system's output on a Google image of the class *building*, where the text adds significant semantic information.

It can be concluded that the integration of video text detection with visual or audio computations is one of the coming trends in video analysis. In some sense, detected video texts can be considered as the semantic descriptions of video data. Therefore, the exploration of video text-related multimodal analysis models will benefit the current video analysis methods and broaden the ranges of their potential applications.

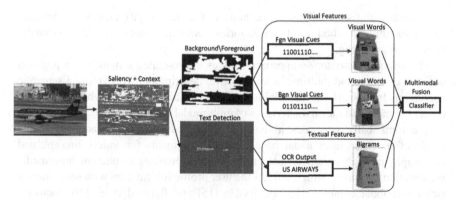

Fig. 9.3 The detected text is converted to characters and words, which in turn are used in a bag-of-character-bigrams text classifier. This text classifier is further combined with a bag-of-visual-words image representation [12]

Fig. 9.4 The system's output on a Google image of the class *building*, where the *text* adds significant semantic information: *Yellow dashed-line boxes* denote the output; the *red dashed-line boxes* are not recognized [12]

9.2 Video Text-Related Multimodality Analysis Models

In this section we give a brief overview on the recent models for multimodal analysis. The details of using these multimodal analysis models that are related with video text detection will be explained by the typical applications in Sect. 9.3.

Generally, the state-of-the-art techniques of multimodality analysis techniques can be roughly classified into two categories: semantic annotation and cross-media correlation modeling.

The *semantic annotation* approach bridges the so-called semantic gap problem between contents and multimodality low-level descriptors by providing a semantic annotation framework for describing and representing knowledge both about the content domain and the characteristics of multimodal data themselves. For example, [13] automatically generates a dynamic multimedia document adapted to the needs of the user from a database of XML fragments for video, images, and paragraphs through parameter selecting. [14] personalizes a coherent multimedia presentation document which reflects the user profile information with semantically rich multimodal content. Blei and Jordan [15] and Barnard et al. [16] focus on automatically labeling unannotated multimodal data using textual models. They first represent a visual or auditory feature cluster with the dictionary index and then construct a linked representation to obtain image-text, audio-text, and other cross-media translation results. Despite its success, their methods still suffer from several weaknesses. First, representing each local visual or auditory feature by a dictionary index can result in severe loss of information. Second, cross-media index actually focuses on the annotation problem, ignoring semantics reasoning among multimodal data. Sidhom and David [17] further attach annotation defined as textual, graphic, or sound to multimedia document source in the context of natural language processing, automatic indexing, and knowledge representation. Recently, [18] allows for linking low-level MPEG-7 descriptors to conventional semantic web ontologies and annotations. Similarly, [19] organizes heterogeneous multimedia items and their context through semantic knowledge with the help of semantic web technologies. Unfortunately, the ontology is difficult to define in a uniform way and thereby still remains a long way to go, especially toward multimodality video analysis.

Generally, the *cross-media correlation modeling* approach [20, 21] explores statistical relationship between cross modalities. Yamamoto et al. [22] present a picture scheme on utilizing media toward understanding of multimedia documents. After extracting visual and auditory features, the known canonical correlation (CC) is computed between the feature matrices to learn their correlation [6], and accordingly, a hierarchical manifold space can be calculated to make the correlations more accurate [23]. Yue-ting et al. [5] use transductive learning to mine the semantic correlations among media objects of different modalities so as to achieve cross-media retrieval, by which the query examples and the returned results can be of different modalities, e.g., to query images by an example of audio in multimedia documents. Iria and Magalhaes [24] exploit cross-media correlations in the categorization of multimedia web page documents by converting every document into a canonical document-graph representation. Similarly, Wang et al. [25] present an iterative similarity propagation approach to explore the interrelationships between web images and their textual annotations. They first consider web images as one type of objects and their surrounding texts as another and then construct their links' structure via web page analysis to iteratively reinforce the similarities between images. However, difficulties still exist due to the heterogeneous feature space and the non-corresponding visual or textual contexts.

In addition, cross-media analysis has a lot of interesting applications. For example, [26] proposes an automatic approach for personalized music sports video document generation by using multimodal feature analysis to detect the semantics of events. In [27], Lu et al. investigate how to integrate multimodal features for story boundary detection in broadcast news documents. They use a diverse collection of features from text, audio, and video modalities and thereby formulate the detection problem as a classification task on the multimodal features. Poignant et al. [28] present a video OCR system that detects and recognizes overlaid texts in video as well as its application to person identification in video documents. Theoretically, it can be found that cross-media analysis is indispensable in these multimedia document understanding applications.

We will show the details by some typical applications to further explain the multimodal analysis techniques or models that are related with video text detection in Sect. 9.3.

9.3   Text Detection for Multimodal Video Content Analysis

In this section, we show several video text-related multimodal approaches, including text detection and OCR for person identification from broadcast videos, multimodal content-based structure analysis of karaoke, text detection for multimodal movie abstraction and retrieval, and web video category by using text modality.

9.3.1   Text Detection and Multimodal Analysis in Broadcast Videos

The textual modality is widely used in broadcast videos and correspondingly plays an important role in broadcast video content analysis. A recent interesting topic is person search in audiovisual broadcast video using the text available because the availability of text can help disambiguate a name that is cited or understand the context of the video stream. Moreover, a classical text-based information retrieval (IR) system could be adopted to take advantage of the extracted texts by further using external information such as electronic newspapers and web pages that are related to specific textual keywords.

In order to search for the appearance of a certain person in video, the simplest approach is to look for the person's name. The Name-it [29] associates names and faces based on their co-occurrences in news video. A face image is labeled with the name that has the largest temporal overlap with a group of images containing faces similar to the given one. With a given name, the face images are found in a similar way. This method can thus be used for both person naming and person finding. Poignant et al. [30] focus their study on the transcription of named entities from the video frames. Proper names and positions of a person become their target to highlight the interest of video text to recognize people. To do this, they perform video text detection on each frame in order to have a follow-up of each text box. Only the boxes sufficiently stable over time are kept in their method. They thus have, for each kept box, a range of presence (starting and ending frames). The box images are then processed by the Otsu algorithm for binarization. An average image is computed for every ten frames, and candidate images for the same text can be obtained. Each of these candidate images is sent to the Google *Tesseract* free software for text recognition. Note that *Tesseract* is quite sensitive to the resolution of the input video frames; thus, a bi-cubic interpolation is applied to obtain the required resolution. In this way, a text-based person search system can be finally developed: when a user types a person's name or a position (job, title, etc.) and a date (e.g., between February 2 and March 31, 2007), the system localizes a part of a newscast where the person is likely to appear on the screen, as shown in Fig. 9.5. Similarly, Chen et al. [31] employ text, timing, anchor person, and face information to find a specific person from news video. They use the text information to search for the seed shots containing the name of the person. Time relationship between the mentioning of the name and the appearance of the person are then used to propagate the text research results into nearby shots. Anchor person detection and face recognition are also used to further improve the result. The final prediction is based on the linear combination and face recognition.

Video text detection can also be integrated with visual or auditory modalities rather than a single modality for person identification in news video. For example, except for video OCR output, textual features can also include automatic speech recognition (ASR) output. Thus, the visual appearance of a person will be accordingly correlated to the appearances of the name text that is obtained by either video OCR or video ASR. It is, however, possible that the appearance may not

Fig. 9.5 Text localization/recognition in a video frame for person search [30]

coincide with the shots in which the name is mentioned as discussed in [32]. In addition, there are cases where the name may not be mentioned in the ASR or more possibly is missing due to ASR recognition errors. On the other hand, although video OCR or ASR potentially has the ability to provide robust recognition results of the appearance of a specific person, most occurrences of person's faces in video stream actually do not have corresponding video text tags. Thereby, there are two main problems in utilizing video OCR or ASR for name text matching to facilitate multimodal video analysis: reducing the recognition error in video OCR and avoiding temporal misalignment in video ASR.

To overcome the problems, Zhao et al. [32] employ the minimum edit distance (MED) to correct the insertion, deletion, and mutation errors in video OCR. They use the distribution statistics collected from the training data that model the probability between the shot where the name appears and those that the face actually occurs to correct the errors. A multimodal and multifaceted approach to person detection in news videos is thus given by making use of multimodal features extracted from text, visual, and audio inherent. They also incorporate multiple external sources of news from the web and parallel news archives to extract location and temporal profile of the person. They call this second source of information the multifaceted context. The multimodal, multifaceted information is then fused using a Rank Boosting approach.

To show the effectiveness of their multimodal person search approach, Zhao et al. choose ten people to be detected based on the queries of TRECVID 2003 and 2004 search task [7]. Given a multimedia query, the participants are required to submit a ranked list of shots. The query consists of a short text description and may be accompanied by short video clips and/or images. Mean average precision (MAP) is used to measure the performance and a significant improvement in performance from text-based retrieval to "text + context"-based retrieval. Moreover, the MAP increases by about 50 % after further combining multimodal features using the linear-weighted sum as reported. This can be attributed to the use of Video OCR and face detector. The major jump in precision is attributed to a better ranking of shots as textual features alone are not sufficient to determine whether a face is present in a shot according to their analysis. In addition, video OCR also improves the precision by providing precise timing information of the appearance of the person's name on the screen.

Another interesting example is text-integrated multimodal analysis for story boundary detection from broadcast videos. Generally, a broadcast video episode contains various news stories or reports, each addressing a particular topic. Story boundary detection aims to identify where one story ends and another begins in a stream of text, speech, or video [33]. It potentially serves as a necessary prepro-cessing stage to various broadcast video tasks, such as semantic concept detection, broadcast indexing and retrieval, video information extraction and editing, etc. For example, a typical broadcast video retrieval system should be able to locate the particular positions in a repository that match the user's query, simultaneously determining where the user-interested stories begin and end.

For detecting story boundaries in broadcast videos, various boundary features have been studied in different modalities. Lu et al. [27] use a diverse collection of features from text, audio, and visual modalities in video streams: lexical features capturing the semantic shifts of broadcast topics and audio/video features reflecting the editorial rules of broadcast news. Generally, the extracted features of the three modalities play different roles in broadcast news video analysis and thereby have their own characteristics in using. For example, word similarity measures will be frequently used as boundary indicators toward revealing topic shifts or semantic topic variations, while audio/video cues are more heuristic and rely on editorial rules that are very different from textual features. Thereby, Lu et al. formulate the detection problem as a classification task, i.e., classifying each candidate into boundary/non-boundary based on a set of multimodal features and perform a comprehensive evaluation for six popular classifiers of decision tree (DT), Bayesian network (BN), naïve Bayesian (NB) classifier, multilayer perception (MLP), support vector machines (SVM), and maximum entropy (ME) classifier. Their results show that BN and DT can generally achieve superior performances over other classifiers and BN offers the best F1 measure on the CCTV broadcast news corpus [33], which contains 71 Mandarin broadcast news videos (over 30 h in duration).

9.3.2 Lyrics Analysis for Interpreting Karaoke Music Video

Karaoke is a video type for entertainment, in which the lyrics are embedded in video frames and the time of text color changes is in general synchronized to the music [43]. Amateur singers can sing along the playback of the music accompaniment. Karaoke is very popular, and today a large number of karaoke music videos can be found available both from music shops or the Internet for home and commercial use. Correspondingly, how to use the karaoke music video data more efficiently rather than simply playing back or singing along has become a new and interesting demand, especially with the rapid development of multimedia hardware devices and media computing technologies.

Automatically detecting the multimodality structures of the song inside a karaoke video helps users interact with karaoke music video in a more convenient way to practice singing the song [44]. For example, a user may want to search for a particular song of interest by directly browsing visual summaries of the lyrics and video. Thus, lyrics text extraction and its visual color change tracking becomes a feasible approach to analyze the content in karaoke video. However, lyrics text detection has the following differences against the existing video graphics text detection approaches:

- Graphics text remains nearly static over all the frames of its occurrence, but the visual characteristics (e.g., color and contrast) of lyrics text always change over time while the background in general contains large variation and dynamics. It makes the existing techniques presented to detect graphics text hardly capable of handling the problem of lyrics extraction from karaoke music video.

- Most of the current video text detection techniques, including graphics text detection and scene text detection, seldom consider multimodality analysis in video streams. Actually, multimodal analysis is helpful and sometimes necessary to detect lyrics text that changes to the music.

Zhu et al. [34] propose a multimodality approach for content-based structure analysis of karaoke music video. They present a video text analysis technique to extract the bitmaps of lyrics video text from the frames and track the time of its color changes that are synchronized to the singing voice. A music structure (chorus/verse/phrase) analysis technique is further proposed based on multimodality contents: lyrics text from video and original singing audio as well as accompaniment audio from the two audio channels. The choruses and verses are detected by analyzing the patterns of repetition of both the lyrics text and the melody. The singing phrase segmentation is based on the time alignment of the lyrics text with the detected singing voice. In their karaoke music retrieval system, the input from the karaoke music data consists of video frame sequence and the audio signals for both the music accompaniment and the original singing. A lyrics text analysis model extracts the bitmaps of lyrics text from the video frames and tracks the text color changes. Music structure detection operates on the lyrics and the audio contents and derives the music structures, i.e., choruses, verses, and phrases. As a result, the detected music structures can be used for content-based indexing, retrieval, and summarizing of karaoke music videos.

In their method, the lyrics text detection technique is proposed from the karaoke video frames to track the color changes of the text over time, which is represented as the time sequences of the extracted characters. They utilize the characteristic of the occurrence of lyrics text on the video frame:

- The lyrics present as text lines alternatively on two (or occasionally three) text boxes with fixed sizes and locations.
- The color of a text line changes in a way like a vertical bar scanning gradually from the left to the right during the occurrence of the text line (called text object).
- In each text object, the text colors keep static (unchanged) before or after the color changes taking place.

Figure 9.6 shows text boxes, text lines, text objects, and color changes of a text line in their method, where Fig. 9.6a gives the text boxes that have fixed positions in the video frame. In most karaoke videos, the text in the upper text box is aligned to the left, whereas the text in the lower text box is aligned to the right. The left half of the upper text box and the right half of the lower text box, as indicated by gray color, are mostly occupied by the texts. Three text objects for a single text box are shown in Fig. 9.6b. Each text object contains only one text line, and the color of the text in a text line change from the left to the right as in Fig. 9.6c.

Fig. 9.6 Illustration of text box, text line, text object, and text color change in karaoke video [34]

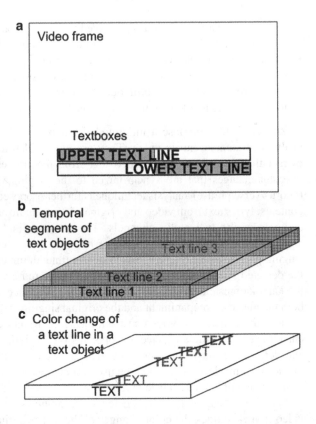

Following these techniques, their steps of multimodal music structure analysis for karaoke video are as follows:

- Locate the positions of the text boxes for the whole karaoke music title, and detect the presence of text lines in the text boxes for each video frame.
- Detect the temporal boundaries of text objects, and track the color changes of a text line in a text object.
- Extract the bitmaps of the lyrics texts based on the dynamic characteristics of the text: the pixel value keeps static either before or after the color change occurs.
- Based on the extracted bitmaps, the individual characters can be separated by estimating the character size and space size, which are typically uniform for the whole title. By employing the text color change trace, a spatial sequence of characters can be converted to a temporal sequence of characters.
- Analyze music structure based on multimodal contents of karaoke music through using the extracted lyrics text bitmaps to detect verse and chorus that are considered as the main sections of songs. Specifically, the repetition of lyrics will be detected based on similarity matching of the text bitmaps, and the

repletion of melody is computed based on harmonic similarity matching of the original singing audio. Moreover, the time alignment of lyrics and singing voice is explored to segment the song lyrics into singing phrases.

As a result, the main sections of songs will be located and identified by analyzing the repetitions of lyrics and melody of the songs for karaoke music video semantic understanding. Zhu et al. have encoded the tiles in MPEG-1 NTSC format, i.e., video has 352×240 frame size and 29.97 frame rate and audio has two channels with 44.1 kHz sampling rate and 16 bits sample size. They use the MPEG Developing Class Toolbox to assist on the video analysis and manual annotation. The audio stream are extracted from the MPEG system stream and decoded to waveform for separate analysis. Time synchronization of video and audio is done by using the video frame rate and audio sampling rate. Adobe Audition software is used to help annotate the singing phrase boundaries. Note that in their system, the positions of the text boxes are manually annotated by the coordinates of the vertical and horizontal bounds, and the durations that lyrics text lines are presented in each text box are similarly annotated by the starting and ending frame numbers for evaluation. Figure 9.7 shows the lyrics text bitmap images of the karaoke title *paint my love*. Correspondingly, all the choruses are correctly located and identified,

```
FROM MY YOUNGEST YEARS              SINCE YOU CAME
    TILL THIS MOMENT HERE   INTO MY LIFE
I'VE NEVER SEEN                    THE DAYS BEFORE
    SUCH A LOVELY QUEEN    ALL FADE TO
FROM THE SKIES ABOVE              BLACK AND WHITE
    TO THE DEEPEST LOVE   SINCE YOU CAME
I'VE NEVER FELT                    INTO MY LIFE
        CRAZY LIKE THIS   EVERYTHING HAS CHANGED
BEFORE                            PAINT MY LOVE
        PAINT MY LOVE     YOU SHOULD PAINT MY LOVE
YOU SHOULD PAINT MY LOVE      IT'S THE PICTURE OF
    IT'S THE PICTURE OF   A THOUSAND SUNSETS
THOUSAND SUNSETS                 IT'S THE FREEDOM OF
    IT'S THE FREEDOM OF   A THOUSAND DOVES
A THOUSAND DOVES                 BABY YOU SHOULD
        BABY YOU SHOULD   PAINT MY LOVE
PAINT MY LOVE                     PAINT MY LOVE
    BEEN AROUND THE WORLD  YOU SHOULD PAINT MY LOVE
THEN I MET YOU GIRL           IT'S THE PICTURE OF
    IT'S LIKE COMING HOME  A THOUSAND SUNSETS
TO A PLACE I'VE KNOWN            IT'S THE FREEDOM OF
        PAINT MY LOVE      THOUSAND DOVES
YOU SHOULD PAINT MY LOVE          BABY YOU SHOULD
    IT'S THE PICTURE OF    PAINT MY LOVE
A THOUSAND SUNSETS
    IT'S THE FREEDOM OF
A THOUSAND DOVES
        BABY YOU SHOULD
PAINT MY LOVE
```

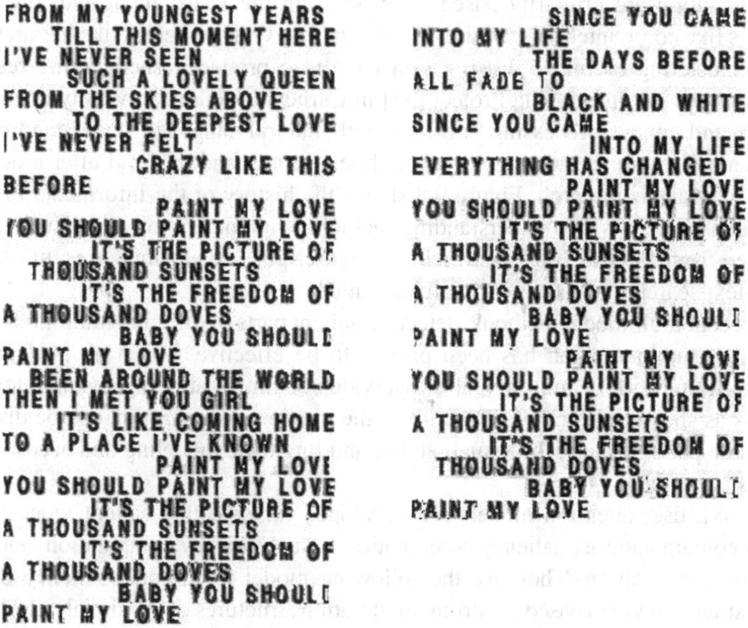

Fig. 9.7 Lyrics text extraction result for *paint my love* for multimodal content-based structure analysis of karaoke, which can be easily modified to automatically work for other configurations, such as one or three text boxes and/or center aligned texts [34]

and 18 verses are correctly detected, illustrating the performance of the proposed multimodal approach is better than the method based only on audio content analysis.

Essentially, the multimodal approach by integrating video text, visual features, and other modalities can be considered as a recent effort toward the development of a music video retrieval or analysis system, which in general allows a user to browse karaoke music content by the form of textual lyrics directly. Actually, the application of the lyrics text analysis technique is not limited to music structure analysis. It can also be potentially used for music summarization and automatic customized songs recommendation. In addition, the overall multimodality approach for music structure analysis can also be applied to the analysis of generic video types in which graphic text is synchronized to audio even without color changes.

9.3.3   Multimodal Video Summarization

Video summarization is believed useful to provide users with a short version of the video by showing important information in understanding the video content briefly [35]. Video summarization serves as an overview of the video, thus becomes a central task to achieve machine understanding of its contents. Earlier works on video summarization are primarily based on processing the visual input and low-level features like color, intensity, texture, or motion [36]. Other schemes like hierarchical frame clustering or fuzzy classification have also produced encouraging results. For example, the Informedia Project [37] in Carnegie Mellon University combines speech and image processing together with natural language understanding to automatically summarize videos for intelligent search and retrieval after a decade of video analysis research. Figure 9.8 shows the history of the Informedia Project with all aspects of video understanding including summarization and visualization of video from 1994 to 2005, in which text transcripts, visual summaries, titles, and a free text search interface are initially included.

In recent multimodal methods, detecting salient parts of different multimodalities for video summarization has been proved to be effective. Ma et al. [41] give a general framework of multimodal movie/video summarization by fusing attention models as shown in Fig. 9.9. The core of the movie summarization can be divided into three parts, namely, the visual, audio, and linguistic modeling and accordingly the fusion of them.

In [38], user attention models are developed for detecting salient video parts, which contain auditory saliency computation, visual saliency computation, and text saliency computation. They use the following model to compute saliency of the audio stream in video based on strong modulation structures of the signal waveform:

$$s(t) = \sum_{k=1}^{K} \alpha_k(t) \cos\left(\phi_k(t)\right) \qquad (9.1)$$

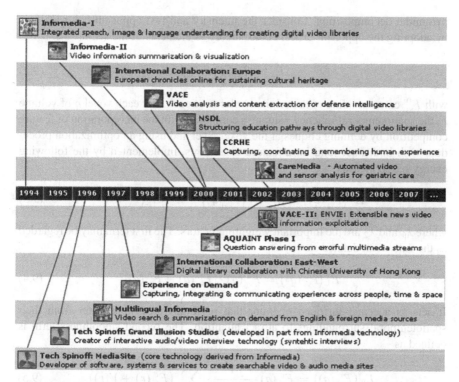

Fig. 9.8 A graphic timeline of major Informedia Project efforts, mainly containing an early manually transcribed/synchronized/indexed stage and a later stage to provide single video abstractions to summarize and visualize multiple videos through combining speech and image processing together with natural language understanding [37]

Fig. 9.9 The framework by fusing user attention models for movie summarization [41]

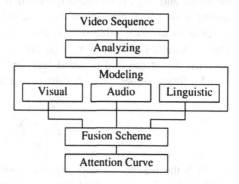

where $\alpha_k(t)$ is the instantaneous amplitude and $d\phi_k(t)/dt$ is the frequency, which can be estimated from a set of Gabor filters $h_k(t)$ by applying the nonlinear energy operator and the energy separation algorithm. For visual saliency computation, the video volume is initially decomposed into a set of feature volumes consisting of intensity, color, and spatiotemporal orientations on multiple scales by using pyramidal decomposition. Consider the intensity and two opponent color features by adopting the opponent process color theory as elements of the vector

$$\overrightarrow{F}_v = [F_{v1}, F_{v2}, F_{v3}] \tag{9.2}$$

with $F_{v_k}^0$ corresponding to the original volume of each. For each voxel q of volume F, the spatiotemporal saliency volume is computed with the incorporation of feature competition by defining cliques at the voxel level and using an optimization procedure with both inter- and intra-feature constraints, implemented by the following energy-based measure:

$$E_v\left(F_{v_k}^c(q)\right) = \lambda_1 \cdot E_1\left(F_{v_k}^c(q)\right) + \lambda_2 \cdot E_2\left(F_{v_k}^c(q)\right) \tag{9.3}$$

where λ_1 and λ_2 are the important weighting factors. The first term may be regarded as the data term, defined as

$$E_1\left(F_{v_k}^c(q)\right) = F_{v_k}^c(q) \cdot \left|F_{v_k}^c(q) - F_{v_k}^h(q)\right| \tag{9.4}$$

It acts as a center-surround operator that promotes areas that differ from their spatiotemporal surroundings to attract attention. The second smoothness term is defined as

$$E_2\left(F_{v_k}^c(q)\right) = F_{v_k}^c(q) \cdot \frac{1}{|N(q)|} \cdot \sum_{r \in N(q)} \left(F_{v_k}^c(r) + V(r)\right) \tag{9.5}$$

where V is the spatiotemporal orientation volume that indicates motion activity in the scene and $N(q)$ is the 26-neighborhood of voxel q. This involves competition among voxel neighborhoods of the same volume and accordingly allows a voxel to increase its saliency value only if the activity of its surroundings is low enough. Thus, a saliency volume S will be created by averaging the conspicuity feature volumes $F_{v_k}^1$ at the first pyramid level by iterative energy minimization. Finally, visual saliency values for each video frame are obtained by

$$S_v = \sum_{k=1}^{3} \omega_k \sum_q S(q) \cdot F_{v_k}^1(q) \tag{9.6}$$

in which the feature volumes are first normalized into [0, 1] and then pointwise multiplied by the saliency volume $S(q)$ to suppress low saliency voxels.

To compute text saliency, a decision-tree-based probabilistic part-of-speech (POS) tagger is used to classify each word into the corresponding part-of-speech, and then text saliency weights are assigned to each word based on the POS tag assigned to the word. The most salient POS tags are proper nouns, followed by nouns, noun phrases, and adjectives, while verbs can specify semantic restrictions on their pre-arguments and post-arguments which usually belong to the aforementioned

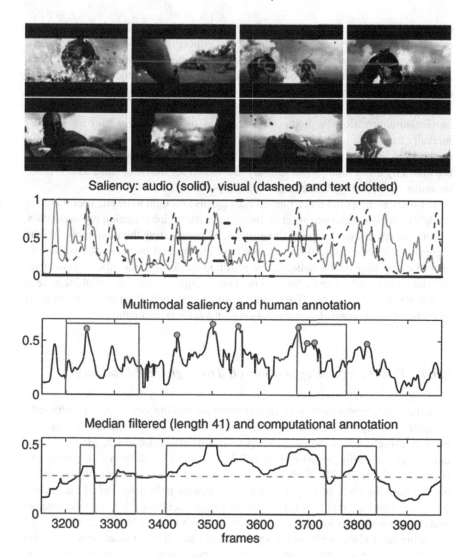

Fig. 9.10 Video abstraction using multimodal saliency and human annotation [38]

classes. Finally, there is a list of words that have very little semantic content and referred as *stop words* and will be filtered out in natural language processing.

For a video stream, audio, visual, and text attention is finally modeled by constructing a composite temporal index of saliency using a linear or nonlinear fusion scheme. Figure 9.10 shows video abstraction or summarization results using multimodal saliency curves and human annotation.

In [39], a keyframe-based video summarization method by using visual attention clues is presented. It describes a new *visual attention index* (VAI) descriptor based on a visual attention model to bridge the semantic gap between low-level descriptors used by computer systems and the high-level concepts perceived by human users, which is divided into three parts, namely, dynamic attention computation, static attention computation, and the fusion of both. However, the main advantage of this method is the ability to control the keyframe density according to the content variation of the whole clip. Jin et al. [45] further proposes a multimodal movie summarization by both using a visual modality curve and an auditory modality curve. By considering the relationships of the two types of curves, the method successfully extracts keyframes as movie summarizations. Another similar algorithm by using multimodal saliency and fusion for movie summarization based on audio, visual, and text attention can refer [44].

In other cases, spatial and temporal cues are also thought to be one useful kind of modality. In [40], Vasconcelos et al. introduce a truly global motion representation, in both the spatial and temporal dimensions, by augmenting the motion model with a generic temporal constraint that avoids oscillation and increases the robustness against competing interpretations. The resulting model is parametric in both space and time and thereby can be fitted to the entire sequence with marginal increase in computational complexity. The results illustrate that their algorithm obtains more meaningful video content summarization than the previous methods.

9.3.4 Web Video Category/Search Through Text Modality

With the rapid development of computer hardware and the techniques of multimedia computing, compressing, and communication, web video services are now becoming increasingly hot on the web. A report on Informa Telecoms & Media [8] said that the global online video market will be worth $37 billion in 2017, driven by popularity of services like Netflix and YouTube, and video services delivered online will account for 10 % of total TV or video revenues before the end of the decade. Moreover, from the report of Online Publishers Association [9], 5 % of the Internet users watch web videos daily and 24 % watch web videos at least once a week.

Facing such a large web video corpus, how to find a desired video or an interested category of videos is becoming increasingly necessary. This situation is similar to the one in searching for web pages. When the amount of web pages increases, people invented two ways for web video search: one is via text-based search engine and the other is by web directory. The latter is inspired by the fact that currently video category information is initially labeled by the user when he/she is uploading the video onto most of the video-sharing websites. However, this manner still has three disadvantages [42]. First, the users have very different understandings of video categories; thus, their labeled categories are in general inconsistent with each other. Second, the categorizations provided by video websites are usually to categorize the genres of videos such as film, news, and sports. They are insufficient to differentiate the rich content of web videos. Figure 9.11 shows the category definitions excerpted from two popular video-sharing websites. Finally, the labeling will cost much

a

Autos & Vehicles

Recent Video
KITT replica

Last Updated:
1 day ago

Comedy

Recent Video
Bug Problem!...

Last Updated:
8 hours ago

Entertainment

Recent Video
Goodnight Bu...

Last Updated:
14 hours ago

Film & Animation

Recent Video
Bad Yoghurt

Last Updated:
14 hours ago

Gadgets & Games

Recent Video
Blunty's vid...

Last Updated:
1 day ago

Howto & DIY

Recent Video
Win a game o...

Last Updated:
10 hours ago

Music

Recent Video
Architecture...

Last Updated:
2 hours ago

News & Politics

Recent Video
You Choose S...

Last Updated:
1 day ago

People & Blogs

Recent Video
Who Has Nalt...

Last Updated:
10 hours ago

Pets & Animals

Recent Video
Sea Lion Iri...

Last Updated:
16 hours ago

Sports

Recent Video
Tour De France

Last Updated:
9 hours ago

Travel & Places

Recent Video
Overlander.t...

Last Updated:
16 hours ago

b

Animals

Animation

Autos

Blogs

Comedy

Commercials

Entertainment

Games

Movies

Music

People

Politics

Screencast

Sports

Technology

Travel

Fig. 9.11 Category definitions excerpted from two popular video-sharing websites [42]. (**a**) YouTube categories (http://youtube.com/categories). (**b**) Soapbox categories (http://soapbox.msn. com)

human efforts and hence create a poor user experience especially for such a large number of web videos. As a result, automatic web video category/search through text modality search engine remains to be a feasible and efficient approach.

Automatic web video category still faces a lot of difficulties. Unlike "movie" or "broadcast" videos, a web video here means a *user video* from video-sharing websites and has the following two main differences [42]. First, web videos have high diversity in terms of category, style, content, subject, format, genre, and so on, especially compared with professional videos. Second, a lot of web videos are captured using handheld devices like mobile phones or camcorders with a relatively low quality of low resolutions under weak light. The differences simultaneously make text detection unreliable for web videos comparing with movies or TV broadcasts. It accordingly makes web video category analysis an equally or more challenging problem.

Fortunately, web videos have rich information from multiple channels especially the surrounding text (the titles, descriptions, and tags of web videos), and the social information (i.e., the relationship among videos through user textual recommendations) can be applied. Such surrounding text information, even not directly detected from videos themselves, can also facilitate semantic analysis of videos in the web page. Among this information, titles, descriptions, and tags are the most important and direct explanation for the corresponding video. For example, Aradhye et al. [46] do not assume any explicit manual annotation other than the weak labels already available in the form of video title, description, and tags on large real-world corpora of user-uploaded video such as YouTube. Their method begins with an empty vocabulary and then analyzes audiovisual features of 25 million YouTube.com videos by searching for consistent correlation between these features and text metadata. Their method autonomously extends the label vocabulary as and when it discovers concepts it can reliably identify, thus eventually leading to a vocabulary with thousands of labels. Wu et al. [47] explore the Google challenge from a new perspective by combining contextual and social information under the scenario of social web. The semantic meaning of text, video relevance from related videos, and user interest induced from user videos are integrated together to determine the video category.

Sometimes web video texts have intrinsic properties, for example, there are in general many candidate words to tag a specific category of videos [42]. An example is that the video which is tagged "soccer" should be related to the video with the tag "sports." The word similarity computed using the JCN word similarity measure on WordNet [11] can be a choice in order to discover the relationship between word terms. Given a word dictionary containing n words $(k_1, k_2, \ldots, k_n)$, a word similarity matrix W can be constructed with the entry $W(i, j)$ being the word similarity between terms k_i and k_j computed based on WordNet. In other situations, the surrounding text of a web video may be extremely sparse. Machine learning algorithms like manifold ranking can then be adopted to propagate the word-video similarity to other related terms. Nevertheless, these properties should be well considered in a text-modality-integrated web video category task.

Both the detected texts from video itself and the surrounding texts in web pages play a critical role in developing web video category or web video search applications. With the development of mobile devices and Internet hardware, using the textual modality and further fusing it with other modalities will become one of the major interests of researchers.

9.4 Summary

Video text adds semantic information to video scenes. They are usually designed to attract human attentions and to reveal scene information where they exist. Text in video adds identification on the brand or type of a product, specifies which buildings serve a particular service, and gives sites by road signs. In this sense, video text can be considered as a useful modality in developing various video-based applications. For example, the task of efficient visual or auditory retrieval in videos can be potentially improved by narrowing the search space from a large number of raw video data after detecting the texts that indicate video semantics or categories as discussed.

Theoretically, the combination of video text modality together with other modalities in video can better facilitate video analysis tasks due to the multimodal nature of video data. Sometimes a single name, a street, or a building text has the ability to provide clear cues about the information of a video scene, rather than solving the relatively difficult mono-modal computational problem like visual object recognition or audio recognition which may be hard to accurately figure out. A video retrieval system that exploits both modalities of audio, image, and text can also achieve better performance in both accuracy and efficiency than one which exploits either one or the other due to the fact that each modality may compensate for weakness of the other. Therefore, it is interesting to exploit the semantic relationship between video text and other modalities to improve automatic video analysis where visual or auditory cues may not prove sufficient.

In this chapter, we introduce the relevance of text and other modalities in video and give a brief overview on the recent multimodal correlation models especially integrating the textual modality for video analysis. Several video applications for text detection and multimodal analysis in broadcast videos, lyrics analysis for interpreting karaoke music videos, multimodal video summarization, and web video category/search through text modality are discussed to introduce the details of multimodal analysis after integrating the video text modality. It is noted that it is still the state-of-the-art problem but will become more important for video analysis in the next decade.

References

1. Beal M, Attias H, Jojic N (2002) Audio-video sensor fusion with probabilistic graphical models. In: Heyden A et al (eds) Computer vision – ECCV 2002. Springer, Berlin, pp 736–50
2. Lin W, Lu T, Su F (2012) A novel multi-modal integration and propagation model for cross-media information retrieval. In: Schoeffmann K et al (eds) Advances in multimedia modeling. Springer, Berlin, pp 740–749
3. Yu B et al (2003) Video summarization based on user log enhanced link analysis. In: Proceedings of the eleventh ACM international conference on multimedia, ACM, Berkeley, pp 382–391
4. Datta R, Li J, Wang JZ (2005) Content-based image retrieval: approaches and trends of the new age. In: Proceedings of the 7th ACM SIGMM international workshop on multimedia information retrieval. ACM, Hilton, Singapore, pp 253–262
5. Yue-ting Z, Yi Y, Fei W (2008) Mining semantic correlation of heterogeneous multimedia data for cross-media retrieval. IEEE Trans Multimed 10(2):221–229
6. Zhang H, Zhuang Y, Wu F (2007) Cross-modal correlation learning for clustering on image-audio dataset. In: Proceedings of the 15th international conference on multimedia. ACM, Augsburg, pp 273–276
7. Fei W, Yanan L, Yueting Z (2009) Tensor-based transductive learning for multimodality video semantic concept detection. IEEE Trans Multimed 11(5):868–878
8. Hongchuan Y, Bennamoun M (2006) 1D-PCA, 2D-PCA to nD-PCA. In: ICPR 2006. 18th international conference on pattern recognition, 2006
9. Snoek CGM, Worring M, Smeulders AWM (2005) Early versus late fusion in semantic video analysis. In: Proceedings of the 13th annual ACM international conference on multimedia. ACM, Hilton, Singapore, pp 399–402
10. Westerveld T et al (2003) A probabilistic multimedia retrieval model and its evaluation. EURASIP J Appl Sig Process 2003:186–198
11. Zhu Q, Yeh M-C, Cheng K-T (2006) Multimodal fusion using learned text concepts for image categorization. In: Proceedings of the 14th annual ACM international conference on multimedia. ACM, Santa Barbara, pp 211–220
12. Karaoglu S, Gemert J, Gevers T (2012) Object reading: text recognition for object recognition. In: Fusiello A, Murino V, Cucchiara R (eds) Computer vision – ECCV 2012. Workshops and demonstrations. Springer, Berlin, pp 456–465
13. Jourdan M, Bes F (2001) A new step towards multimedia documents generation. In: International conference on media futures
14. Scherp A (2008) Canonical processes for creating personalized semantically rich multimedia presentations. Multimedia Systems 14(6):415–425
15. Blei DM, Jordan MI (2003) Modeling annotated data. In: Proceedings of the 26th annual international ACM SIGIR conference on research and development in informaion retrieval. ACM, Toronto, pp 127–134
16. Barnard K et al (2003) Matching words and pictures. J Mach Learn Res 3:1107–1135
17. Sidhom S, David A (2006) Automatic indexing of multimedia documents as a starting point to annotation process. In: Proceedings of the 9th International ISKO Conference
18. Bloehdorn S et al (2005) Semantic annotation of images and videos for multimedia analysis. In: Gómez-Pérez A, Euzenat J (eds) The semantic web: research and applications. Springer, Berlin, pp 592–607
19. Mitschick A (2010) Ontology-based indexing and contextualization of multimedia documents for personal information management applications. Int J Adv Softw 3(1 and 2):31–40
20. Wang X-J et al (2004) Multi-model similarity propagation and its application for web image retrieval. In: Proceedings of the 12th annual ACM international conference on multimedia, ACM, New York, pp 944–951
21. Kyperountas M, Kotropoulos C, Pitas I (2007) Enhanced Eigen-audioframes for audiovisual scene change detection. IEEE Trans Multimed 9(4):785–97

22. Yamamoto M et al (2005) Towards understanding of multimedia documents: a trial of picture book analysis and generation. In: Proceedings of the seventh IEEE international symposium on multimedia

23. Yi Y et al (2008) Harmonizing hierarchical manifolds for multimedia document semantics understanding and cross-media retrieval. IEEE Trans Multimed 10(3):437–46

24. Iria J, Magalhaes J (2009) Exploiting cross-media correlations in the categorization of multimedia web documents. In: Proceedings of the CIAM 2009

25. Wang J et al (2003) ReCoM: reinforcement clustering of multi-type interrelated data objects. In: Proceedings of the 26th annual international ACM SIGIR conference on research and development in information retrieval. ACM, Toronto, pp 274–281

26. Jinjun W et al (2007) Generation of personalized music sports video using multimodal cues. IEEE Trans Multimed 9(3):576–588

27. Mi-Mi L et al (2010) Multi-modal feature integration for story boundary detection in broadcast news. In: Proceedings of the 7th international symposium on Chinese spoken language processing (ISCSLP), 2010

28. Poignant J et al (2012) From text detection in videos to person identification. In: Proceedings of the IEEE international conference on multimedia and expo (ICME), 2012

29. Satoh S, Kanade T (1997) Name-It: association of face and name in video. In: Proceedings of the IEEE computer society conference on computer vision and pattern recognition, 1997

30. Poignant J et al (2011) Text detection and recognition for person identification in videos. In: 9th international workshop on content-based multimedia indexing (CBMI), 2011

31. Ming-yu C, Hauptmann A (2004) Searching for a specific person in broadcast news video. In: ICASSP '04. Proceedings of the IEEE international conference on acoustics, speech, and signal processing, 2004

32. Ming Z et al (2006) Multi-faceted contextual model for person identification in news video. In: Proceedings of the 12th international conference on multi-media modelling, 2006

33. Zhang J et al (2009) A subword normalized cut approach to automatic story segmentation of Chinese Broadcast News. In: Lee G et al (eds) Information retrieval technology. Springer, Berlin, pp 136–148

34. Zhu Y, Chen K, Sun Q (2005) Multimodal content-based structure analysis of karaoke music. In: Proceedings of the 13th annual ACM international conference on multimedia, ACM, Hilton, Singapore, pp 638–647

35. Ying L et al (2006) Techniques for movie content analysis and skimming: tutorial and overview on video abstraction techniques. IEEE Sig Process Mag 23(2):79–89

36. Yueting Z et al (1998) Adaptive key frame extraction using unsupervised clustering. In: ICIP 98. Proceedings of the 1998 international conference on image processing, 1998

37. Hauptmann A (2005) Lessons for the future from a decade of informedia video analysis research. In: Leow W-K et al (eds) Image and video retrieval. Springer, Berlin, pp 1–10

38. Evangelopoulos G et al (2009) Video event detection and summarization using audio, visual and text saliency. In: ICASSP 2009. Proceedings of the IEEE international conference on acoustics, speech and signal processing, 2009

39. Jiang P (2010) Keyframe-based video summary using visual attention clues. In: Qin X-L (ed), pp 64–73

40. Vasconcelos N, Lippman A (1998) A spatiotemporal motion model for video summarization. In: Proceedings of the IEEE computer society conference on computer vision and pattern recognition, 1998

41. Ma Y-F et al (2002) A user attention model for video summarization. In: Proceedings of the tenth ACM international conference on multimedia. ACM, Juan-les-Pins, France, pp 533–542

42. Yang L et al (2007) Multi-modality web video categorization. In: Proceedings of the international workshop on workshop on multimedia information retrieval. ACM, Augsburg, Bavaria, Germany, pp 265–274

43. Kan MY, Wang Y, Iskandar D, New TL, Shenoy A (2008) LyricAlly: automatic synchronization of textual lyrics to acoustic music signals. IEEE Trans Audio Speech Lang Process 16(2):338–349

44. Mayer R, Rauber A (2010) Multimodal aspects of music retrieval: audio, song lyrics – and beyond? Adv Music Inf Retr Stud Comput Intell 274:333–363

45. Jin YK, Lu T, Su F (2012) Movie keyframe retrieval based on cross-media correlation detection and context model. In: IEA/AIE', pp 816–825

46. Aradhye H, Toderici G, Yagnik J. Video2Text: learning to annotate video content. In: ICDWW'09, pp 144–151

47. Wu X, Zhao WL, Ngo CW (2009) Towards google challenge: combining contextual and social information for web video categorization. In: ACM multimedia, pp 1109–1110

48. Lu T, Jin YK, Su F, Shivakumara P, Tan CL. Content-oriented multimedia document understanding through cross-media correlation. Multimed Tools Appl, to appear

Chapter 10
Performance Evaluation

Performance of a computer system or algorithm means how well it works. It can include many aspects, such as computation speed, storage requirements, accuracy of computation, etc. Performance evaluation is an empirical study of the performance of a computer system or algorithm under consideration. Though manual checking and evaluation is frequently used and sometimes is the only feasible option, it is too subjective and too inefficient. Thus, automatic evaluation is more and more preferred due to the large volume of test data and the objectivity and comprehensiveness of the evaluation required.

In pattern recognition, such as video text detection and recognition, we are more interested in the accuracy that a machine (system/algorithm) can detect/recognize the objects of interest and quite a few metrics have been used to measure the accuracy of a pattern recognition system/algorithm, such as ROC curves, true-/false-positive rates (TPR/FPR), precision/recall, and F measures.

As a trend, empirical study of the performances of pattern recognition systems/algorithms is becoming an indispensable part of pattern recognition research and industrial practice. Such empirical study can be used to automatically find the best parameter set or configuration of an algorithm/system. In addition, more and more new systems/algorithms developed in such area are required to conduct thorough empirical evaluation before consideration for publication or deployment. Especially, they are required to be superior to previous or existing algorithms in certain aspects of performance (in certain metrics). This is because theoretical analysis is not sufficient and sometimes not possible. For part of this reason, many contests and competitions, such as ICPR contests and ICDAR competitions, are organized periodically in these major events.

As a problem of pattern recognition, video text detection/recognition should undergo performance evaluation too. Quite a few protocols and benchmark databases have been established for this purpose. In this chapter, we will present state-of-the-art work in this area.

© Springer-Verlag London 2014
T. Lu et al., *Video Text Detection*, Advances in Computer Vision
and Pattern Recognition, DOI 10.1007/978-1-4471-6515-6_10

10.1 Performance Evaluation Protocols

A protocol for performance evaluation is a set of rules used to compare the performances (or accuracy in this chapter particularly) of two or more systems/algorithms under such comparison, which are also referred to as participants in this chapter. The protocol is similar to the regulations in other kind of competition or contest. All participants should agree on and follow such regulations as part of the agreement. The set of rules in such a protocol usually consists of three parts:

1. A benchmark database. This database consists of test data that the participants should work on (as input data). The database also consists of the ideal/expected output (aka ground truth) for each corresponding input.
2. A method for comparing the actual output and the corresponding ground truth of a given input. The method defines the way of how to match and compare the actual output with the ground truth.
3. The performance metrics (or indices) indicating how good an actual output result of a participant is in particular aspects when certain input is used, or how well the system/algorithm works on an input in such aspects. Sometimes, an overall metrics (index) is also needed to indicate the overall performance of a single participant.

The protocol of such performance evaluation should be designed with a purpose. It is very clear that the purpose should be to measure and compare the performances of the participants. However, what kind or aspect of performance is of our interest is the key concern when designing such performance evaluation protocol. Liu and Dori [1] set a few parameters in their protocol which can be adjusted for different purposes. In their idea of goal-oriented evaluation, Wolf and Jolion [2] also argue for that the participants should be measured according to the same purpose as the participating algorithms/systems are designed for. Hence, various protocols have been designed even though the participants are all designed for video/image text detection. In the next three sections, we will present a few well-known ones among them in terms of each of the three components, respectively.

10.2 Benchmark Databases for Video Text Detection

Earlier researchers on video/image text detection usually use their own private benchmark databases [3–5] when evaluating their algorithms/systems due to the lack of publicly assessable databases. These private benchmark databases either are a selection from a bigger public database, e.g., MPEG-7, or simply recorded by researchers themselves. In either case, these databases should undergo manual or semiautomatic annotation for ground truthing. For example, Hua et al. [6] developed a semiautomatic tool for ground truthing their private collection of dataset, which consists of 45 MPEG-7 video clips (128 text boxes) and 90 CNN new video clips (36,615 text boxes). The ground truth of each text box may contain various information which may affect its detection result, including the location coordinates, height and width, orientation and skew angle, text string and length, character density and height variation, color and texture, contrast and background complexity, detectability and recognizability, detection difficulty, etc. Particularly, detectability and recognizability are annotated manually and are useful for those areas which are hardly recognizable and will not be counted for misses and false alarms. The detection difficulty can be calculated based on all the above factors. We will mention these factors again when defining performance metrics.

As more and more contests and competitions are held, there are a few public benchmark databases accessible to all researchers. As early as in 2003, a text locating competition was organized during the 7th International Conference on Document Analysis and Recognition (ICDAR) [7] to test participants' abilities to locate text regions in scene images. The benchmark database used is still available at http://algoval.essex.ac.uk/icdar/datasets.html and has been extended [8] and used again for a few times during the ICDAR competitions later. Particularly, the 2013 edition of the ICDAR Robust Reading Competitions [9] also included video text detection and provided 28 video clips (13 for training and 15 for testing) in addition to adding the pixel-level ground truths for text segmentation from images.

MSRA Text Detection 500 Database (MSRA-TD500) [10] (available at http:// www.iapr-tc11.org/mediawiki/index.php/MSRA_Text_Detection_500_Database_ (MSRA-TD500)) is a publically accessible database containing 500 natural images taken from indoor and outdoor scenes using a pocket camera. The challenge of this dataset includes mixture of text languages, complexity of background, and greater variation of text fonts, sizes, colors, and orientations. The ground truth information, including the detection difficulty, is arranged for each text line.

So far the most comprehensive and publically available dataset for video text detection and tracking is probably the one developed for the US Government Video Analysis and Content Extraction (VACE) program [11]. It can be downloaded from its public website at http://doi.ieeecomputersociety.org/10.1109/TPAMI.2008.57. In this work, text is treated as a special kind of objects in video for detection and tracking. The ground truth dataset for video text detection and tracking consists of 50 video clips for training and 50 video clips for testing (about 450,000 frames in total), which are completely annotated at the I-frame level.

10.3 Matching Detected Text Boxes with Ground Truths

Matching detected text boxes with ground truths is relatively simple. Some methods use area centroid as the matching factor. For example, Landais et al. [12] consider two text box areas matched if and only if each centroid falls inside the other. Most other methods use the spatial overlap of text pixels or the two text box areas as the sole factor for matching. The difference only exists in the overlapping threshold setting (e.g., 80 % as used by Lienhart and Wernicked [4]) and whether multiple matching is allowed. Some also use different thresholds for matching when calculating detection precision and recall separately [9].

Instead of using absolute threshold values of overlapping area to control matching, Hua et al. [6] consider two text boxes as matched as long as they overlap, even though with a relatively small percentage. They actually control meaningful matching using the so-called detection quality of the overlapped area, which depends on not only the size of the area but also the number of Sobel edge points inside the area.

Detection fragmentation and detection merge are two very common types of detection errors. Detection fragmentation means one ground truth text area is detected as a set of separate smaller text areas. Detection merge means a few ground truth text areas (that may or may not be very close to each other) are detected as one integrated text area. Such detection errors will definitely affect further processing. However, whether these errors are measured depends on the purposes of the detection algorithms and the evaluation protocols. Some researchers argue that detection fragmentation and detection merge are still better than false negatives and should be given some credits. Hence, multiple matching (e.g., many-to-one matching for detection merge, one-to-many matching for detection fragmentation, and many-to-many for both) should be allowed.

Kasturi et al. [11] systematically solve the problem of matching detected text boxes with ground truths as an assignment problem and therefore can benefit from many existing solutions (such as in [13]). They use a simple but very clear way to handle the issue that the number of detected text boxes and the number of ground truth text boxes are not equal and find out the unmatched ones. They simply add some imaginary or dummy text boxes in both sides and those text boxes matched with imaginary text boxes are considered unmatched. An imaginary text box matching with a ground truth text box means a miss in detection and an imaginary text box matching with a detected text box means a false positive.

Hua et al. [6] consider not only detection merge cases but also detection fragmentation cases when multiple ground truth text boxes are combined as one detected text box or one ground truth text box is brokenly detected as multiple text boxes. The detection fragmentation degree is measured as we will present in the next section.

10.4   Performance Metrics for Video Text Detection

The first comprehensive performance evaluation protocol for video text detection is probably the one developed by Hua et al. [6]. Before that, most papers of video or image text detection algorithms/systems simply evaluate their performances using the precision/recall rates or similar rates (e.g., TPR/FPR) [3–5]. Li et al. [3] simply calculate the frame-based precision and recall by counting the number of detected frames containing any text.

If we treat each frame of a video clip as a single image, a video text detection algorithm/system outputs exactly the same information (i.e., the text box, which is the bounding box to represent the location, size, and orientation of a detected text area) as an image text detection algorithm/system does. In this sense, the accuracy of the detected text box is what we concern most.

Instead of measuring the accuracy of detected text boxes, Wu et al. [5] measure the detection accuracy using the recall rate of the detected characters/words, which are completely covered by the detected text box. In addition, they also test how much of the detected character/words are able to be recognized by a specified OCR system. Lienhart and Wernicked [4] measure the accuracy of their text detection result at both pixel level (similar to the pixel-based indices in [1]) and text box level. The pixel-based hit rate is actually the recall rate of character pixels, while the text box-based hit rate is actually the recall rate of detected text boxes overlapping more than 80 % of their areas with their corresponding ground truth text boxes. In fact, all these performance indices are special or simpler cases of the ones developed by Hua et al. [6].

Hua et al. [6] propose an objective, comprehensive, and difficulty-tolerant performance evaluation protocol for video/image text detection algorithms based on the protocol originally developed for performance evaluation of text segmentation algorithms from engineering drawings [14]. Actually, text segmentation from document images or engineering drawings is just a simpler case of image/video text detection. They have made remarkable modifications to make it suitable for text detection from video clips. Especially, they proposed the concepts of detection difficulty (DD), detectability index (DI), and detection quality.

Each ground truth text box is assigned a DD value depending on a variety of factors, including text/image mixture, low image quality, character connectivity, background complexity, and variation in text location, size, font, etc., of the text inside the text box. Each ground truth text box is also assigned a DI value depending on both the number and recognizability of the characters inside the text box. Both DD and DI values are part of the ground truth data.

The detection quality of the overlapped area between a matched pair of ground truth text box and detected text box is measured in terms of both the size of the area and the number of Sobel edge points inside the area. It is not only the factor actually controlling meaningful matching but also the basis of the metrics of detection quality (i.e., the basic quality of detection). The detection quality can also be normalized according to the DD value of the ground truth and then a DD-tolerant detection quality can be used more objectively [6].

Both detection fragmentation and detection merge are considered by designing a fragmentation quality index to measure the degree of detection fragmentation of a ground truth text box and the degree of detection merge of a detected text box [6].

The fragmentation quality of a ground truth text box measures the degree to which the ground truth text box are split into the detected text boxes. It is related to the total number of detected text boxes that fully or partially overlap the ground truth text box and the size uniformity of the fragmentation. Namely, the more detected text boxes are resulted, the bad fragmentation quality is obtained, and the less uniformly the text box is split, the bad fragmentation quality is obtained. The fragmentation quality of a detected text box is similarly designed but is used to measure the detection merge. The total detection quality is a combination of the basic detection quality and the fragmentation quality.

Both positive and negative indices for performance are included and normalized with respect to the text box DD. Therefore, these indices are tolerant to different ground truth difficulty. In addition, an overall detection rate is also included, which is the DI-weighted average of the detection qualities of all ground truth text boxes and is more accurate to reveal the real and stable performance of a participating system/algorithm.

The actual formulas defined in [6] for these metrics are just a few instances following the principles of these metrics. They can be defined in various other forms, especially in simpler forms [4, 5, and 11].

The detection quality of a matched pair of ground truth text box and a detected text box is defined by Kasturi et al. [11] as their overlap ratio, which is the ratio of their overlapped area to their union area. This ratio can also be upgraded to 1 or downgraded to 0 in different threshold settings. The text detection accuracy for each individual frame is then defined as the sum of all these overlap ratios of all matched pairs over the average of the number of ground truth text boxes and detected text boxes. The text detection accuracy for the entire video clip (a sequence of frames) is simply defined as the average of the text detection accuracy over all relevant frames in the video clip. The text tracking accuracy for a video clip is defined similarly except for that matched text boxes should also overlap temporally (e.g., they should have the same identity across frames).

10.5   Dataset and Evaluation of Video Text Recognition

Compared with performance evaluation of video text detection, performance evaluation of video text recognition is seldom explored. One reason is that it is related to OCR, which has been well researched, and many resources are available. However, compared with OCR for scanned documents, video OCR or natural image OCR is much more complex due to varied sizes, fonts, and colors of characters inside, especially captured in various environments affected by factors such as lighting and orientation.

The ground truth data of the well-known ICDAR 2003 Robust Reading dataset [7] contains not only bounding boxes but also text transcriptions. Hence, it can be used to evaluate text recognition results. Compared with the ICDAR 2003 dataset, the Natural Environment OCR (NEOCR) dataset [15] contains much more complex and rich ground truth data, including arbitrary orientations. It contains a total of

659 real-life images with 5,238 text boxes captured and annotated by Nagy and his group members. In addition, it can be customized into a few different subdatasets with simple configurations which can be used to evaluate special characteristics of a participating OCR system/algorithm.

10.6 Summary

Performance evaluation is becoming an indispensable part of pattern recognition research and industrial practice. This chapter focuses on the performance evaluation issues of video text detection systems/algorithms. It first introduces the three basic elements of a performance evaluation protocol and then presents state-of-the-art work in each of these three aspects. Finally, it also introduces two datasets for text recognition from video or natural images. This chapter only introduces basic concepts and principles used in a performance evaluation protocol and leaves the details and variations of individual definitions to the readers to check from the references provided.

References

1. Wenyin L, Dori D (1997) A protocol for performance evaluation of line detection algorithms. Machine Vis Applicat 9(5/6):240–250
2. Wolf C, Jolion J-M (2006) Object count/area graphs for the evaluation of object detection and segmentation algorithms. Int J Doc Anal Recognit 8(4):280–296
3. Li HP, Doermann D (2000) Automatic text detection and tracking in digital video. IEEE Trans Image Process 9(1):147–156
4. Lienhart R, Wernicked A (2002) Localizing and segmenting text in images and videos. IEEE Trans Circ Syst Video Technol 12(4):236–268
5. Wu V, Manmatha R, Riseman EM (1999) Textfinder: an automatic system to detect and recognize text in images. IEEE Trans Pattern Anal Mach Intell 21(11):1224–1229
6. Hua X, Wenyin L, Zhang H (2004) An automatic performance evaluation protocol for video text detection algorithms. IEEE Trans Circ Syst Video Technol 14(4):498–507
7. Lucas S, Panaretos A, Sosa L, Tang A, Wong S, Young R (2003) ICDAR 2003 robust reading competitions. In: Proceedings of the 7th international conference on document analysis and recognition, Edinburgh, UK, pp 682–687
8. Shahab A, Shafait F, Dengel A (2011) ICDAR 2011 Robust reading competition – challenge 2: reading text in scene images. In: Proceedings of the 11th international conference of document analysis and recognition, pp 1491–1496
9. Karatzas D, Shafait F, Uchida S, Iwamura M, Gomez L, Robles S, Mas J, Fernandez D, Almazan J, de las Heras LP (2013) ICDAR 2013 robust reading competition. In: Proceedings of the 12th international conference of document analysis and recognition, pp 1115–1124

10. Yao C, Bai X, Liu W, Ma Y, Tu Z (2012) Detecting texts of arbitrary orientations in natural images. In: Proceedings of the CVPR, pp 1083–1090
11. Kasturi R, Goldgof D, Soundararajan P, Manohar V, Garofolo J, Bowers R, Boonstra M, Korzhova V, Zhang J (2009) Framework for performance evaluation of face, text, and vehicle detection and tracking in video: data, metrics, and protocol. IEEE Trans Pattern Anal Mach Intell 31(2):319–336
12. Landais R, Vinet L, Jolion J-M (2005) Evaluation of commercial OCR: a new goal directed methodology for video documents. In: Proceedings of the 3rd international conference on advances in pattern recognition, vol I, pp 674–683
13. Knuth DE (1993) The Stanford GraphBase: a platform for combinatorial computing. ACM Press, New York
14. Wenyin L, Dori D (1998) A proposed scheme for performance evaluation of graphics/text separation algorithms. In: Tombre K, Chhabra A (eds) Graphics recognition – algorithms and systems, Lecture notes in computer science, vol 1389. Springer, Berlin, pp 359–371
15. Nagy R, Dicker A, Meyer-Wegener K (2011) NEOCR A configurable dataset for natural image text recognition. In: Proceedings of the CBDAR 2011, pp 53–58

Index

© Springer-Verlag London 2014
T. Lu et al., *Video Text Detection*, Advances in Computer Vision
and Pattern Recognition, DOI 10.1007/978-1-4471-6515-6

Printed in the United States
By Bookmasters